CHRISTIAN CAVANAUGH

SQL Server™ 2005 DBA
Street Smarts

D1298045

SQL Server™ 2005 DBA
Street Smarts
A Real World Guide to
SQL Server 2005 Certification Skills

Joseph L. Jorden

BICENTENNIAL
1807
WILEY
2007
BICENTENNIAL

Wiley Publishing, Inc.

CHRISTIAN CAVANAUGH

Acquisitions and Development Editor: Maureen Adams
Technical Editor: Rick Tempestini
Production Editor: Rachel Meyers
Copy Editor: Kim Wimpsett
Production Manager: Tim Tate
Vice President and Executive Group Publisher: Richard Swadley
Vice President and Executive Publisher: Joseph B. Wikert
Vice President and Publisher: Neil Edde
Book Designers: Judy Fung, Bill Gibson
Compositor: Laurie Stewart, Happenstance Type-O-Rama
Proofreader: Nancy Riddiough
Indexer: Nancy Guenther
Cover Designer: Ryan Sneed
Anniversary Logo Design: Richard Pacifico

Copyright © 2007 by Wiley Publishing, Inc., Indianapolis, Indiana

Published simultaneously in Canada

ISBN-13: 978-0-4700-8349-9
ISBN-10: 0-470-08349-2

No part of this publication may be reproduced, stored in a retrieval system or transmitted in any form or by any means, electronic, mechanical, photocopying, recording, scanning or otherwise, except as permitted under Sections 107 or 108 of the 1976 United States Copyright Act, without either the prior written permission of the Publisher, or authorization through payment of the appropriate per-copy fee to the Copyright Clearance Center, 222 Rosewood Drive, Danvers, MA 01923, (978) 750-8400, fax (978) 646-8600. Requests to the Publisher for permission should be addressed to the Legal Department, Wiley Publishing, Inc., 10475 Crosspoint Blvd., Indianapolis, IN 46256, (317) 572-3447, fax (317) 572-4355, or online at http://www.wiley.com/go/permissions.

Limit of Liability/Disclaimer of Warranty: The publisher and the author make no representations or warranties with respect to the accuracy or completeness of the contents of this work and specifically disclaim all warranties, including without limitation warranties of fitness for a particular purpose. No warranty may be created or extended by sales or promotional materials. The advice and strategies contained herein may not be suitable for every situation. This work is sold with the understanding that the publisher is not engaged in rendering legal, accounting, or other professional services. If professional assistance is required, the services of a competent professional person should be sought. Neither the publisher nor the author shall be liable for damages arising herefrom. The fact that an organization or Website is referred to in this work as a citation and/or a potential source of further information does not mean that the author or the publisher endorses the information the organization or Website may provide or recommendations it may make. Further, readers should be aware that Internet Websites listed in this work may have changed or disappeared between when this work was written and when it is read.

For general information on our other products and services or to obtain technical support, please contact our Customer Care Department within the U.S. at (800) 762-2974, outside the U.S. at (317) 572-3993 or fax (317) 572-4002.

Wiley also publishes its books in a variety of electronic formats. Some content that appears in print may not be available in electronic books.

Library of Congress Cataloging-in-Publication Data is available from the publisher.

TRADMARKS: Wiley, the Wiley logo, and the Sybex logo are trademarks or registered trademarks of John Wiley & Sons, Inc. and/or its affiliates, in the United States and other countries, and may not be used without written permission. SQL Server is a trademark of Microsoft Corporation in the United States and/or other countries. All other trademarks are the property of their respective owners. Wiley Publishing, Inc., is not associated with any product or vendor mentioned in this book.

10 9 8 7 6 5 4 3 2 1

This is dedicated to the most important person in my life—my wife, Rachelle.
—Joseph L. Jorden

Acknowledgments

I've authored and tech edited a number of books for Sybex over the years, and each one is more exciting than the last. I can't possibly take all the credit for this book, though; a lot of work goes into these books, and I did only part of it. I always think of my acquisitions editor, Maureen Adams, first. She got the ball rolling and kept the momentum. I would also like to thank the production editor, Rachel Meyers, and the tech editor, Rick Tempestini, for all their hard work in bringing this book to production.

I owe my friends and family special thanks because even though they're not always sure what I'm writing about, they're always excited to see the book. First, my family: my mother, Mary; Buddy and Shelly Jorden; and Janet, Colin, and Leian McBroom—thanks to all of you. Also, when I started babbling on about technical stuff, there were those who patiently sat and listened until I stopped talking: I need to thank everyone at Jelly Belly. As I always say, there is no better place to work than a candy company. For tolerating my offbeat sense of humor and ninja-like stealth, I have to thank Andrea Elliott (watch out, I may be behind you right now). Thanks also to Mark and Marlin Chappell for getting up early and missing their cartoons to work with me all those Saturday mornings. Most important, though, thanks to my wife, Rachelle Jorden, once again for her patience and understanding as I wrote yet another book. Finally, thanks to all of you for reading this work—may it serve you well.

About the Author

Joseph L. Jorden (MCP, MCSE, MCTS) is the Lead Developer for Jelly Belly Candy Company where he spends a great deal of his time developing database applications and assisting the DBA with SQL Server administration tasks. Joseph was one of the first 100 people to achieve the MCSE+I certification from Microsoft, one of the first 2,000 people to earn the MCSE certification on Windows 2000 and he is a charter member of the MCTS certification program. Joseph also spent a few years as an MCT during which time he taught Microsoft Official Curriculum courses about SQL Server 6.5, 7.0, and 2000. He has spoken at PASS conferences and Comdex about SQL Server and other computing subjects. Joseph has also written a number of articles for various publications, and he has written and tech edited several books for Sybex, most of them on the subject of SQL Server.

Contents at a Glance

Contents

Introduction

Microsoft's new generation of certifications is designed not only to emphasize your proficiency with a specific technology but also to prove you have the skills needed to perform a specific role. In other words, you need to know how to use SQL Server 2005 in theory *and* in practice. This makes the MCTS: SQL Server 2005 certification a powerful credential for career advancement.

Obtaining this certification requires you to pass only one exam, Exam 70-431, which is called TS: Microsoft SQL Server 2005 – Implementation and Maintenance. Although I developed this book based on the exam objectives, its purpose is to serve more as a reference than an exam prep book. It guides you through procedures and tasks that solidify related concepts, allowing you to devote your memorization efforts to more abstract theories because you've mastered the more practical topics through doing. So, keep this book handy, because it will serve as a valuable reference during your career as a SQL Server 2005 professional.

The Microsoft Certified Technology Specialist Program

Since the inception of its certification program, Microsoft has certified millions of people. Over the years, Microsoft has learned what it takes to help people show their skills through certification. Based on that experience, Microsoft has introduced a new generation of certifications:

- Microsoft Certified Technology Specialist (MCTS)
- Microsoft Certified IT Professional (MCITP)
- Microsoft Certified Professional Developer (MCPD)
- Microsoft Certified Architect (MCA)

The MCTS certification program is designed to validate core technology and product skills for a specific product. It helps you prove you are capable of implementing, building, troubleshooting, and debugging that product.

The new generation of exams offers a shorter certification path than previous iterations. For example, to become a Microsoft Certified Database Administrator, you had to pass four exams. To obtain an MCTS certification, you need to pass only one exam.

Is This Book for You?

SQL Server 2005 DBA Street Smarts: A Real World Guide to SQL Server 2005 Certification Skills was designed to give you some insight into the world of a typical database administrator by walking you through some of the daily tasks you can expect on the job. You should invest in some equipment to get the full effect from this book; you might even consider using Microsoft's Virtual PC or Virtual Server software (both are available for free download at the time of this writing). However, you can derive much value from simply reading through the tasks without performing the steps on live equipment. Organized classes and study groups are the ideal structures for obtaining and practicing with the recommended equipment.

The *MCTS: Microsoft SQL Server 2005 Implementation and Maintenance Study Guide* (Sybex, 2006) is a recommended companion to this book in your studies for the MCTS: SQL Server 2005 certification.

How This Book Is Organized

This book is organized into four phases of database administration.

Each phase is separated into individual tasks. The phases represent broad categories under which related responsibilities are grouped. The tasks within each phase lead you step-by-step through the processes required for successful completion. When performed in order, the tasks in this book approximate those required by a database administrator over an extended period of time. The four phases and their descriptions follow:

- *Phase 1, "Installing and Configuring Microsoft SQL Server 2005,"* gives you guidance on how to install and configure SQL Server 2005 for the first time. You will then see how to create and secure a variety of database objects.

- *Phase 2, "Implementing High Availability and Disaster Recovery,"* provides practical advice on keeping SQL Server 2005 up and running using database mirroring, log shipping, and database snapshots. You will also see how to prepare for, and recover from, disaster through the backup and restore process. Finally, you will see how to use replication as a powerful high-availability tool.

- *Phase 3, "Maintaining and Automating SQL Server,"* helps you leave work on time by showing you how to automate tasks. You will even see how to get SQL Server to e-mail you with reports and problems.

- *Phase 4, "Monitoring and Troubleshooting SQL Server,"* offers a wealth of information on finding problems before the users find them. Once you've found the issues through monitoring, you'll get some good advice on troubleshooting as well.

Each task in this book is organized into sections aimed at giving you what you need when you need it. The first section introduces you to the task and any key concepts that can assist you in understanding the underlying technology and the overall procedure. Descriptions of the remaining sections follow:

- *The "Scenario"* section places you in the shoes of the database administrator, describing a situation in which you will likely find yourself. The scenario is closely related to and solved by the task at hand.

- *The "Scope of Task"* section is all about preparing for the task. It gives you an idea of how much time is required to complete the task, what setup procedures are needed before beginning, and any concerns or issues that may arise.

- *The "Procedure"* section is the actual meat of the task. This section informs you of the equipment required to perform the task in a lab environment. It also gives you the ordered steps to complete the task.
- *The "Criteria for Completion"* section briefly explains the outcome you should expect after completing the task. Any deviation from the result described is an excellent reason to perform the task again and watch for sources of the variation.

How to Contact the Publisher

Sybex welcomes feedback on all of its books. Visit the Sybex website at www.sybex.com or the Wiley website at www.wiley.com for book updates and additional certification information. You'll also find forms you can use to submit comments or suggestions regarding this or any other Sybex book.

How to Contact the Author

Joseph L. Jorden welcomes your questions and comments. You can reach him by e-mail at JLJorden@comcast.net.

The TS: Microsoft SQL Server 2005 – Implementation and Maintenance Exam Objectives

The following are the areas in which you must be proficient in order to pass the TS: Microsoft SQL Server 2005 – Implementation and Maintenance exam.

- Installing and configuring SQL Server 2005
    - Verify prerequisites.
    - Upgrade from a previous version of SQL Server.
    - Create a named instance.
    - Configure log files and data files.
    - Configure the SQL Server SQLiMail subsystem.
    - Choose a recovery mode for the database.
    - Configure server security principals.
    - Configure server securables.
    - Identify the external data source.
    - Identify the characteristics of the data source.
    - Identify the security model of the data source.
- Implementing high availability
    - Distinguish between replication types.

- Configure a publisher, a distributor, and a subscriber.
- Configure replication security.
- Configure conflict resolution settings for merge replication.
- Monitor replication.
- Prepare databases for mirroring.
- Create endpoints.
- Specify database partners.
- Specify a witness server.
- Configure an operating mode.
- Initialize a secondary database.
- Configure log-shipping options.
- Configure a log-shipping mode.
- Configure monitoring.
- Create a snapshot.
- Revert a database from a snapshot.
- Supporting data consumers
  - Construct SQL queries to return data.
  - Format the results of SQL queries.
  - Identify collation details.
  - Insert update and delete data.
  - Handle exceptions and errors.
  - Manage transactions.
  - Identify the specific structure needed by a consumer.
  - Retrieve XML data.
  - Modify XML data.
  - Convert between XML data and relational data.
  - Create an XML index.
  - Load an XML schema.
  - Create an HTTP endpoint.
  - Secure an HTTP endpoint.
  - Create services.
  - Create queues.
  - Create contracts.

- Create conversations.
- Create message types.
- Send messages to a service.
- Set a database to the Bulk-Logged recovery model to avoid inflating the transaction log.
- Run the `bcp` utility.
- Perform a bulk insert task.
- Import bulk XML data by using the `OPENROWSET` function.
- Copy data from one table to another by using the SQL Server 2005 Integration Services (SSIS) Import and Export Wizard.

- Maintaining databases
  - Set a job owner.
  - Create a job schedule.
  - Create job steps.
  - Configure job steps.
  - Disable a job.
  - Create a maintenance job.
  - Set up alerts.
  - Configure operators.
  - Modify a job.
  - Delete a job.
  - Manage index fragmentation.
  - Manage statistics.
  - Shrink files.
  - Perform database integrity checks by using `DBCC CHECKDB`.
  - Perform a full backup.
  - Perform a differential backup.
  - Perform a transaction log backup.
  - Initialize a media set by using the `FORMAT` option.
  - Append or overwrite an existing media set.
  - Create a backup device.
  - Identify which files are needed from the backup strategy.
  - Restore a database from a single file and from multiple files.
  - Choose an appropriate restore method.
  - Choose an appropriate method for moving a database.

- Monitoring and troubleshooting SQL Server performance
  - Start a new trace.
  - Save the trace logs.
  - Configure SQL Server Profiler trace properties.
  - Configure a System Monitor counter log.
  - Correlate a SQL Server Profiler trace with System Monitor log data.
  - Build a workload file by using SQL Server Profiler.
  - Tune a workload file by using the Database Engine Tuning Advisor.
  - Save recommended indexes.
  - Identify the cause of a block by using the `sys.dm_exec_requests` system view.
  - Terminate an errant process.
  - Configure SQL Server Profiler trace properties.
  - Connect to a nonresponsive server by using the Dedicated Administrator Connection (DAC).
  - Review SQL Server start-up logs.
  - Review error messages in event logs.
  - Identify the cause of a failure.
  - Identify outcome details.
  - Find out when a job last ran.
- Creating and implementing database objects
  - Specify column details.
  - Specify the file group.
  - Assign permissions to a role for tables.
  - Specify a partition scheme when creating a table.
  - Create an indexed view.
  - Create an updateable view.
  - Assign permissions to a role or schema for a view.
  - Create a trigger.
  - Create DDL triggers for responding to database structure changes.
  - Identify recursive triggers.
  - Identify nested triggers.
  - Create a function.
  - Identify deterministic versus nondeterministic functions.
  - Create a stored procedure.

- Recompile a stored procedure.
- Assign permissions to a role for a stored procedure.
- Specify the scope of a constraint.
- Create a new constraint.
- Specify the filegroup.
- Specify the index type.
- Specify relational index options.
- Specify columns.
- Specify a partition scheme when creating an index.
- Disable an index.
- Create an online index by using an `ONLINE` argument.
- Create a Transact-SQL user-defined type.
- Specify details of the data type.
- Create a CLR user-defined type.
- Create a catalog.
- Create an index.
- Specify a full-text population method.

Phase
1

Installing and Configuring Microsoft SQL Server 2005

Many people are so excited to start working with their new software that they just start installing it without verifying they meet the prerequisites; you may have even done this yourself in the past. To ensure a successful installation of SQL Server 2005, though, you need to make sure you have the right hardware and software in place first; otherwise, you will end up with a mess. Once you have installed SQL Server 2005, you then need to configure it before you can let your users start working with it. The tasks in this phase will show you how to successfully install and configure SQL Server 2005.

Task 1.1: Verifying Prerequisites and Installing the Default Instance

In this task, you will verify that your machine meets the prerequisites for installing SQL Server 2005, and then you will install the default instance.

Scenario

You are the database administrator (DBA) for a midsize company with offices in various cities throughout the United States and Canada. The company has decided to use SQL Server 2005 for data storage and retrieval, and you have been asked to install the software and get it running.

As an experienced DBA, you understand the importance of installing the software right the first time, because if you install SQL Server incorrectly or on the wrong hardware, it will work slowly or not at all. Therefore, you have decided to verify the prerequisites and then install the software.

Scope of Task

Duration

This task should take less than one hour.

Setup

This task requires little setup. All you need is access to a copy of SQL Server 2005 Enterprise Edition and a computer that meets the requirements to run it.

Caveat

It seems redundant, but SQL Server 2005 runs better on faster hardware. So, remember that the minimum requirements listed later in this task are just that, minimum. If you have access to a faster machine with more random access memory (RAM), use it.

Procedure

In this task, you will verify that your computer meets the requirements for running SQL Server 2005 and then install the default instance.

Equipment Used

Although several editions of SQL Server 2005 exist, you will be working with the Enterprise Edition in this book because it has the widest range of available features. You can download a 180-day trial copy of Enterprise Edition from the Microsoft website (`http://www.microsoft.com/sql`). You will also need access to a machine that meets the prerequisites for Enterprise Edition.

Details

First, you must make certain your server meets the requirements for installing SQL Server 2005. Table 1.1 lists the prerequisites for installing the Standard, Developer, and Enterprise Editions.

TABLE 1.1   Developer/Standard/Enterprise Edition Requirements

Component	32-bit	x64	Itanium
Processor	600MHz Pentium III–compatible or faster processor; 1GHz or faster processor recommended	1GHz AMD Opteron, AMD Athlon 64, Intel Xeon with Intel EM64T support, Intel Pentium IV with EM64T support processor	1GHz Itanium or faster processor
Memory	512MB of RAM or more; 1GB or more recommended	512MB of RAM or more; 1GB or more recommended	512MB of RAM or more; 1GB or more recommended
Disk drive	CD or DVD drive	CD or DVD drive	CD or DVD drive

TABLE 1.1   Developer/Standard/Enterprise Edition Requirements *(continued)*

Component	32-bit	x64	Itanium
Hard disk space	Approximately 350MB of available hard disk space for the recommended installation with approximately 425MB of additional space for SQL Server BOL, SQL Server Mobile BOL, and sample databases	Approximately 350MB of available hard disk space for the recommended installation with approximately 425MB of additional space for SQL Server BOL, SQL Server Mobile BOL, and sample databases	Approximately 350MB of available hard disk space for the recommended installation with approximately 425MB of additional space for SQL Server BOL, SQL Server Mobile BOL, and sample databases
Operating system	Microsoft Windows 2000 Server with SP4 or newer; Windows 2000 Professional Edition with SP4 or newer; Windows XP with SP2 or newer; Windows Server 2003 Enterprise Edition, Standard Edition, or Datacenter Edition with SP1 or newer; Windows Small Business Server 2003 with SP1 or newer	Microsoft Windows Server 2003 Standard x64 Edition, Enterprise x64 Edition, or Datacenter x64 Edition with SP1 or newer; Windows XP Professional x64 Edition or newer	Microsoft Windows Server 2003 Enterprise Edition or Datacenter Edition for Itanium-based systems with SP1 or newer

Second, after you have verified that your machine can handle SQL Server 2005, you can begin the installation. Follow these steps (which are for installing Enterprise Edition, but the steps are similar for all editions):

1. You need to create a service account, so create a user account named SqlServer, and make it a member of the Administrators local group. You can perform this task using one of these tools:

   - On a Windows member server or on Windows XP, use Computer Management.

   - On a Windows domain controller, use Active Directory Users and Computers.

2. Insert the SQL Server CD, and wait for the automenu to open.

3. Under Install, choose Server Components ➢ Tools ➢ Books Online ➢ Samples.

4. You will then be asked to read and agree with the end user license agreement (EULA); check the box to agree, and click Next.

5. If your machine does not have all the prerequisite software installed, the setup will install them for you at this time. Click Install if you are asked to do so. When complete, click Next.

6. Next you will see a screen telling you that the setup is inspecting your system's configuration again, and then the welcome screen appears. Click Next to continue.

7. Another, more in-depth system configuration screen appears letting you know whether any configuration settings will prevent SQL Server from being installed. You need to repair errors (marked with a red icon) before you can continue. You can optionally repair warnings (marked with a yellow icon), which will not prevent SQL Server from installing. Once you have made any needed changes, click Next.

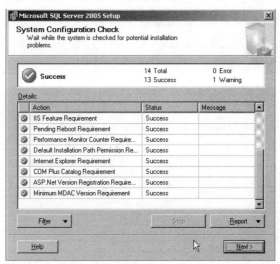

8. After a few configuration setting screens, you will be asked for your product key. Enter it, and click Next.

9. On the next screen, you need to select the components you want to install. Check the boxes next to the SQL Server Database Services option and the Workstation Components, Books Online and Development Tools option.

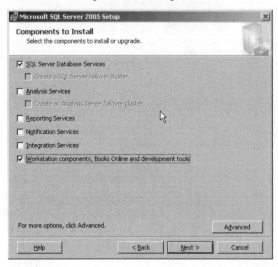

10. Click the Advanced button to view the advanced options for the setup.

11. Expand Documentation ➤ Samples ➤ Sample Databases. Then click the button next to Sample Databases, select Entire Feature Will Be Installed on Local Hard Drive, and then click Next. (This will install the AdventureWorks database you will be using later in this book.)

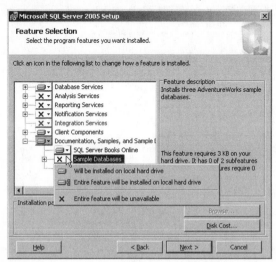

12. On the Instance Name screen, choose Default Instance, and click Next.

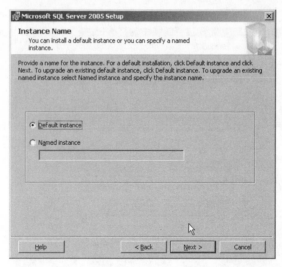

13. On the next screen, enter the account information for the service account you created in step 1. You will be using the same account for each service. When finished, click Next.

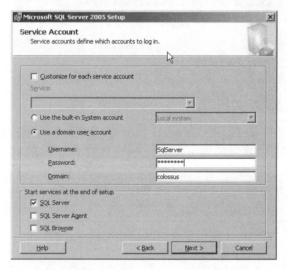

14. On the Authentication Mode screen, select Mixed Mode, enter a password for the sa account, and click Next.

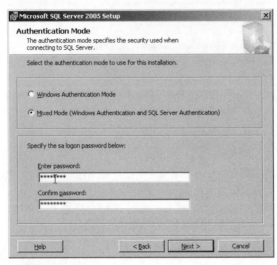

15. Select the Latin1_General collation designator on the next screen, and click Next.

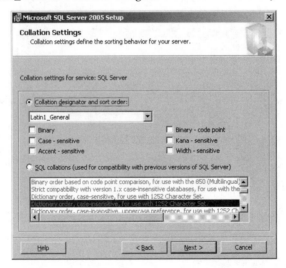

16. On the following screen, you can select to send error and feature usage information directly to Microsoft. You will not be enabling this function here. So, leave the defaults, and click Next.

17. On the Ready to Install screen, review your settings, and then click Install.

18. The setup progress appears during the install process. When the setup is finished (which may take several minutes), click Next.

19. The final screen gives you an installation report, letting you know whether any errors occurred and reminding you of any post-installation steps to take. Click Finish to complete your install.

20. Reboot your system if requested to do so.

Criteria for Completion

You have completed this task when you have a running instance of SQL Server 2005 installed on your system. To verify this, select Start ➢ All Programs ➢ Microsoft SQL Server 2005 ➢ Configuration Tools ➢ SQL Server Configuration Manager. Select SQL Server 2005 Services, and check the icons. If the icon next to SQL Server (MSSQLServer) service is green, then your installation is a success (see Figure 1.1).

FIGURE 1.1   Check SQL Server Configuration Manager to see whether your services are running after installation.

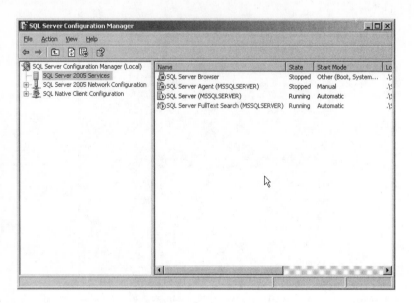

Task 1.2: Installing a Second Instance

Using a technique called *instancing*, you can have more than one copy of SQL Server 2005 running on the same computer at the same time. Each instance has its own set of system databases and its own security system in place. This is useful if you need a server for production and another for testing but you do not have enough hardware for two separate physical machines or you need to have two or more systems with disparate security settings. Throughout this book, you will be using a named instance in order to get some practice with the more advanced features of SQL Server 2005 (such as replication). In this task, you will install a second instance of SQL Server 2005 on the same machine as the default instance.

Scenario

You are the database administrator (DBA) for a midsize company with offices in various cities throughout the United States and Canada. You know you need an instance of SQL Server 2005 for testing new service packs, new database schemas, and the like, but your company does not have the budget for new hardware at this time. The only way for you to have a test copy of SQL Server is to install a named instance.

Scope of Task

Duration

This task should take less than one hour.

Setup

Again, all you need for this task is the machine you used in Task 1.1 and the same copy of SQL Server 2005 you used in Task 1.1.

Caveat

This task doesn't have any caveats.

Procedure

In this task, you will install a second instance of SQL Server on the same machine used in Task 1.1.

Equipment Used

All you need for this task is the machine you used in Task 1.1 and the same copy of SQL Server 2005 you used in Task 1.1.

Details

Follow these steps to create a second instance of SQL Server on the same machine as the default instance:

1. Insert the SQL Server CD, and wait for the automenu to open.

2. Under Install, choose Server Components ➤ Tools ➤ Books Online ➤ Samples.

3. You will then be asked to read and agree with the end user license agreement (EULA); check the box to agree, and click Next.

4. If your machine does not have all the prerequisite software installed, the setup will install them for you at this time. Click Install if you are asked to do so. When complete, click Next.

5. Next you will see a screen telling you the setup is inspecting your system's configuration again, and then the welcome screen appears. Click Next to continue.

6. Another, more in-depth system configuration screen appears letting you know whether any configuration settings will prevent SQL Server from being installed. You need to repair errors (marked with a red icon) before you can continue. You can optionally repair warnings (marked with a yellow icon), which will not prevent SQL Server from installing. Once you have made any needed changes, click Next.

7. After a few configuration setting screens, you will be asked for your registration information. Enter it, and click Next.

8. On the next screen, you need to select the components you want to install. Check the box next to SQL Server Database Services, and click Next.

9. On the Instance Name screen, choose Named Instance, and in the text box enter **Second**. Then click Next.

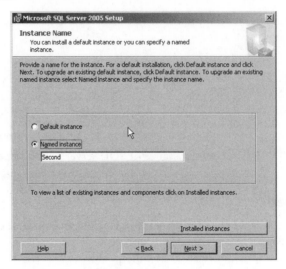

10. On the next screen, enter the account information for the service account you created in step 1 of Task 1.1. You will be using the same account for each service. When finished, click Next.

11. On the Authentication Mode screen, select Mixed Mode, enter a password for the sa account, and click Next.

12. Select the Latin1_General collation designator on the next screen, and click Next.

13. On the following screen, you can select to send error and feature usage information directly to Microsoft. You will not be enabling this function here. So, leave the defaults, and click Next.

14. On the Ready to Install screen, you can review your settings, and then click Install.

15. The setup progress appears during the install process. When the setup is finished (which may take several minutes), click Next.

16. The final screen gives you an installation report, letting you know whether any errors occurred and reminding you of any post-installation steps to take. Click Finish to complete your install.

17. Reboot your system if requested to do so.

Criteria for Completion

You have completed this task when you have a second running instance of SQL Server 2005 installed on your system. To verify this, select to Start ➢ Microsoft SQL Server 2005 ➢ Configuration Tools ➢ SQL Server Configuration Manager. Select SQL Server 2005 Services, and refer to the icons. If the icon next to SQL Server (Second) instance is green, then your installation is a success (see Figure 1.2).

FIGURE 1.2   Check SQL Server Configuration Manager to see whether your services are running for the Second instance.

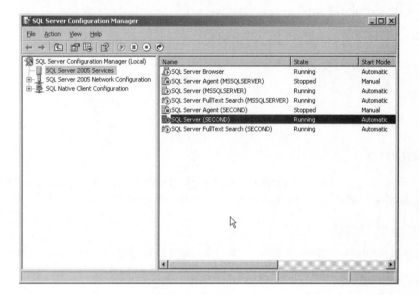

Task 1.3: Designing and Creating a Database

SQL Server 2005 stores your database information in two types of files: one or more database files and one or more transaction log files. As a database administrator (DBA), it is your duty to design and create databases to store user data and other objects. As part of your role as a database creator, you must decide how large to make these database files and what type of growth characteristics they should have, as well as their physical placement on your system.

In this task, you will decide where to put the data and log files and then create a database.

Scenario

You are the DBA for a midsize company with offices in various cities throughout the United States and Canada. You have just installed a new instance of SQL Server, and now you need to create a database to hold data for your sales department.

Scope of Task

Duration

This task should take approximately 30 minutes.

Setup

All you need for this task is access to the machine you installed SQL Server 2005 on in Task 1.1.

Caveat

This task doesn't have any caveats.

Procedure

In this task, you will create a database that will hold data for the sales department. You will use this database in later tasks for storing other database objects as well.

Equipment Used

All you need for this task is access to the machine you installed SQL Server 2005 on in Task 1.1.

Details

First, you must decide where to put the data and log files. Here are some guidelines to use:

- Data and log files should be on separate physical drives so that, in case of a disaster, you have a better chance of recovering all data.

- Transaction logs are best placed on a RAID-1 array because this has the fastest sequential write speed.

- Data files are best placed on a RAID-5 array because they have faster read speed than other RAID-arrays.

- If you have access to a RAID-10 array, you can place data and log files on it because it has all the advantages of RAID-1 and RAID-5.

Next, you must decide how big your files should be. Data files are broken down into 8KB pages and 64KB extents (eight contiguous pages). To figure out how big your database will need to be, you must figure out how big your tables will be. You can do that using these steps:

1. Calculate the space used by a single row of the table.

   a. To do this, add the storage requirements for each datatype in the table.

   b. Add the null bitmap using this formula: `null_bitmap = 2 + ((number of columns + 7) /8)`.

   c. Calculate the space required for variable length columns using this formula: `variable_datasize = 2 + (num_variable_columns X 2) + max_varchar_size`.

   d. Calculate the total row size using this formula: `Row_Size = Fixed_Data_Size + Variable_Data_Size + Null_Bitmap + Row_Header`.

NOTE   The row header is always 4 bytes.

2. Calculate the number of rows that will fit on one page. Each page is 8,192 bytes with a header, so each page holds 8,096 bytes of data. Therefore, calculate the number of rows using this formula: `8096 ÷ (RowSize + 2)`.

3. Estimate the number of rows the table will hold. No formula exists to calculate this; you just need to have a good understanding of your data and user community.

4. Calculate the total number of pages that will be required to hold these rows. Use this formula: `Total Number of Pages = Number of Rows in Table / Number of Rows Per Page`.

Once you have decided where to put your files and how big they should be, follow these steps to create a database named Sales (you will be creating the files on a single drive for simplicity):

1. Start SQL Server Management Studio by selecting Start ➢ Programs ➢ Microsoft SQL Server 2005 ➢ Management Studio.

2. Connect to your default instance of SQL Server.

3. Expand your Databases folder.

4. Right-click either the Databases folder in the console tree or the white space in the right pane, and choose New Database from the context menu.

5. You should now see the General tab of the Database properties sheet. Enter the database name **Sales**, and leave the owner as <default>.

6. In the data files grid, in the Logical Name column, change the name of the primary data file to **Sales_Data**. Use the default location for the file, and make sure the initial size is 3.

7. Click the ellipsis button (the one with three periods) in the Autogrowth column for the Sales_Data file. In the dialog box that opens, check the Restricted File Growth radio button, and restrict the filegrowth to 20MB.

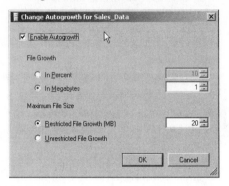

8. To add a secondary data file, click the Add button, and change the logical name of the new file to **Sales_Data2**. Here too use the default location for the file, and make sure the initial size is 3.

9. Restrict the filegrowth to a maximum of 20MB for Sales_Data2 by clicking the ellipsis button in the Autogrowth column.

10. Leave all of the defaults for the Sales_Log file.

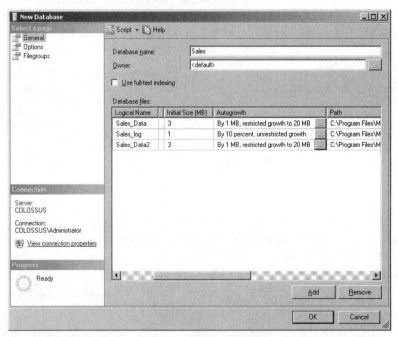

11. Click OK when you are finished. You should now have a new Sales database.

Criteria for Completion

You have completed this task when you have a database named Sales that you can see in SQL Server Management Studio, as shown in Figure 1.3.

FIGURE 1.3   You should see a database named Sales in SQL Server Management Studio.

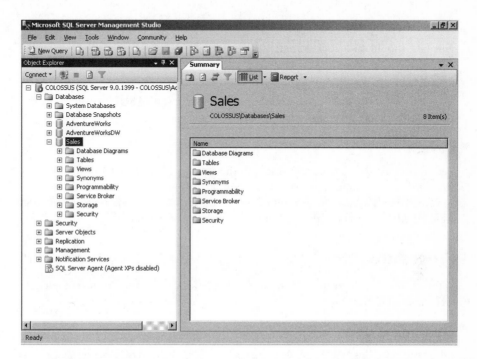

Task 1.4: Designing and Creating a Table

All of the data in a database is logically organized into tables. Each table in turn is divided into columns and rows (or fields and records). Each table holds a grouping of related data. For example, if you are creating a database to hold sales information, you may have one table for available products, another table for orders placed, another for salesperson territories, and so on.

To create a table, you need to know what data will be stored in the table so you can decide which columns should be in the table and what datatype each column should be. These decisions are different for each database in each company. In this task, you will be creating some tables in your Sales database.

Scenario

You have just created a database for your sales department, and now you need to create some tables to hold customer, product, and order data.

Scope of Task

Duration

This task should take approximately 30 minutes.

Setup

All you need for this task is access to the machine you installed SQL Server 2005 on in Task 1.1 and the Sales database you created in Task 1.3.

Caveat

Remember that this is just an exercise. In the real world, you would probably have multiple tables for each of these categories. For example, you would have an OrderHeader table and an OrderDetails table to store multiple line items for a single order. You are creating a single table for each category in this task only for the sake of simplicity.

Procedure

In this task, you will create three tables in your Sales database: a Products table, a Customers table, and an Orders table.

Equipment Used

All you need for this task is access to the machine you installed SQL Server 2005 on in Task 1.1 and the Sales database you created in Task 1.3.

Details

You will be creating three tables based on these criteria, as shown in Table 1.2, Table 1.3, and Table 1.3.

TABLE 1.2   Products Table Fields

Field Name	Datatype	Contains
ProdID	Int, Identity	A unique ID number for each product that can be referenced in other tables to avoid data duplication

TABLE 1.2   Products Table Fields *(continued)*

Field Name	Datatype	Contains
Description	Nvarchar(100)	A brief text description of the product
InStock	Int	The amount of product in stock

TABLE 1.3   Customers Table Fields

Field Name	Datatype	Contains
CustID	Int, Identity	A unique number for each customer that can be referenced in other tables
Fname	Nvarchar(20)	The customer's first name
Lname	Nvarchar(20)	The customer's last name
Address	Nvarchar(50)	The customer's street address
City	Nvarchar(20)	The city where the customer lives
State	Nchar(2)	The state where the customer lives
Zip	Nchar(5)	The customer's ZIP code
Phone	Nchar(10)	The customer's phone number without hyphens or parentheses (to save space, those will be displayed but not stored)

TABLE 1.4   Orders Table Fields

Field Name	Datatype	Contains
CustID	Int	References the customer number stored in the Customers table so you don't need to duplicate the customer information for each order placed
ProdID	Int	References the Products table so you don't need to duplicate product information
Qty	Int	The amount of product sold for an order
OrdDate	Smalldatetime	The date and time the order was placed

Follow these steps to create the Products table in the Sales database:

1. Open SQL Server Management Studio. In Object Explorer, expand your server, and expand Databases ➢ Sales.

2. Right-click the Tables icon, and select New Table to open the table designer.

3. In the first row, under Column Name, enter **ProdID**.

4. Just to the right of that, under Data Type, select Int.

5. Make certain Allow Nulls isn't checked. The field can be completely void of data if this option is checked, and you don't want that here.

6. In the bottom half of the screen, under Column Properties, in the Table Designer section, expand Identity Specification, and change (Is Identity) to Yes.

7. Just under ProdID, in the second row under Column Name, enter **Description**.

8. Just to the right of that, under Data Type, enter **nvarchar(100)**.

9. Make certain Allow Nulls is cleared.

10. Under Column Name in the third row, enter **InStock**.

11. Under Data Type, select Int.

12. Uncheck Allow Nulls.

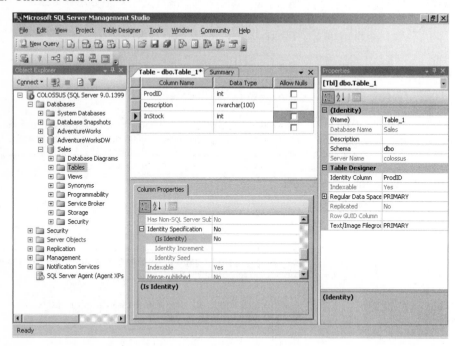

13. Click the Save button on the left side of the toolbar (it looks like a floppy disk).

14. In the Choose Name box that opens, enter **Products**, then click OK.

15. Close the table designer by clicking the *X* in the upper-right corner of the window.

Now, follow these steps to create the Customers table:

1. Right-click the Tables icon, and select New Table to open the table designer.

2. In the first row, under Column Name, enter **CustID**.

3. Under Data Type, select Int.

4. Make certain Allow Nulls isn't checked.

5. Under Column Properties, in the Table Designer section, expand Identity Specification, and change (Is Identity) to Yes.

6. Just under CustID, in the second row under Column Name, enter **Fname**.

7. Just to the right of that, under Data Type, enter **nvarchar(20)**.

8. Make certain Allow Nulls is unchecked.

9. Using the parameters displayed earlier, fill in the information for the remaining columns. Don't allow nulls in any of the fields.

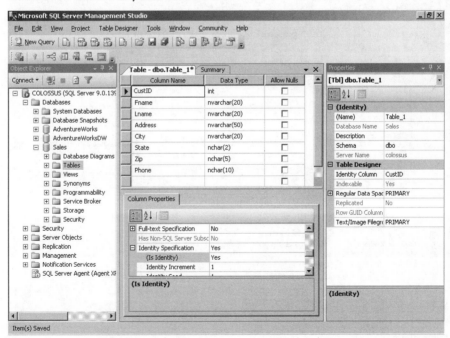

10. Click the Save button.

11. In the Choose Name box that opens, enter **Customers**, then click OK.

12. Close the table designer.

Now follow the same steps to create the Orders table:

1. Right-click the Tables icon, and select New Table to open the table designer.

2. In the first row, under Column Name, enter **CustID**.

3. Under Data Type, select Int.

4. Make certain Allow Nulls isn't checked.

5. This won't be an identity column like it was in the Customers table, so don't make any changes to the Identity Specification settings.

6. Just under CustID, in the second row under Column Name, enter **ProdID** with a datatype of int. Don't change the Identity Specification settings. Don't allow null values.

7. Just below ProdID, create a field named Qty with a datatype of int that doesn't allow nulls.

8. Create a column named OrdDate with a datatype of smalldatetime. Don't allow null values.

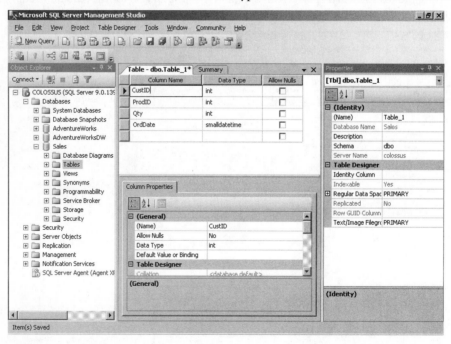

9. Click the Save button.

10. In the Choose Name box that opens, enter **Orders**, then click OK.

11. Close the table designer.

Criteria for Completion

You have completed this task when you have the Products, Customers, and Orders tables in your database with the columns defined in the exercise. To verify this, just expand your Sales database in SQL Server Management Studio and then expand Tables; you should see all three tables, as shown in Figure 1.4.

FIGURE 1.4   You should see the Products, Customers, and Orders tables in your Sales database.

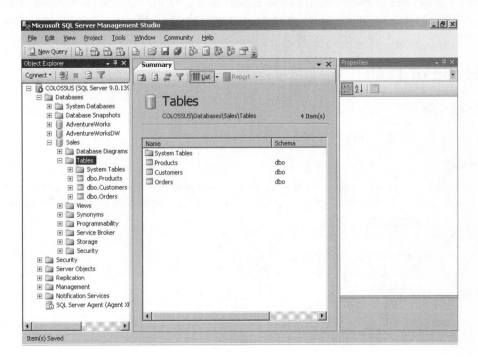

Task 1.5: Designing and Creating a Constraint

When you first create a table, it's wide open to your users. It's true that they can't violate datatype restrictions by entering characters in an int type field and the like, but that is really the only restriction. It's safe to say you probably want more restrictions than that. For example, you probably don't want your users to enter **XZ** for a state abbreviation in a State field (because

XZ isn't a valid state abbreviation), and you don't want them entering numbers for someone's first name. You need to restrict what your users can enter in your fields, which you can do by using constraints. In this task, you will create constraints on your Customers table in the Sales database.

Scenario

You have just created tables in your new Sales database, one of which holds customer information. You want to make certain that users enter only valid ZIP codes in the Zip field of the Customers table, so you decide to create a constraint to restrict the data that can be entered in the field.

Scope of Task

Duration

This task should take approximately 15 minutes.

Setup

For this exercise, you need access to the machine you installed SQL Server 2005 on in Task 1.1, the Sales database you created in Task 1.3, and the Customers table you created in Task 1.4.

Caveat

This task doesn't have any caveats.

Procedure

In this task, you will create a constraint on the Customers table to prevent users from entering invalid ZIP codes. Specifically, you will prevent users from entering letters; they can enter only numbers.

Equipment Used

For this exercise, you need access to the machine you installed SQL Server 2005 on in Task 1.1, the Sales database you created in Task 1.3, and the Customers table you created in Task 1.4.

Details

Follow these steps to create a constraint on the Zip field of the Customers table:

1. In Object Explorer, expand the Sales database, and expand Tables ➤ dbo.Customers.

2. Right-click Constraints, and click New Constraint.

3. In the New Constraint dialog box, enter **CK_Zip** in the (Name) text box.

4. In the Description text box, enter **Check for valid zip codes**.

5. To create a constraint that will accept only five numbers that can be zero through nine, enter the following code in the Expression text box:

```
(zip like '[0-9][0-9][0-9][0-9][0-9]')
```

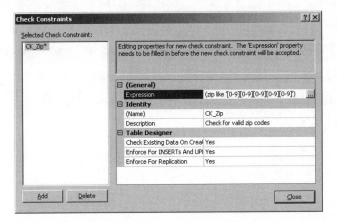

6. Click Close.

7. Click the Save button at the top left of the toolbar.

8. Close the table designer (which was opened when you started to create the constraint).

Criteria for Completion

This task is complete when you have a constraint that prevents users from entering letters in the Zip field of the Customers table. To test your new constraint, follow these steps:

1. In SQL Server Management Studio, and click the New Query button.

2. Enter the following code in the query window:

```
USE Sales
INSERT Customers
VALUES ('Greg','Scott','111 Main','Provo'
,'UT','88102','5045551212')
```

3. Click the Execute button just above the query window to execute the query, and notice the successful results.

4. To see the new record, click the New Query button, and execute the following code:

```
SELECT * FROM customers
```

5. Notice that the record now exists with a CustID of 1 (because of the identity property discussed earlier, which automatically added the number for you).

6. To test the check constraint by adding characters in the Zip field, click the New Query button, and execute the following code (note the letters in the Zip field):

```
USE Sales
INSERT customers
VALUES ('Amanda','Smith','817 3rd','Chicago','IL','AAB1C','8015551212')
```

7. Notice in the results pane that the query violated a constraint and so failed.

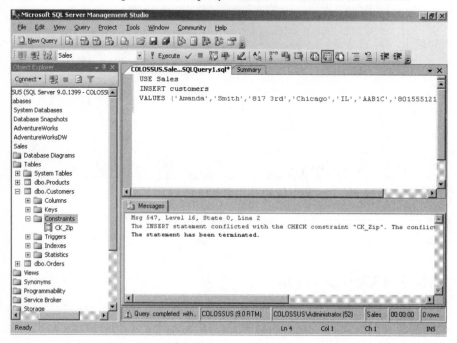

Task 1.6: Designing and Creating a View

Microsoft describes a *view* as a virtual table or a stored SELECT query. Views do not hold any data themselves; they represent the data that is stored in a table. Of course, views offer more advantages than just looking at the data stored in a table. For instance, you may want to see only a subset of records in a large table, or you may want to see data from multiple tables in a single query. Both of these are good reasons to use a view. In this task, you will create a view based on the Person.Contact table in the AdventureWorks database.

Scenario

You have a database that has been in use for some time and has a number of records in the Contacts table. Your users have asked you to break this data down for them by area code. You have decided that the easiest way to accomplish this goal is to create a view that displays only a subset of data from the table based on the area code.

Scope of Task

Duration

This task should take approximately 15 minutes.

Setup

For this exercise, you need access to the machine you installed SQL Server 2005 on in Task 1.1 and the AdventureWorks database that is installed with the sample data.

Caveat

Realistically, views won't be this simplistic in the real world; this is just to keep the exercise simple.

Procedure

In this task, you will create a view based on the Person.Contact table in the AdventureWorks database. Specifically, you will create a view that displays only those customers in the 398 area code.

Equipment Used

For this task, you need access to the machine you installed SQL Server 2005 on in Task 1.1 and the AdventureWorks database that is installed with the sample data.

Details

Follow these steps to create the Contacts_in_398 view:

1. Open SQL Server Management Studio by selecting it from the Microsoft SQL Server 2005 group under Programs on your Start menu, and connect with Windows Authentication if requested.

2. In Object Explorer, expand your server, and then expand Databases ➤ AdventureWorks. Right-click Views, and select New View.

3. In the Add Table dialog box, select Contact (Person), and click Add.

4. Click Close, this opens the view designer.

5. In the Transact-SQL syntax editor text box, under the column grid, enter the following:

```
SELECT LastName, FirstName, Phone
FROM Person.Contact
WHERE (Phone LIKE '398%')
```

6. Click the Execute button (the red exclamation point) on the toolbar to test the query.

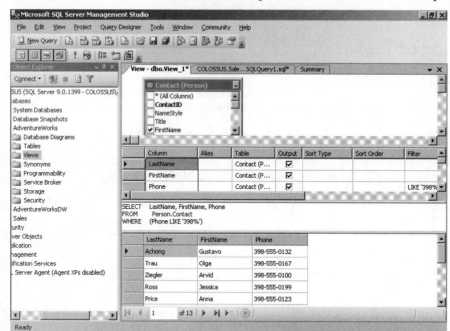

7. Choose File ➢ Save View – dbo.View_1.

8. In the Choose Name dialog box, enter **Contacts_in_398**, and click OK.

9. To test the view, click the New Query button, and execute the following code:

```
USE AdventureWorks
SELECT * FROM dbo.Contacts_in_398
```

10. To verify that the results are accurate, open a new query, and execute the code used to create the view:

```
USE AdventureWorks
SELECT lastname, firstname, phone from Person.Contact
WHERE phone LIKE '398%'
```

Criteria for Completion

This task is complete when you can query the Contacts_in_398 view and retrieve the correct results. To test your view, execute this code:

```
USE AdventureWorks
SELECT * FROM dbo.Contacts_in_398
```

You should see the results shown in Figure 1.5.

FIGURE 1.5   You should see only those contacts in the 398 area code.

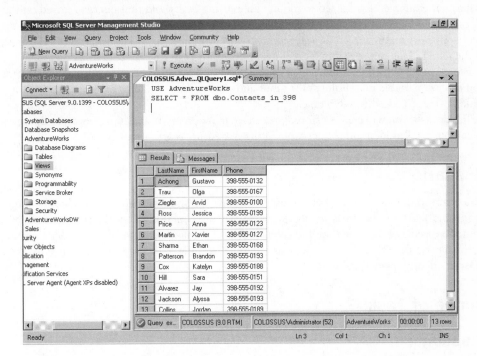

Task 1.7: Designing and Creating a Stored Procedure

A *stored procedure* is a query that is stored in a database on SQL Server rather than being stored in the front-end code on the client machine (also called an *ad hoc query*). Several good reasons exist for doing this.

One advantage of using stored procedures is that when SQL Server receives a query, it compiles it. In other words, it reads the query, looks at such things as JOINs and WHERE clauses, and compares that query with all the available indexes to see which index (if any) would return data to the user fastest. Once SQL Server determines which indexes will function best, it creates a set of instructions telling SQL Server how to run the query (called an *execution plan*), which is stored in memory. Ad hoc queries must be compiled nearly every time they're run whereas stored procedures are precompiled. This means stored procedures have gone through the compilation process and have a plan waiting in memory; therefore, they execute faster than ad hoc queries.

Another advantage of using stored procedures is that they can make database management easier. For example, if you need to modify an existing query and that query is stored on the users' machines, you must make those changes on all of the users' machines. If you store the query centrally on the server, as a stored procedure, you need to make the changes only once, at the server. This can save you a great deal of time and effort.

Stored procedures can also accept variable input and produce variable output. This means you can use variable placeholders for input and output data, which is extremely useful for making stored procedures dynamic.

In this task, you will create a stored procedure that accepts an input parameter and returns data from the Production.Product table in the AdventureWorks database.

Scenario

You have a database that has been in use for some time and has a number of records in the Product table. Your users frequently query the table for data based on the SellStartDate column. To speed up execution time and enhance ease of management, you have decided to create a stored procedure that accepts a date as an input parameter and returns a result set of the most frequently queried columns.

Scope of Task

Duration

This task should take approximately 15 minutes.

Setup

For this task, you need access to the machine you installed SQL Server 2005 on in Task 1.1 and the AdventureWorks database that is installed with the sample data.

Caveat

This task doesn't have any caveats.

Procedure

In this task, you will create a stored procedure based on the Production.Product table in the AdventureWorks database. Specifically, you will create a stored procedure that returns product data based on an input parameter.

Equipment Used

For this task, you need access to the machine you installed SQL Server 2005 on in Task 1.1 and the AdventureWorks database that is installed with the sample data.

Details

Follow these steps to create the Production.Show_Products stored procedure:

1. Open SQL Server Management Studio. In Object Explorer, expand your server, and then expand Databases ➤ AdventureWorks ➤ Programmability.

2. Right-click the Stored Procedures icon, and select New Stored Procedure to open a new query window populated with a stored procedure template.

3. In the Transact-SQL syntax box, change the code to look like this:

```
CREATE PROCEDURE Production.Show_Products
    @Date datetime
AS
BEGIN
    SELECT Name, Color, ListPrice, SellStartDate
    FROM Production.Product
    WHERE SellStartDate > @Date
    ORDER BY SellStartDate, Name
END
GO
```

4. Click the Execute button on the toolbar to create the procedure.

5. Close the query window.

Criteria for Completion

This task is complete when you can execute the Production.Show_Products stored procedure using an input parameter and have it return the correct results. Execute the following code in a new query window to test your stored procedure:

```
USE AdventureWorks
EXEC Production.Show_Products '1/1/1998'
```

You should see the results shown in Figure 1.6.

FIGURE 1.6   You should see only those products that are available after January 1, 1998.

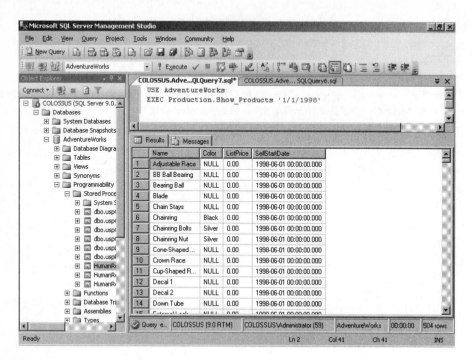

Task 1.8: Designing and Creating an *INSERT* Trigger

As I discuss later in this book, you can control access to data by assigning permissions for objects (such as tables) to users. You can use these permissions to prevent users from inserting new data or modifying or deleting existing data. If you want more granular control than that, you can use triggers.

A *trigger* is a collection of SQL statements that looks and acts a great deal like a stored procedure. The only real difference between the two is that a trigger can't be executed directly; they are activated (or *fired*) when a user executes a Transact-SQL statement. Data Manipulation Language (DML) triggers fire on INSERT, UPDATE, and

DELETE statements; and Data Definition Language (DDL) triggers fire on CREATE, ALTER, and DROP statements.

INSERT triggers fire every time someone tries to create a new record in a table using the INSERT command. As soon as a user tries to insert a new record into a table, SQL Server copies the new record into a table in the database called the *trigger table* and a special table stored in memory called the *inserted* table. SQL Server then determines whether the data being inserted into your table meets the criteria defined in your trigger. If so, the record is inserted; if not, the record is not inserted.

You can even record what your users are doing by adding the RAISERROR() command to your trigger, which will write an error to the Windows event log. As you will see later in this book, the SQL Server Agent service can read this log entry and fire an alert, which can be used to send e-mail and text messages and even execute subsequent code.

In this task, you will create an INSERT trigger that prevents users from overselling a product in the Products table of the Sales database. If a user tries to do so, you will use the RAISERROR() command to write an event to the Windows event log.

Scenario

You have created a database for your sales department that contains information about orders customers have placed. The sales manager needs to know what is in stock at all times, so she would like to have the quantity of an item that is in stock decremented automatically when a user places an order. You have decided that the best way to accomplish this is by using a trigger on the Orders table.

Scope of Task

Duration

This task should take approximately 30 minutes.

Setup

For this task, you need access to the machine you installed SQL Server 2005 on in Task 1.1, the Sales database you created in Task 1.3, and the Products table you created in Task 1.4.

Caveat

When executing a trigger, SQL Server uses two special tables: inserted and deleted. The inserted table holds new records that are about to be added to the table, and the deleted table holds records that are about to be removed. You will be using the inserted table in this task.

Procedure

In this task, you will create a trigger that automatically decrements the InStock quantity in the Products table when a user places an order.

Equipment Used

For this task, you need access to the machine you installed SQL Server 2005 on in Task 1.1, the Sales database you created in Task 1.3, and the Products table you created in Task 1.4.

Details

First, you need to add some data to the Customers and Products tables:

1. Open SQL Server Management Studio by selecting it from the Microsoft SQL Server 2005 group in Programs on the Start menu, and log in using either Windows Authentication or SQL Server Authentication.

2. Open a new SQL Server query window, and enter and execute the following code to populate the Customers table with customer information:

```
USE Sales
INSERT customers
VALUES ('Andrea','Elliott','111 Main','Oakland','CA','94312','7605551212')
INSERT customers
VALUES ('Tom', 'Smith', '609 Georgia', 'Fresno', 'CA', '33045', '5105551212')
INSERT customers
VALUES ('Janice', 'Thomas', '806 Star', 'Phoenix', 'AZ', '85202',
'6021112222')
```

3. To populate the Products table with product and inventory information, enter and execute the following code:

```
INSERT Products
VALUES ('Giant Wheel of Brie', 200)
INSERT Products
VALUES ('Wool Blankets', 545)
INSERT Products
VALUES ('Espresso Beans', 1527)
INSERT Products
VALUES ('Notepads', 2098)
```

4. Close the query window.

   Next, follow these steps to create the new InvUpdate trigger:

1. In Object Explorer, expand your server, and then expand Databases ➢ Sales ➢ Tables ➢ dbo.Orders.

2. Right-click the Triggers folder, and select New Trigger.

3. In the Transact-SQL syntax box, enter and execute the following code to create the trigger:

```
CREATE TRIGGER dbo.InvUpdate
    ON  dbo.Orders
    FOR INSERT
AS
BEGIN
UPDATE p
SET p.instock = (p.instock - i.qty)
FROM Products p JOIN inserted i
ON p.prodid = i.prodid
END
GO
```

4. Close the query window.

Criteria for Completion

This task is complete when you have a trigger that automatically updates the InStock column of the Products table whenever a record is inserted in the Orders table. To test your new trigger, follow these steps:

1. Open a new SQL Server query, and execute the following code to verify the InStock quantity for item 1 (it should be 200):

```
USE Sales
SELECT prodid, instock
FROM Products
```

2. To cause the INSERT trigger to fire, you need to insert a new record in the Orders table. To do this, open a new query window, and enter and execute the following code, which assumes you're selling 15 quantities of product 1 to customer ID 1 on today's date (GETDATE( ) is used to return today's date):

```
USE Sales
INSERT Orders
VALUES (1,1,15,getdate())
```

3. To verify that the INSERT trigger fired and removed 15 from the InStock column of the Products table, click the New Query button, and enter and execute the following code:

```
USE Sales
SELECT prodid, instock
FROM Products
```

4. Notice that the exact quantity you sold customer 1 (15) was subtracted from the total InStock quantity of product ID 1. You now have 185 instead of 200.

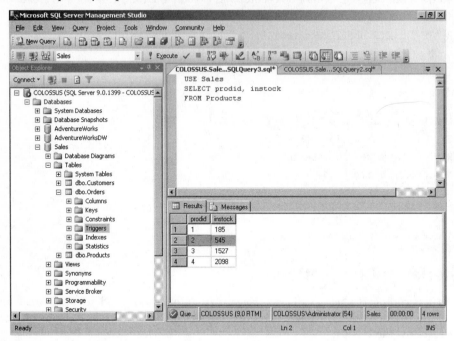

5. Close the query windows.

Task 1.9: Designing and Creating a *DELETE* Trigger

Ordinarily, when a user executes a DELETE statement, SQL Server removes the record from the table, and the record is never heard from again. That behavior changes when you add a DELETE trigger to the table. With a DELETE trigger in place, SQL Server moves the record being deleted to a logical table in memory called *deleted*; the records aren't entirely gone, and you can still reference them in your code. This comes in handy for complex business logic.

The special deleted table can easily be compared to the Recycle Bin in the Windows operating system, where deleted files are moved before they're deleted from the system. The biggest difference is that the deleted table is automatically purged of records after a transaction is complete whereas the Recycle Bin must be purged manually.

Suppose you want to keep your users from deleting customers who have more than $10,000 in credit with your company. Without a DELETE trigger in place, a user could successfully delete any record they wanted, regardless of the amount of credit the customer had. With a DELETE trigger in place, however, SQL Server places the record in question in the deleted table, so you can still reference the credit limit column and base the success of the transaction on the value therein.

In this task, you will create a DELETE trigger that prevents users from deleting customers based in Arizona.

Scenario

You have created a database for your sales department that contains information about orders customers have placed. One of your biggest customers is in Arizona, and they have recently had to stop placing regular orders with you, which makes them look inactive. Your sales manager is concerned that someone new may accidentally delete important information about this customer, and she has asked you to prevent that from happening. You have decided that the best way to accomplish this is by using a trigger on the Customers table.

Scope of Task

Duration

This task should take approximately 15 minutes.

Setup

For this task, you need access to the machine you installed SQL Server 2005 on in Task 1.1, the Sales database you created in Task 1.3, and the Customers table you created in Task 1.4.

Caveat

When executing a trigger, SQL Server uses two special tables named *inserted* and *deleted*. The inserted table holds new records that are about to be added to the table, and the deleted table holds records that are about to be removed. You will be using the deleted table in this task.

Procedure

In this task, you will create a DELETE trigger that prevents users from deleting customers based in Arizona.

Equipment Used

For this task, you need access to the machine you installed SQL Server 2005 on in Task 1.1, the Sales database you created in Task 1.3, and the Products table you created in Task 1.4.

Details

Follow these steps to create the new AZDel trigger:

1. In Object Explorer, expand your server, and then expand Databases ➤ Sales ➤ Tables ➤ dbo.Orders.

2. Right-click the Triggers folder, and select New Trigger.

3. In the Transact-SQL syntax box, enter and execute the following code to create the trigger:

```
CREATE TRIGGER dbo.AZDel
    ON   dbo.Customers
    FOR DELETE
AS
BEGIN
IF (SELECT state FROM deleted) = 'AZ'
BEGIN
PRINT 'Cannot remove customers from AZ'
PRINT 'Transaction has been cancelled'
ROLLBACK
END
END
GO
```

4. Close the query window.

Criteria for Completion

This task is complete when you have a trigger that prevents you from deleting customers who reside in Arizona. To test your new trigger, follow these steps:

1. Open a new SQL Server query, and execute the following code to verify you have customers from Arizona (for example, Janice Thomas should be in Arizona):

```
USE Sales
SELECT * FROM customers
```

2. To cause the DELETE trigger to fire, try to delete Janice from the Customers table. To do this, open a new query, and enter and execute the following code (you should see an error message upon execution):

```
USE Sales
DELETE from Customers
WHERE Lname = 'Thomas'
```

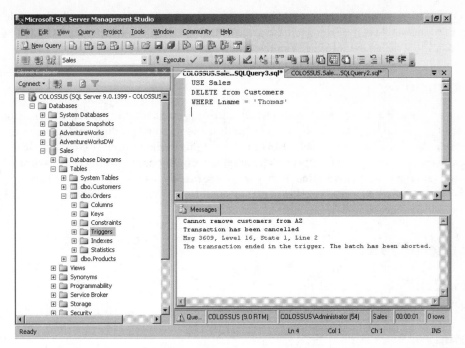

3. To verify that Janice has not been deleted, enter and execute the following code (you should still see Janice):

```
USE Sales
SELECT * FROM customers
```

4. Close the query window.

Task 1.10: Designing and Creating an *UPDATE* Trigger

As discussed in the previous task, a trigger is a collection of SQL statements that fires when a user performs an action against a record in a table. An UPDATE trigger fires when a user executes an UPDATE statement against a table.

What makes this type of trigger unique is that it uses the same functionality as both DELETE and INSERT triggers. When an UPDATE statement is executed, SQL Server actually deletes the record in question from the table and holds it in the deleted table; it then inserts a new record in the table and holds a duplicate copy in the inserted table. So, both the inserted and updated tables are available to UPDATE triggers.

In this task, you will create an UPDATE trigger that prevents users from overselling a product in the Products table of the Sales database. If a user tries to do so, you will use the RAISERROR() command to write an event to the Windows event log.

Scenario

You have created a database for your sales department that contains product information. Some of the new sales personnel have accidentally oversold some product, and the sales manager has asked you for a technical means to prevent this in the future. You have decided to put a trigger in place that prevents users from selling any amount of product that will set the InStock column to a negative value. If they try to execute such a transaction, you have opted to use the RAISERROR() command to write an event to the Windows event log for tracking and reporting purposes.

Scope of Task

Duration

This task should take approximately 30 minutes.

Setup

For this task, you need access to the machine you installed SQL Server 2005 on in Task 1.1, the Sales database you created in Task 1.3, and the Products table you created in Task 1.4.

Caveat

When executing a trigger, SQL Server uses two special tables named *inserted* and *deleted*. The inserted table holds new records that are about to be added to the table, and the deleted table holds records that are about to be removed. You will be using the inserted table in this task.

Procedure

In this task, you will create a trigger that prevents users from updating a record in the Products table if that update would set the InStock column to a negative amount. If they try to execute such a query, you will use the RAISERROR() command to write an event to the Windows event log.

Equipment Used

For this task, you need access to the machine you installed SQL Server 2005 on in Task 1.1, the Sales database you created in Task 1.3, and the Products table you created in Task 1.4.

Details

Follow these steps to create the new CheckStock trigger:

1. Expand your server, and then expand Databases ➢ Sales ➢ Tables ➢ dbo.Products.
2. Right-click the Triggers folder, and select New Trigger.
3. In the Transact-SQL syntax box, enter and execute the following code to create the trigger:

```
CREATE TRIGGER dbo.CheckStock
   ON  dbo.Products
   FOR UPDATE
AS
BEGIN

   IF (SELECT InStock from inserted) < 0
   BEGIN
      PRINT 'Cannot oversell Products'
      PRINT 'Transaction has been cancelled'
      ROLLBACK
      RAISERROR('Cannot oversell products', 10, 1) WITH LOG
   END
END
GO
```

4. Close the query window.

Criteria for Completion

This task is complete when you have a trigger that prevents you from entering a negative value in the InStock column of the Products table in the Sales database and also writes an event to the Windows event log if you try. To test your new trigger, follow these steps:

1. Open a new SQL Server query, and execute the following code to verify the quantity in stock on available products (product ID 2 should have 545 in stock currently):

```
USE Sales
SELECT prodid, instock FROM Products
```

2. To cause the UPDATE trigger to fire, you'll try to sell 600 units of product ID 2 (wool blankets) to a customer. Open a new SQL Server query, and enter and execute the following code (you should see an error message upon execution):

```
USE Sales
UPDATE Products
SET InStock = (Instock - 600)
WHERE prodid = 2
```

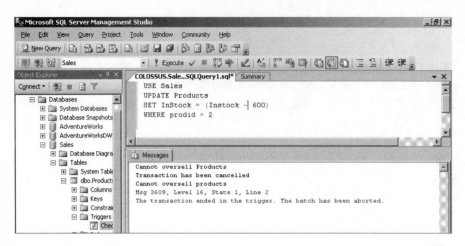

3. To verify that the transaction was disallowed and that you still have 545 wool blankets in stock, click the New Query button, and enter and execute the following code (you should still see 545 of product ID 2):

```
USE Sales
SELECT prodid, instock FROM Products
```

4. Now, open Event Viewer, and look in the Application log for the event written by RAISERROR().

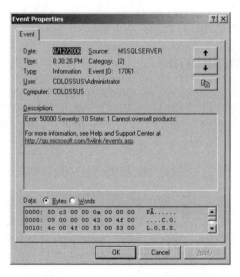

5. Close the query window.

Task 1.11: Designing and Creating an *INSTEAD OF* Trigger

In Task 1.6, I discussed views, which you can use to display only a few of the columns in a table, only a subset of the rows in a table, or data from more than one table at a time. This works great when you want to see just the data, but you can have problems when you try to modify data through a view.

Because views may not display all the columns in a table, data modification statements can fail. For example, suppose you have a Customers table like the one in your Sales database that contains customer information such as name, address, city, state, ZIP code, and so on. Then suppose you have created a view that displays all the columns except the City field. If you try to update the Customers table through the new view, the update will fail because the City field (which is a required field) is not available through the view. Using an INSTEAD OF trigger can make this type of update successful.

In this task, you will create an INSTEAD OF trigger that can insert a value that is not available through a view into a table. To accomplish this, you will first create a view that does not display the City column (which is a required column for updates), and then you will try to update through this column. Next you will create an INSTEAD OF trigger that can insert the missing value for you, after which you will try the insert again.

Scenario

You have created a database for your sales department with a table that contains customer information. Your sales manager has asked you to make it easier for sales representatives to find the customer data they need, so you have decided to create a view that displays only the necessary data. You need to make sure the sales representatives can insert new data through the view, and because the view does not show all the required columns, you need to create an INSTEAD OF trigger to modify the INSERT statement so that INSERT statements on the view will succeed.

Scope of Task

Duration

This task should take approximately 30 minutes.

Setup

For this task, you need access to the machine you installed SQL Server 2005 on in Task 1.1, the Sales database you created in Task 1.3, and the Customers table you created in Task 1.4.

Caveat

This task doesn't have any caveats.

Procedure

In this task, you will create a view that shows only a subset of columns from the Customers table in the Sales database. Then you will create a trigger that intercepts an INSERT statement and modifies the statement so that all required columns are filled in.

Equipment Used

For this task, you need access to the machine you installed SQL Server 2005 on in Task 1.1, the Sales database you created in Task 1.3, and the Customers table you created in Task 1.4.

Details

First, you need to create a view based on the Customers table that does not display the City field (which is a required field for an INSERT). Follow these steps to create the PHX_Customers view:

1. In SQL Server Management Studio, open a new query, and enter and execute the following code:

```
USE Sales
GO
CREATE VIEW PHX_Customers AS
SELECT fname, lname, address, state, zip, phone
FROM Customers
WHERE City = 'Phoenix'
```

2. To verify that the view displays only the columns you want, click the New Query button, and enter and execute the following query:

```
USE Sales
SELECT * FROM PHX_Customers
```

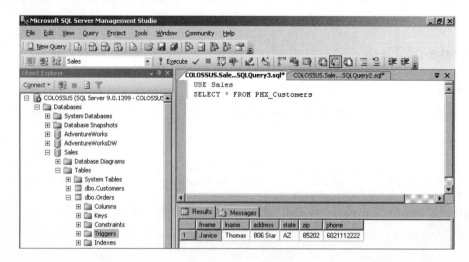

3. Now you will try to insert a new customer through the view. Select New Query with Current Connection from the Query menu, and enter and execute the following code:

```
USE Sales
INSERT PHX_Customers
VALUES ('Timothy', 'Calunod', '123 Third', 'CA', '95023', '9252221212')
```

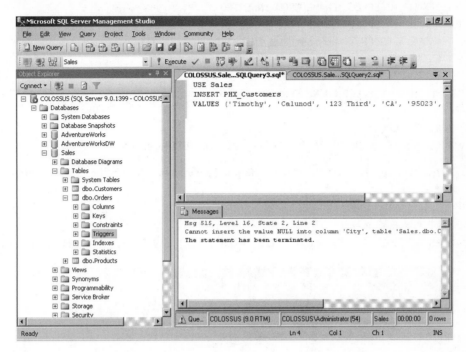

Next, you can create an INSTEAD OF trigger that inserts the missing value for you when you insert through the view:

1. Expand your server, and then expand Databases ➢ Sales ➢ Views ➢ dbo.PHX_Customers.

2. Right-click the Triggers folder, and select New Trigger.

3. In the Transact-SQL syntax box, enter and execute the following code to create the trigger:

```
CREATE TRIGGER Add_City ON PHX_Customers
INSTEAD OF INSERT
AS
DECLARE
 @FNAME VARCHAR(20),
 @LNAME VARCHAR(20),
 @ADDR VARCHAR(50),
 @CITY VARCHAR(20),
 @STATE NCHAR(2),
```

```
@ZIP CHAR(5),
@PHONE CHAR(10)

SET @CITY = 'Phoenix'

SET @FNAME = (SELECT FNAME FROM INSERTED)
SET @LNAME = (SELECT LNAME FROM INSERTED)
SET @ADDR = (SELECT ADDRESS FROM INSERTED)
SET @STATE = (SELECT STATE FROM INSERTED)
SET @ZIP = (SELECT ZIP FROM INSERTED)
SET @PHONE = (SELECT PHONE FROM INSERTED)

INSERT CUSTOMERS
VALUES(@FNAME, @LNAME, @ADDR, @CITY, @STATE, @ZIP, @PHONE)
```

4. To test the trigger, enter and execute the same code from step 3 in the previous series of steps:

```
USE Sales
INSERT PHX_Customers
VALUES ('Timothy', 'Calunod', '123 Third', 'CA', '95023', '9252221212')
```

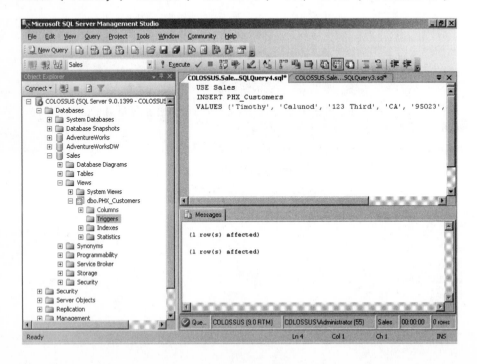

5. To verify that the data was inserted into the Customers table and that the City column was populated, select New Query with Current Connection from the Query menu, and enter and execute the following query:

```
USE Sales
SELECT * FROM Customers
```

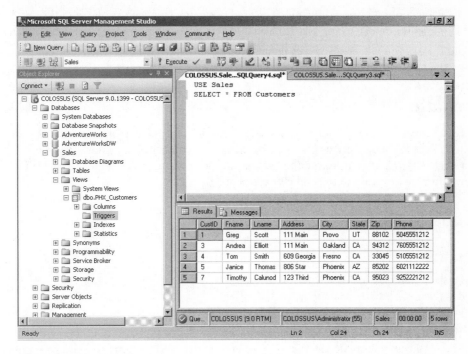

6. Close the query windows.

Criteria for Completion

This task is complete when you have an INSTEAD OF trigger that intercepts an INSERT statement on the PHX_Customers database and adds a value to insert into the City field.

Task 1.12: Designing and Creating a User-Defined Function

A *function* is a grouping of Transact-SQL statements that you can reuse. SQL Server has a large number of built-in functions, but these may not meet all of your needs. For this reason, SQL Server gives you the ability to create your own functions, called *user-defined functions*, to perform any tasks you may need. This is especially useful for performing complex calculations in your business logic. You can create several types of functions:

- Scalar functions return a single value or the type specified in the RETURN statement, such as a single int value.

- Table-valued functions return a table datatype.

- CLR functions are special functions created using any language available in the .NET Framework (that is, C# or Visual Basic .NET). These can return scalar or table values.

In this task, you will create a user-defined function that determines which customer has placed the largest order for a given product.

Scenario

You have created a database for your sales department with a table that contains order information. Your sales manager wants to know the largest number of items for a given product on a single order. She wants to run this calculation every week, so you decide to create a user-defined function for ease of use and management.

Scope of Task

Duration

This task should take approximately 15 minutes.

Setup

For this task, you need access to the machine you installed SQL Server 2005 on in Task 1.1, the Sales database you created in Task 1.3, and the Orders and Customers tables you created in Task 1.4.

Caveat

This task doesn't have any caveats.

Procedure

In this task, you will create a user-defined function that calculates the largest number of items for a given product on a single order. First you will add some orders to the database, and then you will create a function to calculate the sales; finally, you will verify the function.

Equipment Used

For this task, you need access to the machine you installed SQL Server 2005 on in Task 1.1, the Sales database you created in Task 1.3, and the Orders and Customers tables you created in Task 1.4.

Details

First, you need to place some orders in the Orders table so the function has some data to work with:

1. Open a new SQL Server query, and execute the following code to insert some new records in the Orders table:

```
USE Sales
INSERT Orders
VALUES (3,2,15,getdate())
GO
INSERT Orders
VALUES (1,2,10,getdate())
GO
INSERT Orders
VALUES (1,1,20,getdate())
GO
INSERT Orders
VALUES (4,3,25,getdate())
GO
```

2. To verify that the new orders exist, enter and execute this code in a new query window:

```
USE Sales
SELECT * FROM Orders
```

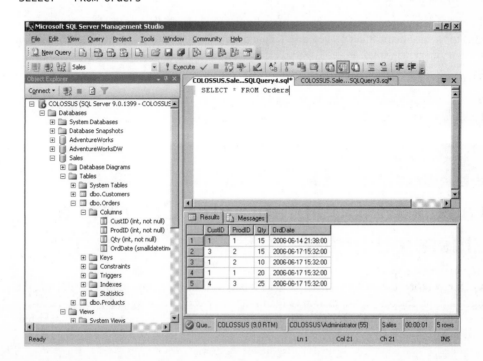

Next, you are ready to create a user-defined function to calculate the largest number of items for a given product on a single order:

1. In SQL Server Management Studio, open a new query, and enter and execute the following code:

```
USE Sales
GO
CREATE FUNCTION ItemOrderCount
  (@ProductID int)
RETURNS int
AS
BEGIN
  RETURN (SELECT MAX(Qty) FROM Orders WHERE ProdID = @ProductID)
END
```

 I'm using the GO statement here because the CREATE FUNCTION statement must be the first statement in a batch. GO separates the statements into separate batches.

Criteria for Completion

This task is complete when you have created a function that tells you the largest amount of items for a specific product placed on a single order. To test your function, execute this code in a new query window:

```
USE Sales
GO
SELECT dbo.ItemOrderCount(1)
```

As shown in Figure 1.7, you should get a value of 20; this was the most items placed on a single order for product ID 1.

Task 1.13: Designing and Creating a Clustered Index

SQL Server stores data on the hard disk in 8KB pages inside the database files. By default, these pages and the data they contain aren't organized in any way. To bring order to this chaos, you must create an index. You can create two types of indexes on a table: clustered and nonclustered.

FIGURE 1.7   The ItemOrderCount() function should return a value of 20 for product ID 1.

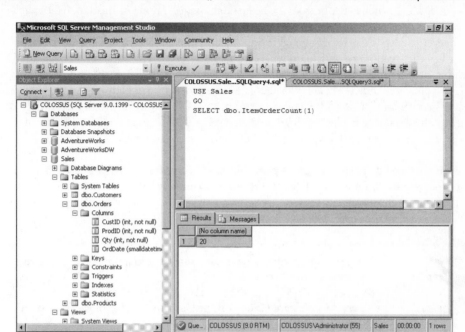

Clustered indexes physically rearrange the data that users insert in your tables. The arrangement of a clustered index on disk is comparable to that in a dictionary, because they both use the same storage paradigm. If you needed to look up a word in the dictionary—for example, *satellite*—how would you do it? You would turn right to the *S* section of the dictionary and continue through the alphabetically arranged list until you found the word *satellite*. The process is similar with a clustered index; a clustered index on a Lastname column would place *Adams* physically before *Burns* in the database file. This way, SQL Server can more easily pinpoint the exact data pages it wants.

It might help to visualize an index in SQL Server as an upside-down tree. In fact, the index structure is called a *B-tree* (binary-tree) structure. At the top of the B-tree structure, you find the *root page*; it contains information about the location of other pages further down the line called *intermediate-level pages*. These intermediate pages contain yet more key values that can point to still other intermediate-level pages or data pages. The pages at the bottom of a clustered index, the *leaf pages*, contain the actual data, which is physically arranged on disk to conform to the constraints of the index.

Because all the data is arranged physically in the database, clustered indexes are a good choice when users search for a range of data.

On a table without a clustered index in place (called a *heap*), new data is inserted at the end of the table, which is the bottom of the last data page. If none of the data pages has any room, SQL Server allocates a new extent and starts filling it with data. Because you've told SQL Server to physically rearrange your data by creating a clustered index, SQL Server no longer has the freedom to stuff data wherever it finds room. The data must physically be placed in order. To accomplish this, you need to leave some room at the end of each data page on a clustered index. This blank space is referred to as the *fill factor*. A higher fill factor gives less room, and a lower fill factor gives more room. If you specify a fill factor of 70, for example, the data page is filled with 70 percent data and 30 percent blank space. If you specify 100, the data page is filled to nearly 100 percent, having room for only one record at the bottom of the page.

When you need to insert data into a page that has become completely full, SQL Server performs a *page split*. This means SQL Server takes approximately half the data from the full page and moves it to an empty page, thus creating two half-full pages, leaving plenty of room for new data.

 Because clustered indexes physically rearrange the data, you can have only one clustered index per table.

In this task, you will create a clustered index on the Customers table of the Sales database.

Scenario

You have created a database for your sales department with a table that contains customer information. Your sales representatives have started complaining about slow access times. You know that the sales representatives look up customers based on their ZIP codes quite often, so you decide to create a clustered index on the Zip column of the Customers table to improve data access times.

Scope of Task

Duration

This task should take approximately 15 minutes.

Setup

For this task, you need access to the machine you installed SQL Server 2005 on in Task 1.1, the Sales database you created in Task 1.3, and the Customers tables you created in Task 1.4.

Caveat

Because this is just a test system and Customers is a small table with little data, you will not see a significant improvement in data access time.

Procedure

In this task, you will create a clustered index on the Customers table based on the Zip column.

Equipment Used

For this task, you need access to the machine you installed SQL Server 2005 on in Task 1.1, the Sales database you created in Task 1.3, and the Customers table you created in Task 1.4.

Details

To create the new idx_cl_Zip clustered index, follow these steps:

1. Open SQL Server Management Studio, and connect using Windows Authentication.
2. In Object Explorer, expand your server, and then expand Databases ➢ Sales ➢ Tables ➢ dbo.Customers.
3. Right-click Indexes, and select New Index.
4. In the Index name box, enter **idx_cl_Zip**.
5. Select Clustered for the index type.
6. Click the Add button next to the Index Key Columns grid.
7. Check the box next to the Zip column.

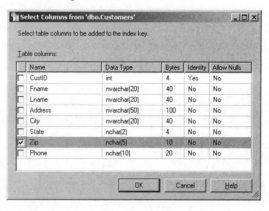

8. Click OK to return to the New Index dialog box.

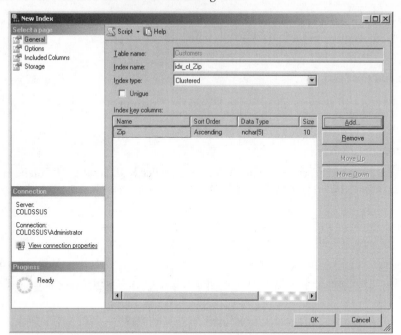

9. Click OK to create the index.

Criteria for Completion

This task is complete when you have a clustered index on the Zip column of the Customers table in the Sales database. To verify that the index is there, expand Databases ➢ Sales ➢ Tables ➢ dbo.Customers ➢ Indexes, and you should see the idx_cl_Zip index listed, as shown in Figure 1.8.

Task 1.14: Designing and Creating a Nonclustered Index

Like its clustered cousin, a *nonclustered* index is a B-tree structure having a root page, intermediate levels, and a leaf level. However, two major differences separate the index types. The first is that the leaf level of the nonclustered index doesn't contain the actual data; it contains pointers to the data stored in data pages. The second big difference is that the nonclustered index doesn't physically rearrange the data. It functions more like the index at the back of a topically arranged book.

FIGURE 1.8   The new idx_cl_Zip clustered index shows up in Object Explorer after it has been created.

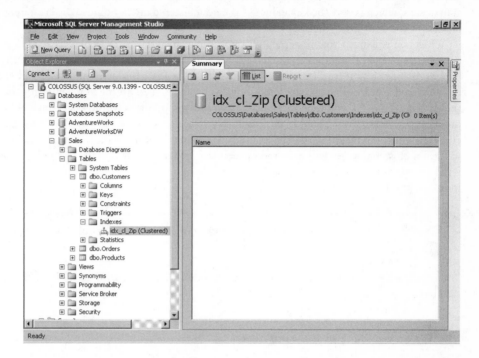

When you search for data on a table with a nonclustered index, SQL Server first queries the sysindexes table looking for a record that contains your table name and a value in the indid column from 2 to 251 (0 denotes a heap, and 1 is for a clustered index). Once SQL Server finds this record, it looks at the root column to find the root page of the index (just like it did with a clustered index). Once SQL Server has the location of the root page, it can begin traversing the B-tree in search of your data.

If you're searching a nonclustered index that is based on a heap (a table with no clustered index in place), SQL Server uses the pointer in the leaf-level page to jump right to the data page and return your data.

If your table has a clustered index in place, the nonclustered index leaf level contains a pointer to the clustered index key value. This means once SQL Server is done searching your nonclustered index, it has to traverse your clustered index as well. SQL Server searches two indexes because it can actually be faster when you consider how data is updated through a nonclustered index.

When inserting data using a nonclustered index on a heap, SQL Server inserts the data wherever it finds room and adds a new key value that points to the new record of the associated index pages.

When you insert data into a table with a nonclustered index and a clustered index in place, SQL Server physically inserts the data where it belongs in the order of the clustered index and updates the key values of the nonclustered index to point to the key values of the clustered index. When one of the data pages becomes full and you still have more data to insert, a page split occurs, which is why the key values of the nonclustered index point to the clustered index instead of the data pages themselves.

When you're using a nonclustered index without a clustered index in place, each index page contains key values that point to the data. This pointer contains the location of the extent, as well as the page and record number of the searched-for data. If a page split occurred and the nonclustered index didn't use clustered index key values, then all the key values for the data that had been moved would be incorrect because all the pointers would be wrong. The entire nonclustered index would need to be rebuilt to reflect the changes. However, because the non-clustered index references the clustered index key values (not the actual data), all the pointers in the nonclustered index will be correct even after a page split has occurred, and the nonclus-tered index won't need to be rebuilt. That is why you reference the key values of a clustered index in a nonclustered index.

    You can have 249 nonclustered indexes per table, though in practice you will not have nearly that many.

In this task, you will create a nonclustered index on the Customers table of the Sales database.

Scenario

You have created a database for your sales department with a table that contains customer information. You want to make sure data access is as fast as possible. After some investigation, you have discovered that your sales representatives consistently search for customer informa-tion by searching for a last name. Because they search only for a single record at a time, you decide to create a nonclustered index on the Lname column of the Customers table to improve data access times.

Scope of Task

Duration

This task should take approximately 15 minutes.

Setup

For this task, you need access to the machine you installed SQL Server 2005 on in Task 1.1, the Sales database you created in Task 1.3, and the Customers table you created in Task 1.4.

Caveat

Because this is just a test system and Customers is a small table with little data, you will not see a significant improvement in data access time.

Procedure

In this task, you will create a nonclustered index on the Customers table based on the Zip column.

Equipment Used

For this task, you need access to the machine you installed SQL Server 2005 on in Task 1.1, the Sales database you created in Task 1.3, and the Customers table you created in Task 1.4.

Details

To create the new idx_ncl_Lname nonclustered index, follow these steps:

1. Open SQL Server Management Studio, and connect using Windows Authentication.

2. In Object Explorer, expand your server, and then expand Databases ➢ Sales ➢ Tables ➢ dbo.Customers.

3. Right-click Indexes, and select New Index.

4. In the Index Name box, enter **idx_ncl_Lname**.

5. Select Nonclustered for the index type.

6. Click the Add button next to the Index Key Columns grid.

7. Check the box next to the Lname column.

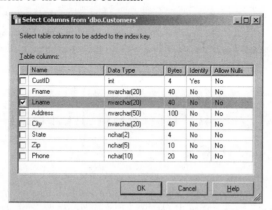

8. Click OK to return to the New Index dialog box.

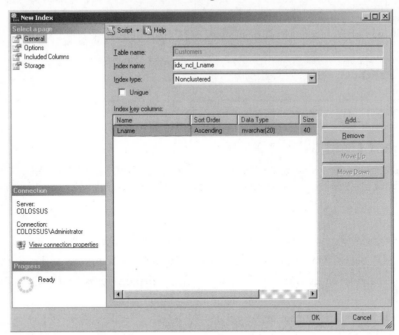

9. Click OK to create the index.

Criteria for Completion

This task is complete when you have a nonclustered index on the Lname column of the Customers table in the Sales database, as shown in Figure 1.9. To verify that the index is there, expand Databases ➢ Sales ➢ Tables ➢ dbo.Customers ➢ Indexes, and you should see the idx_ncl_Lname index listed.

Task 1.15: Designing and Creating a Full-Text Index

Databases are excellent containers for all sorts of data, including massive amounts of text. Many companies, in fact, have entire libraries of corporate documents stored in their databases. New datatypes, such as nvarchar(max), were devised to store such large amounts of text. Because the standard SELECT statement wasn't designed to handle such large amounts of text, something else had to be devised—something more robust. Enter *full-text search*.

FIGURE 1.9   The new idx_ncl_Lname nonclustered index shows up in Object Explorer after it has been created.

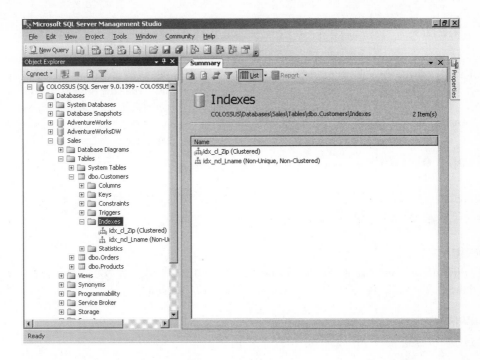

Full-text search is a completely separate program that runs as a service (called the SQL Server FullText Search service, or msftesq) and can index all sorts of information from most of the BackOffice (or even non-Microsoft) products. Thus, when you perform a full-text search, you are telling SQL Server to make a request of the FullText Search service. To perform a full-text search, you need only use the `CONTAINS`, `CONTAINSTABLE`, `FREETEXT`, or `FREETEXTTABLE` clause in your `SELECT` query.

You can find a detailed discussion of `CONTAINS`, `CONTAINSTABLE`, `FREETEXT`, and `FREETEXTTABLE` in *Mastering SQL Server 2005* (Sybex, 2006).

Before you can start using this powerful tool, you need to configure it. The first step you need to take is to create a full-text index. You create full-text indexes with SQL Server tools, such as SQL Server Management Studio, but you maintain them with the FullText Search service; and they are stored on the disk as files separate from the database. To keep the full-text indexes organized, they are stored in catalogs in the database. You can create as many catalogs in your databases as you'd like to organize your indexes, but these catalogs cannot span databases.

In this task, you will create a full-text index on the Production.Document table of the AdventureWorks database.

Scenario

One of the databases that your company has been using for some time contains a table that stores large documents. Your users have been using standard SELECT statements to access the documents in this table, but that method is proving too slow now that the table is starting to grow. You want to make sure users can query the table and get results as quickly and easily as possible, so you decide to create a full-text index on the table.

Scope of Task

Duration

This task should take approximately 20 minutes.

Setup

For this task, you need access to the machine you installed SQL Server 2005 on in Task 1.1 and the AdventureWorks database that is installed with the sample data.

Caveat

This task doesn't have any caveats.

Procedure

In this task, you will create a full-text catalog and index on the Production.Document table of the AdventureWorks database.

Equipment Used

For this task, you need access to the machine you installed SQL Server 2005 on in Task 1.1 and the AdventureWorks database that is installed with the sample data.

Details

To create the new full-text catalog and index on the Production.Document table, follow these steps:

1. Open SQL Server Management Studio, and in Object Explorer, expand Databases ➤ AdventureWorks ➤ Tables.

2. Right-click Production.Document, move to Full-Text Index, and click Define Full-Text Index.

3. On the first screen of the Full-Text Indexing Wizard, click Next.

4. Each table on which you create a full-text index must already have a unique index associated with it for the FullText Search service to work. In this instance, select the default PK_Document_DocumentID index, and click Next.

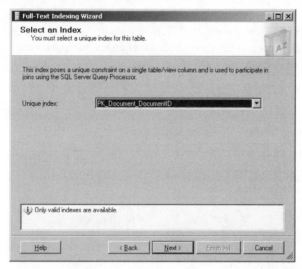

5. On the next screen, you are asked which column you want to full-text index. Document-Summary is the only nvarchar(max) column in the table, so it is the best candidate; select the box next to it, and click Next.

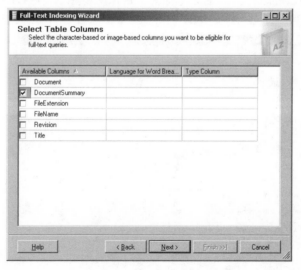

6. On the next screen, you are asked when you want changes to the full-text index applied:

   ▪ Automatically means the full-text index is updated with every change made to the table. This is the fastest, least-hassle way to keep full-text indexes up-to-date, but it can tax the server because it means the changes to the table and index take place all at once.

   ▪ Manually means changes to the underlying data are maintained, but you will have to schedule index population yourself. This is a slightly slower way to update the index, but it is not as taxing on the server because changes to the data are maintained but the index is not updated immediately.

   ▪ Do Not Track Changes means changes to the underlying data are not tracked. This is the least taxing, and slowest, way to update the full-text index. Changes are not maintained, so when the index is updated, the FullText Search service must read the entire table for changes before updating the index.

7. Choose Automatically, and click Next.

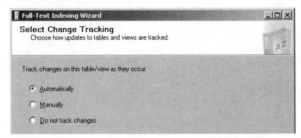

8. The next screen asks you to select a catalog. You'll need to create one here, because you don't have any available. In the Name field, enter **AdventureWorks Catalog**. You can also select a filegroup to place the catalog on; leave this as default, and click Next.

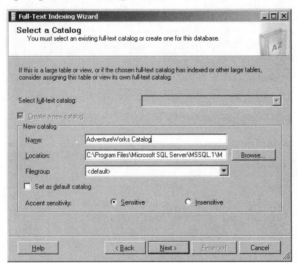

9.   On the next screen, you are asked to create a schedule for automatically repopulating the full-text index. If your data is frequently updated, you will want to do this more often, maybe once a day. If it is read more often than it is changed, you should repopulate less frequently. You can schedule population for a single table or an entire catalog at a time. Here, you will set repopulation to happen just once for the entire catalog by clicking the New Catalog Schedule button.

10. On the New Schedule Properties screen, enter **Populate AdventureWorks**, and click OK.

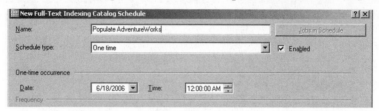

11. When you are taken back to the Full-Text Indexing Wizard, click Next.

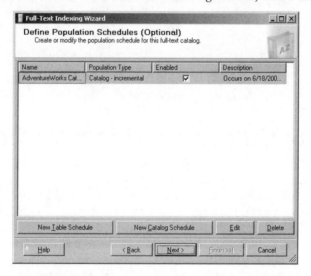

12. On the final screen of the wizard, you are given a summary of the choices you have made. Click Finish to create the index.

Criteria for Completion

This task is complete when you have a full-text index on the Production.Document table of the AdventureWorks database. To verify that the index is there, follow these steps:

1.   To see your new catalog and index, in Object Explorer expand AdventureWorks ➢ Storage ➢ Full Text Catalogs.

2. Double-click the AdventureWorks catalog to open its properties.

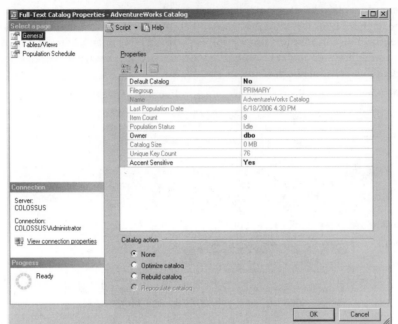

Task 1.16: Creating a Windows Login

It is vitally important to protect the information stored in your databases. Realizing this, the team at Microsoft implemented a world-class security system in SQL Server 2005. The foundation of this security system is the login. Two types of logins exist: Windows and Standard. To fully understand how they work, you need to know about authentication modes.

An *authentication mode* is how SQL Server processes usernames and passwords. SQL Server 2005 provides two such modes: Windows Authentication mode and Mixed mode.

In Windows Authentication mode, a user can sit down at her computer, log in to the Windows domain, and gain access to SQL Server using the Kerberos security protocol. Although an in-depth discussion of Kerberos is beyond the scope of this book, here is a brief overview of how this security protocol works:

1. When the user logs in, Windows performs a DNS lookup to locate a Key Distribution Center (KDC).

2. The user's machine logs in to the domain.

3. The KDC issues a special security token called a Ticket Granting Ticket (TGT) to the user.

4. To access the SQL Server, the user's machine presents the TGT to the SQL Server; if the ticket is accepted, the user is allowed access.

The main advantage of Windows Authentication mode is that users don't have to remember multiple usernames and passwords. This mode also allows you to apply Windows password policies, which perform such tasks as expire passwords, require a minimum length for passwords, keep a history of passwords, and so on.

One of the disadvantages is that only users with Windows accounts can open a trusted connection to SQL Server. This means someone like a Novell client can't use Windows Authentication mode because they don't have a Windows account. If it turns out that you have such clients, you'll need to implement Mixed mode.

Mixed mode allows both Windows Authentication and SQL Server Authentication. SQL Server Authentication works as follows:

1. A user logs in to his network, Windows or otherwise.

2. The user opens a nontrusted connection to SQL Server using a username and password other than those used to gain network access. It's called a *nontrusted* connection because SQL Server doesn't trust the operating system to verify the user's password.

3. SQL Server matches the username and password entered by the user to an entry in the syslogins table.

The primary advantage is that anyone—Mac users, Novell users, Unix users, and the like—can gain access to SQL Server using Mixed mode. You could also consider this to be a second layer of security, because if someone hacks into the network in Mixed mode, it doesn't mean they have automatically hacked into SQL Server at the same time.

Ironically, multiple passwords can be a problem as well as an advantage. When users have multiple sets of credentials, they tend to write them down and thus breach the security system you have worked so hard to create.

In this task, you will create Windows logins for several Windows user and group accounts.

Scenario

You have just installed a new SQL Server at your company, and you need to make sure the right people have access. Some of these users will be using Windows accounts, so you have decided to create Windows logins in SQL Server for these users.

Scope of Task

Duration

This task should take approximately 90 minutes.

Setup

For this task, you need access to the machine you installed SQL Server 2005 on in Task 1.1.

Caveat

You will need administrative access to the machine you will be using for this task, because you will be creating new groups and user accounts on the machine. This task also works best if performed on Windows 2003.

Procedure

In this task, you will create several Windows user and group accounts and then create Windows logins for these accounts in SQL Server.

Equipment Used

For this task, you need access to the machine you installed SQL Server 2005 on in Task 1.1.

Details

You need to create the Windows user and group accounts in Computer Management (or Active Directory Users and Computers if you are in a domain with Domain Admin rights):

1. Open Computer Management in the Administrative Tools group under Programs on the Start menu, expand Local Users and Groups, click Users, and then select Action ➢ New User.

2. Create six new users with the criteria in the following list:

Username	Description	Password	Must Change	Never Expires
MorrisL	IT	Password1	Deselect	Select
RosmanD	Administration	Password1	Deselect	Select
JohnsonK	Accounting	Password1	Deselect	Select
JonesB	Accounting	Password1	Deselect	Select
ChenJ	Sales	Password1	Deselect	Select
SamuelsR	Sales	Password1	Deselect	Select

3. While in Computer Management, create a Local group called Accounting.

4. Add the new users you just created whose Description value is Accounting.

5. While still in Computer Management, create a Local group named Sales.

6. Add all the users whose Description value is Sales.

7. Open Local Security Policy from the Administrative Tools group under Programs on the Start menu.

8. Expand Local Policies, and click User Rights Assignment.

9. Double-click the Allow Log on Locally right, and click Add User or Group.

10. Select the Everyone group, click OK, and then click OK again (on a production machine this is not a best practice; this is only for this exercise).

11. Close the Local Policies tool, and open SQL Server Management Studio.

With your user accounts and groups created, you're ready to create Windows logins for these accounts in SQL Server:

1. Open SQL Server Management Studio, expand your server, and then expand Security ➤ Logins.

2. Right-click Logins, and select New Login.

3. In the Login Name box, enter *Sqldomain\Accounting* (the name of the Local group created earlier).

4. Under Defaults, select AdventureWorks as the default database.

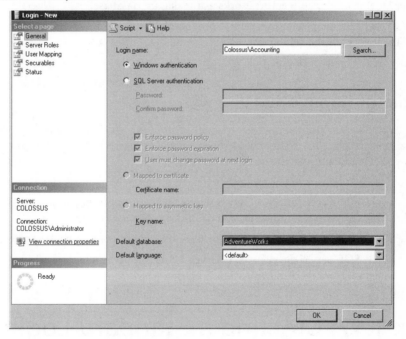

5. On the User Mapping page, select the Map check box next to AdventureWorks to give your user access to the default database.

6. Click OK to create the login.

7. Right-click Logins, and select New Login.

8. In the Login Name box, enter *Sqldomain\Sales* (the name of the Local group created earlier).

9. Under Defaults, select AdventureWorks as the default database.

10. On the User Mapping page, select the Map check box next to AdventureWorks to give your user access to the default database.

11. Click OK to create the login.

12. Right-click Logins, and select New Login.

13. Enter *Sqldomain***RosmanD** in the Login Name field.

14. Under Defaults, select AdventureWorks as the default database.

15. On the User Mapping page, select the Permit check box next to AdventureWorks to give your user access to the default database.

16. Click OK to create the login.

17. Right-click Logins, and select New Login.

18. Enter *Sqldomain***MorrisL** in the Login Name field.

19. Under Defaults, select AdventureWorks as the default database.

20. On the User Mapping page, select the Permit check box next to AdventureWorks to give your user access to the default database.

21. Click OK to create the login.

Criteria for Completion

This task is complete when you have successfully created the Windows login accounts specified in the task. To test this, first you'll log in as a member of one of the groups you created, and then you'll log in as a specific user:

1. Log out of Windows, and log back in as JonesB.

2. Open a new SQL Server query in SQL Server Management Studio, and select Windows Authentication from the Authentication drop-down list.

3. Close SQL Server Management Studio, log out of Windows, and log back in as RosmanD.

4. Open a new SQL Server query in SQL Server Management Studio, and select Windows Authentication from the Authentication drop-down list.

Task 1.17: Creating a Standard Login

In Task 1.16, you learned that only clients with a Windows account can make trusted connections to SQL Server (where SQL Server trusts Windows to validate the user's password). If the user (such as a Macintosh or Novell client) for whom you're creating a login can't make a trusted connection, you must create a Standard login for them. In this task, you'll create two Standard logins that you'll use later in the phase.

Although you can create Standard logins in Windows Authentication mode, you won't be able to use them. If you try, SQL Server will ignore you and use your Windows credentials instead.

Scenario

You have just installed a new SQL Server at your company, and you need to make sure the right people have access. Some of these users run Macintosh and Linux, and they do not have Windows accounts, so you must create Standard logins in SQL Server for these users.

Scope of Task

Duration

This task should take approximately 30 minutes.

Setup

For this task, you need access to the machine you installed SQL Server 2005 on in Task 1.1.

Caveat

This task doesn't have any caveats.

Procedure

In this task, you will create two Standard logins in SQL Server.

Equipment Used

For this task, you need access to the machine you installed SQL Server 2005 on in Task 1.1.

Details

Follow these steps to create the Standard logins in SQL Server:

1. Open SQL Server Management Studio, and expand your server by clicking the + sign next to the icon named after your server.
2. Expand Security, and then expand Logins.
3. Right-click Logins, and select New Login.
4. Select the SQL Server Authentication radio button.

5. In the Name box, enter **SmithB**.

6. In the Password text box, enter **Password1** (remember, passwords are case sensitive).

7. In the Confirm Password text box, enter **Password1** again.

8. Under Defaults, select AdventureWorks as the default database.

9. Uncheck the User Must Change Password at Next Login box.

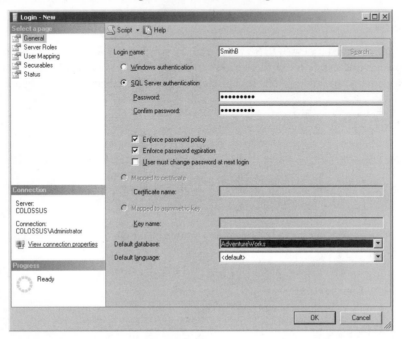

10. On the User Mapping page, select the Map check box next to AdventureWorks to give your user access to the default database.

11. Click OK to create your new login.

12. Right-click Logins, and select New Login.

13. Select the SQL Server authentication radio button.

14. In the Name box, enter **GibsonH**.

15. In the Password text box, enter **Password1**.

16. In the Confirm Password text box, enter **Password1**.

17. Under Defaults, select AdventureWorks as the default database.

18. Uncheck the User Must Change Password at Next Login box.

19. Do not select the Permit check box next to AdventureWorks on the User Mapping page. You'll create a database user account later in this phase.

20. Click OK to create your new login.

Criteria for Completion

This task is complete when you have successfully created the Standard login accounts specified in the task. To test this, follow these steps:

1.   To test the SmithB login, click the New Query button in SQL Server Management Studio.

2.   On the Query menu, hover over Connection, and then click Change Connection.

3.   In the dialog box that opens, select SQL Server Authentication from the Authentication drop-down list.

4.   In the Login Name box, enter **SmithB**.

5.   In the Password box, enter **Password1**.

6.   Click Connect to connect to AdventureWorks.

Task 1.18: Assigning Logins to Fixed Server Roles

You need to make sure your users have only the permissions they need once they are logged in to SQL Server. You can accomplish this goal by assigning logins to fixed server roles, which are specifically designed to allow you to limit the amount of administrative access that a user has once logged in to SQL Server. Some users may be allowed to do whatever they want; other users may be able to manage security only. You can assign users any of eight server roles. The following list starts at the highest level and describes the administrative access granted:

Sysadmin   Members of the sysadmin role have the authority to perform any task in SQL Server. Be careful whom you assign to this role, because people who are unfamiliar with SQL Server can accidentally create serious problems. This role is only for the database administrators (DBAs).

Serveradmin   These users can set serverwide configuration options, such as how much memory SQL Server can use or how much information to send over the network in a single frame. They can also shut down the server. If you make your assistant DBAs members of this role, you can relieve yourself of some of the administrative burden.

Setupadmin   Members here can install replication and manage extended stored procedures (these are used to perform actions not native to SQL Server). Give this role to the assistant DBAs as well.

Securityadmin   These users manage security issues such as creating and deleting logins, reading the audit logs, and granting users permission to create databases. This too is a good role for assistant DBAs.

Processadmin   SQL Server is capable of multitasking; that is, it can do more than one task at a time by executing multiple processes. For instance, SQL Server might spawn one process for writing to cache and another for reading from cache. A member of the processadmin group can end (or *kill*, as it's called in SQL Server) a process. This is another good role for assistant DBAs and developers. Developers especially need to kill processes that may have been triggered by an improperly designed query or stored procedure.

Dbcreator   These users can create and make changes to databases. This may be a good role for assistant DBAs as well as developers (who should be warned against creating unnecessary databases and wasting server space).

Diskadmin   These users manage files on disk. They perform tasks such as mirroring databases and adding backup devices. Assistant DBAs should be members of this role.

Bulkadmin   Members of this role can execute the BULK INSERT statement, which allows them to import data into SQL Server databases from text files. Assistant DBAs should be members of this role.

If you don't want users to have any administrative authority, don't assign them to a server role. This limits them to being normal users.

Builtin\Administrators is automatically made a member of the sysadmin server role, giving SQL Server administrative rights to all your Windows administrators. Because not all your Windows administrators should have these rights, you may want to create a SQLAdmins group in Windows, add your SQL Server administrators to that group, and make the group a member of the sysadmin role. Afterward, you should remove Builtin\Administrators from the sysadmin role.

In this task, you will assign two of the logins you created in the previous two tasks to fixed server roles, thereby limiting their administrative authority.

Scenario

You have just created several new logins on your SQL Server so your users can access the system. You need to ensure that these accounts have the right amount of administrative access, so you have decided to assign two of these logins to fixed server roles.

Scope of Task

Duration

This task should take approximately 15 minutes.

Setup

For this task, you need access to the machine you installed SQL Server 2005 on in Task 1.1 and the logins you created in Tasks 1.16 and 1.17.

Caveat

This task doesn't have any caveats.

Procedure

In this task, you will assign two of the logins you created to fixed server roles to limit their administrative access.

Equipment Used

For this task, you need access to the machine you installed SQL Server 2005 on in Task 1.1 and the logins you created in Tasks 1.16 and 1.17.

Details

Follow these steps to assign the logins to fixed server roles:

1. Open SQL Server Management Studio by selecting it from the SQL Server 2005 group under Programs on the Start menu, expand Security, and expand Server Roles.

2. Double-click the Sysadmin server role to open its properties.

3. Click Add, click Browse, select the check box next to *SqlDomain*\MorrisL, click OK, and then OK again.

4. MorrisL should now appear in the Role Members list.

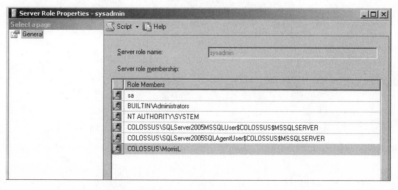

5. Click OK to exit the Server Role Properties dialog box.

6. Double-click Serveradmin Server Role Properties.

7. Click Add, enter **GibsonH**, and click OK.

8. Click OK to exit the Server Role Properties dialog box.

Criteria for Completion

This task is complete when you have successfully added MorrisL to the sysadmins fixed server role (as shown in Figure 1.10) and GibsonH to the serveradmin fixed server role (as shown in Figure 1.11).

FIGURE 1.10   MorrisL should show up in the sysadmins Role Members list.

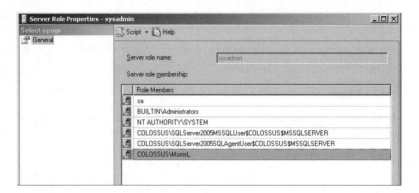

FIGURE 1.11   GibsonH should show up in the serveradmin Role Members list.

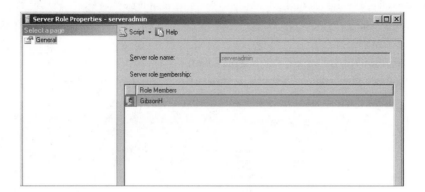

Task 1.19: Creating a Database User Mapping

Once you have created logins for your users so they can access SQL Server, you need to give them access to databases once they have logged in. You do so by creating database user mappings and then assigning permissions to those user mappings (I discuss permissions later in this book).

If you've looked at the existing database security, you may have noticed that two user mappings already exist in your databases when they are first created: DBO and guest. Members of the sysadmin fixed server role automatically become the database owner (DBO) user in every database on the system. In this way, they can perform all the necessary administrative functions in the databases, such as adding users and creating tables. The *guest user* is a catch-all database user mapping for people who have a SQL Server login but not a user account in the database. These users can log in to the server as themselves and access any database where they don't have a user mapping. The guest account should be limited in function, because anybody with a SQL Server login can use it.

In this task, you will create a database user mapping for GibsonH to access the Adventure-Works database.

Scenario

You have just created several new logins on your SQL Server so your users can access the system. You didn't create user mappings for all the logins, though, so you need to create a user mapping for GibsonH to access the AdventureWorks database.

Scope of Task

Duration

This task should take approximately 15 minutes.

Setup

For this task, you need access to the machine you installed SQL Server 2005 on in Task 1.1 and the GibsonH login you created in Task 1.17.

Caveat

This task doesn't have any caveats.

Procedure

In this task, you will create a user mapping for GibsonH to access the AdventureWorks database.

Equipment Used

For this task, you need access to the machine you installed SQL Server 2005 on in Task 1.1 and the GibsonH login you created in Task 1.17.

Details

To create a user mapping for GibsonH in AdventureWorks, follow these steps:

1.   Open SQL Server Management Studio, and expand your server.

2.   Expand Databases by clicking the + sign next to the icon.

3.   Expand the AdventureWorks database.

4.   Expand Security, and click the Users icon.

5.   Right-click Users, and select New User.

6.   Click the ellipsis button next to the Login Name box, and click Browse. View all the available names; note that only logins you've already created are available.

7.   Select the check box next to GibsonH, and click OK twice.

8.   Enter **GibsonH** in the User Name box and **dbo** in the Default Schema box.

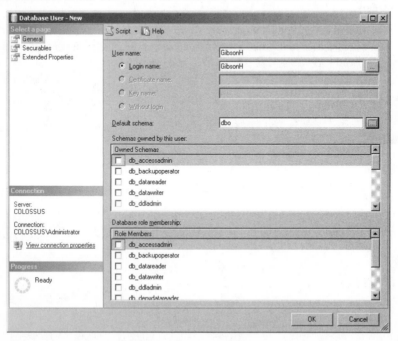

9.   Click OK to create the GibsonH database user account.

Criteria for Completion

This task is complete when you have successfully created a user mapping for GibsonH in the AdventureWorks database, as shown in Figure 1.12.

FIGURE 1.12　　GibsonH should show up in Users list of the AdventureWorks database.

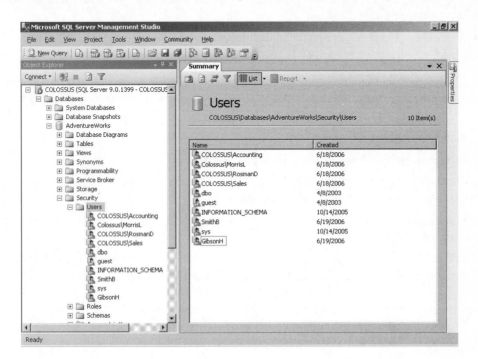

Task 1.20: Assigning User Mappings to Fixed Database Roles

In SQL Server when several users need permission to access a database, it's much easier to give them all permissions as a group rather than try to manage each user separately. That is what *database roles* are for—granting permissions to groups of database users, rather than granting permissions to each database user separately. Three types of database roles exist: fixed, custom, and application.

Fixed database roles have permissions already applied; that is, all you have to do is add users to these roles, and the users inherit the associated permissions. (This is different from custom database roles, as you'll see later.) You can use several fixed database roles in SQL Server to grant permissions:

db_owner   Members of this role can do everything the members of the other roles can do as well as some administrative functions.

db_accessadmin   These users have the authority to say who gets access to the database by adding or removing users.

db_datareader   Members here can read data from any table in the database.

db_datawriter   These users can add, change, and delete data from all the tables in the database.

db_ddladmin   Data Definition Language (DDL) administrators can issue all DDL commands; this allows them to create, modify, or change database objects without viewing the data inside.

db_securityadmin   Members here can add and remove users from database roles, and they can manage statement and object permissions.

db_backupoperator   These users can back up the database.

db_denydatareader   Members can't read the data in the database, but they can make schema changes (for example, add a column to a table).

db_denydatawriter   These users can't make changes to the data in the database, but they're allowed to read the data.

Public   The purpose of this group is to grant users a default set of permissions in the database. All database users automatically join this group and can't be removed.

> Because all database users are automatically members of the Public database role, you need to be cautious about the permissions that are assigned to the role.

In this task, you will add user mappings to fixed database roles.

Scenario

You have just created several new logins on your SQL Server and created user mappings for them in the AdventureWorks database. You now need to make sure these users have only the necessary permissions, so you need to add some of them to fixed database roles.

Scope of Task

Duration

This task should take approximately 15 minutes.

Setup

For this task, you need access to the machine you installed SQL Server 2005 on in Task 1.1, the GibsonH and SmithB logins you created in Task 1.17, the SmithB user mapping you created in Task 1.17, and the GibsonH user mapping you created in Task 1.19.

Caveat

This task doesn't have any caveats.

Procedure

In this task, you will add the SmithB user mapping to the db_denydatawriter fixed database role and the GibsonH user mapping to the db_denydatareader fixed database role.

Equipment Used

For this task, you need access to the machine you installed SQL Server 2005 on in Task 1.1, the GibsonH and SmithB logins you created in Task 1.17, the SmithB user mapping you created in Task 1.17, and the GibsonH user mapping you created in Task 1.19.

Details

To add these user mappings to the fixed database roles, follow these steps:

1. Open SQL Server Management Studio, expand your server, and then expand Databases ➢ AdventureWorks.

2. Expand Security, then Roles, and then Database Roles.

3. Right-click db_denydatawriter, and select Properties.

4. Click Add.

5. Enter **SmithB** in the Enter Object Names to Select box, and click OK.

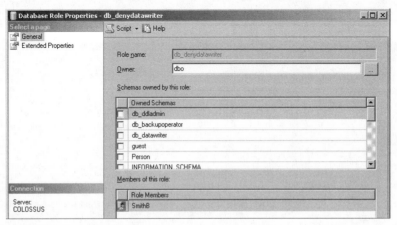

6. Click OK again to return to SQL Server Management Studio.

7. Right-click db_denydatareader, and select Properties.

8. Click Add.

9. Enter **GibsonH** in the Enter Object Names to Select box, and click OK. Then click OK again.

Criteria for Completion

This task is complete when you have successfully added the SmithB user mapping to the db_denydatawriter fixed database role and the GibsonH user mapping to the db_denydatareader fixed database role. Follow these steps to verify you have been successful:

1. Open a new SQL Server query in SQL Server Management Studio.

2. On the Query menu, hover over Connection, and then click Change Connection.

3. Select SQL Server Authentication from the Authentication list box.

4. In the User Name box, enter **SmithB**; in the Password box, enter **Password1,** and click Connect.

5. Enter and execute the following query, which tries to update information in the Human-Resources.Department table (it fails because SmithB is a member of the db_denydatawriter role):

```
INSERT INTO HumanResources.Department (DepartmentID, Name, GroupName,
ModifiedDate) values (200, 'Test','TestGroup',GetDate())
```

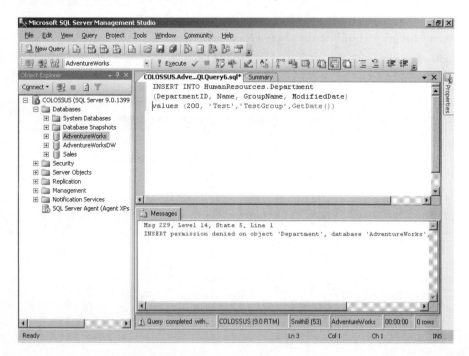

6. On the Query menu, hover over Connection, and then click Change Connection.

7. Select SQL Server Authentication from the Authentication list box.

8. In the User Name box, enter **GibsonH**; in the Password box, enter **Password1,** and click Connect.

9. Enter and execute the following query, which tries to read data from the Human-Resources.Department table (it fails because GibsonH is a member of the db_denydatareader role):

```
SELECT DepartmentID, Name, GroupName, ModifiedDate  FROM
HumanResources.Department
```

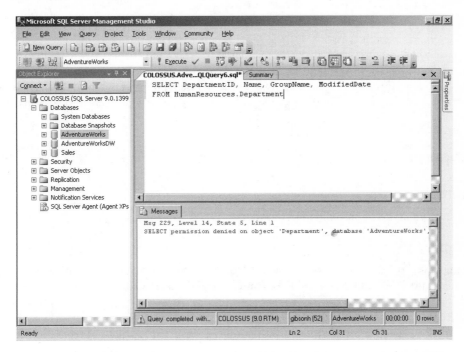

10. Close the query window.

Task 1.21: Creating a Custom Database Role

Although quite a few fixed database roles are at your disposal, they will not always meet your security needs. For example, you may have several users who need Select, Update, and Execute permissions in your database and nothing more. Because none of the fixed database roles give that set of permissions, you need to create a *custom* database role. When you create this new role, you assign permissions to it and then assign users to the role; the users inherit whatever permissions you assign to that role. That is different from the fixed database roles, where you don't need to assign permissions but just need to add users.

 NOTE   You can make your custom database roles members of other database roles. This is referred to as *nesting roles.*

In this task, you will create a custom database role, assign permissions to it, and add user mappings to the new custom role.

Scenario

You have just created several new logins on your SQL Server and created user mappings for them in the AdventureWorks database. You have added some of these users to fixed database roles, but other users require combinations of permissions that none of the fixed database roles offers. To assign the appropriate permissions to these users, you decide to create a custom database role.

Scope of Task

Duration

This task should take approximately 15 minutes.

Setup

For this task, you need access to the machine you installed SQL Server 2005 on in Task 1.1, the AdventureWorks database, and the RosmanD login you created in Task 1.16.

Caveat

In the real world, you would not create a custom database role for just one user, and you would grant more than a single permission.

Procedure

In this task, you will create a custom database role that grants the members permission to select data from the HumanResources.Department table in the AdventureWorks database. You will then add the RosmanD user mapping to the new custom database role.

Equipment Used

For this task, you need access to the machine you installed SQL Server 2005 on in Task 1.1, the AdventureWorks database, and the RosmanD login you created in Task 1.16.

Details

To create a new custom database role and add users to it, follow these steps:

1. Open SQL Server Management Studio, expand your server, and then expand Databases ➤ AdventureWorks.

2. Expand Security and then Roles.

3. Right-click Database Roles, and select New Database Role.

4. In the Role Name box, enter **SelectOnly**, and enter **dbo** in the Owner box.

5. Add *Sqldomain***RosmanD** to the Role Members list.

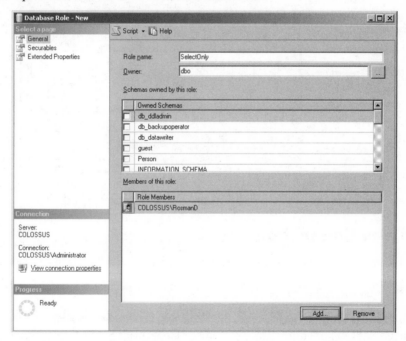

6. On the Securables page, click Add under the Securables list box, select the Specific Objects radio button, and click OK.

7. Click the Objects Type button, select Tables, and click OK.

8. Click Browse, select the HumanResources.Department check box, click OK, and then click OK again.

9. In the Explicit Permissions for HumanResources.Department list, check the Grant check box next to Select, and click OK.

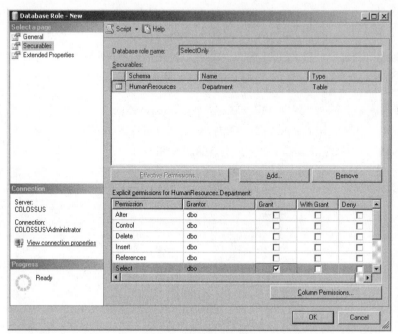

10. Click OK to create the role and return to SQL Server Management Studio.

Criteria for Completion

This task is complete when you have successfully created a new custom database role, assigned permissions, and added the RosmanD user mapping to the new role. Follow these steps to verify you have been successful:

1. Close all programs, log out of Windows, and log back in as RosmanD.

2. Open a new SQL Server query in SQL Server Management Studio, and connect using Windows Authentication.

3. Notice that the following query succeeds because RosmanD is a member of the new SelectOnly role:

```
USE AdventureWorks
SELECT * FROM HumanResources.Department
```

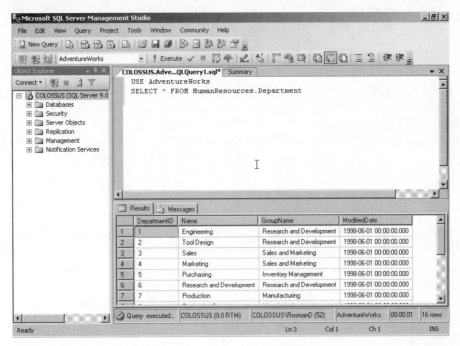

4. Now notice the failure of the next query because RosmanD is a member of a role that is allowed to select only:

```
INSERT INTO HumanResources.Department (DepartmentID, [Name], GroupName,
ModifiedDate) values (200, 'Test','TestGroup',GetDate())
```

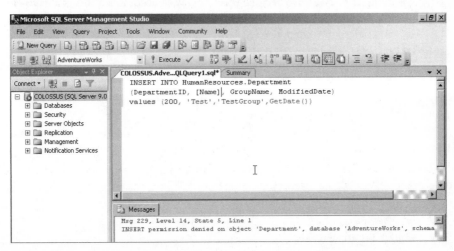

5. Close all programs, log out of Windows, and log back in as yourself.

Task 1.22: Creating an Application Role

Many companies have developed custom applications in-house for manipulating their data; your company may have developed such an application. Such applications can take months, or even years, to build and perfect, so it goes without saying that you want your employees to use the custom application rather than find their own ways to modify the data. That is where application roles come in to play.

An *application* role is a special role that is activated with a password. By implementing this special role, your users can't access data using just their SQL Server login and database account; they must use the proper application. Here is how it works:

1. Create an application role, and assign it permissions.

2. Users open the approved application and are logged in to SQL Server.

3. To enable the application role, the application executes the `sp_setapprole` stored procedure (which is written into the application at design time).

Once the application role is enabled, SQL Server no longer sees users as themselves; it sees users as the application and grants them application role permissions.

In this task, you will create and assign permissions to an application role.

Scenario

Your company has written a custom application for manipulating data in one of your databases. This application has taken hundreds of staff hours and has cost hundreds of thousands of dollars, so management has insisted employees use this custom application to access the database and nothing else. You have decided the best way to accomplish this goal is to create an application role, which your developers can hard code into their application.

Scope of Task

Duration

This task should take approximately 15 minutes.

Setup

For this task, you need access to the machine you installed SQL Server 2005 on in Task 1.1 and the AdventureWorks database.

Caveat

This task doesn't have any caveats.

Procedure

In this task, you will create an application role that grants the members permission to select data from the HumanResources.Department table in the AdventureWorks database.

Equipment Used

For this task, you need access to the machine you installed SQL Server 2005 on in Task 1.1 and the AdventureWorks database.

Details

To create an application role and assign permissions to it, follow these steps:

1. Open SQL Server Management Studio, and expand Databases ➢ AdventureWorks ➢ Security.

2. Right-click Application Roles, and select New Application Role.

3. In the Role Name box, enter **EntAppRole**.

4. Enter **dbo** in the Default Schema box.

5. In the Password and Confirm Password boxes, enter **Password1**.

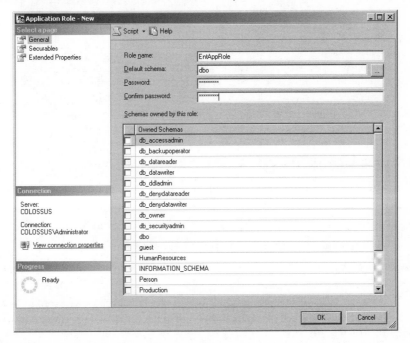

6. On the Securables page, click Add under the Securables list box, select the Specific Objects radio button, and click OK.

7. Click the Objects Type button, select Tables, and click OK.

8. Click Browse, select the HumanResources.Department check box, click OK, and then click OK again.

9. In the Permissions for HumanResources.Department list, select the Grant check box next to Select, and click OK to create the role.

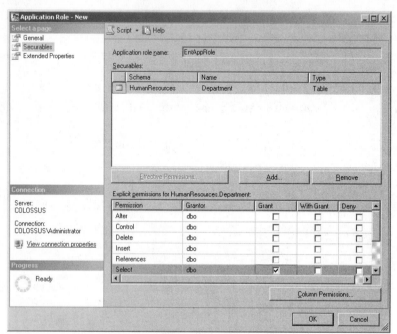

Criteria for Completion

This task is complete when you have successfully created a new application role and assigned permissions. Follow these steps to verify you have been successful:

1. Open a new SQL Server query in SQL Server Management Studio.

2. On the Query menu, hover over Connection, and click Change Connection.

3. Connect using SQL Authentication with GibsonH as the username and Password1 as the password.

4. Enter and execute the following query. Notice that it fails because GibsonH has been denied Select permissions because of membership in the db_denydatareader database role (assigned in Task 1.20):

```
USE AdventureWorks
SELECT * FROM HumanResources.Department
```

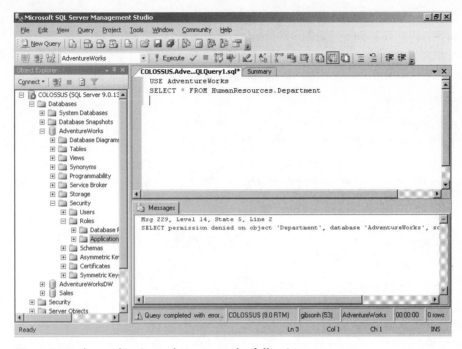

5. To activate the application role, execute the following query:

    ```
    sp_setapprole @rolename='EntAppRole', @password='Password1'
    ```

6. Clear the query window, and execute the following query. Notice that the query is successful this time. This is because SQL Server now sees you as EntAppRole, which has Select permission.

    ```
    SELECT * FROM HumanResources.Department
    ```

7. Close the query window.

Task 1.23: Assigning Permissions

In the past few tasks, you assigned permissions to users by adding them to roles. To understand how these roles work, you need a more complete understanding of what permissions are and how they work.

Any object to which SQL Server regulates access is referred to as a *securable*. Securables can fall under three scopes:

- Server scope
  - Server
  - Endpoint

- SQL Server login
- SQL Server login mapped to a Windows login
- SQL Server login mapped to a certificate
- SQL Server login mapped to an asymmetric key
- Database scope
  - Database users
  - Database users mapped to a Windows login
  - Database users mapped to a certificate
  - Database users mapped to an asymmetric key
  - Database roles
  - Application roles
  - Assemblies
  - Message type
  - Service contract
  - Service
  - Full-text catalog
  - DDL events
  - Schema
- Schema scope
  - Table
  - View
  - Function
  - Procedure
  - Queue
  - Type
  - Rule
  - Default
  - Synonym
  - Aggregate

All of these objects are secured by applying permissions. You can work with two types of permissions: statement and object permissions.

Statement permissions have nothing to do with the actual data; they allow users to create the structure that holds the data. It's important not to grant these permissions haphazardly, because doing so can lead to such problems as wasted server resources. It's best to restrict statement permissions to database administrators (DBAs), assistant DBAs, and developers. These are some good examples of statement permissions:

- Create Database
- Create Table
- Create View
- Create Procedure
- Create Index
- Create Rule
- Create Default

> **NOTE** When you create a new database, a record is added to the sysdatabases system table, which is stored in the master database. Therefore, you can grant the CREATE DATABASE statement only on the master database.

The second type of permissions is *object* permissions, which control how users work with the actual data. Using object permissions, you can control who is allowed to read from, write to, or otherwise manipulate your data. The 12 object permissions are as follows:

Control   This permission gives the principal ownership-like capabilities on the object and all objects under it in the hierarchy. For example, if you grant a user Control permission on the database, then the user has Control permission on all the objects in the database, such as tables and views.

Alter   This permission allows users to create, alter, or drop the securable and any object under it in the hierarchy. The only property the user can't change is ownership.

Take Ownership   This allows the user to take ownership of an object.

Impersonate   This permission allows one login or user to impersonate another.

Create   As the name implies, this permission lets a user create objects.

View Definition   This permission allows users to see the Transact-SQL syntax that was used to create the object being secured.

Select   When granted, this permission allows users to read data from the table or view. When granted at the column level, it lets users read from a single column.

Insert   This permission allows users to insert new rows into a table.

Update   This permission lets users modify existing data in a table but not add new rows to or delete existing rows from a table. When this permission is granted on a column, users can modify data in that single column.

Delete   This permission allows users to remove rows from a table.

References   Tables can be linked together on a common column with a foreign-key relationship, which is designed to protect data across tables. When two tables are linked with a foreign key, this permission allows the user to select data from the primary table without having Select permission on the foreign table.

Execute   This permission allows users to execute the stored procedure where the permission is applied.

All the permissions in SQL Server can exist in one of three states:

Grant   Granting allows users to use a specific permission. For instance, if you grant SmithB Select permission on a table, then SmithB can read the data within. You know a permission has been granted when the Allow check box is selected next to the permission in the permissions list.

Revoke   A revoked permission isn't specifically granted, but a user can inherit the permission if it has been granted to another role of which they are a member. That is, if you revoke the Select permission from SmithB, then SmithB can't use it. If, however, SmithB is a member of a role that has been granted Select permission, SmithB can read the data just as if SmithB had the Select permission. A permission is revoked when neither Allow nor Deny boxes are selected next to a permission.

Deny   If you deny a permission, the user doesn't get the permission—no matter what. If you deny SmithB Select permission on a table, even if SmithB is a member of a role with Select permission, then SmithB can't read the data. You know a permission has been denied when the Deny check box is selected next to the permission in the permissions list.

In this task, you'll get some hands-on experience with assigning permissions and changing the states of those permissions.

Scenario

You have just installed a new SQL Server for your company and want to make sure you fully understand how permissions work, so you have decided to test permissions on your test server before assigning them to users on production databases.

Scope of Task

Duration

This task should take approximately 30 minutes.

Setup

For this task, you need access to the machine you installed SQL Server 2005 on in Task 1.1, the SmithB account you created in Task 1.17, and the AdventureWorks database.

Caveat

In a production environment, for ease of management, you will create custom roles and assign permissions to those roles. You will usually assign permissions to a specific user only when you want to deny a permission to that user.

Procedure

In this task, you will assign permissions to the SmithB user mapping. You will then change the permission state and test the effects of the change.

Equipment Used

For this task, you need access to the machine you installed SQL Server 2005 on in Task 1.1, the SmithB account you created in Task 1.17, and the AdventureWorks database.

Details

To create assign and modify permissions for SmithB, follow these steps:

1. Open SQL Server Management Studio, expand your server, and then expand Databases ➤ AdventureWorks ➤ Security.

2. Expand Users, right-click SmithB, and select Properties.

3. On the Securables page, click Add under the Securables list box, select the Specific Objects radio button, and click OK.

4. Click the Objects Type button, select Tables, and click OK.

5. Click Browse, select the HumanResources.Department check box, and click OK twice.

6. In the Permissions for HumanResources.Department list, select the Grant check box next to Select, and click OK.

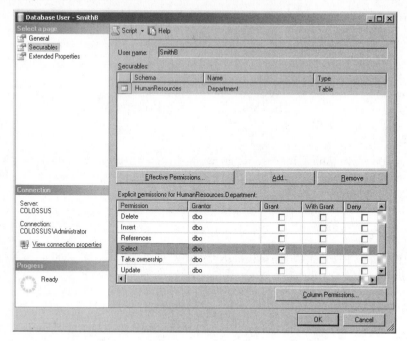

7. Open a new SQL Server query in SQL Server Management Studio.

8. On the Query menu, hover over Connection, and then click Change Connection.

9. Select SQL Server Authentication from the Authentication list box.

10. In the User Name box, enter **SmithB**; in the Password box, enter **Password1,** and click Connect.

11. Execute the following query. It's successful because SmithB has Select permission on the HumanResources.Department table.

```
USE AdventureWorks
SELECT * FROM HumanResources.Department
```

12. Right-click SmithB under Users in the AdventureWorks database, and select Properties.

13. On the Securables page, click Add under the Securables list box, select the Specific Objects radio button, and click OK.

14. Click the Objects Type button, select Tables, and click OK.

15. Click Browse, select the HumanResources.Department check box, and click OK.

16. In the Permissions for HumanResources.Department list, uncheck the Grant check box next to Select (this revokes the permission), and click OK.

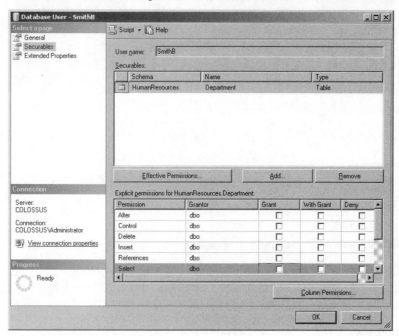

17. Return to the query window, and execute the query in step 11. It fails because SmithB doesn't have explicit Select permission.

18. Right-click SmithB under Users in the AdventureWorks database, and select Properties.

19. Under Role Membership, select the check box next to the db_datareader role.

20. Return to the query window, and rerun the query from step 11. Now it fails because SmithB does not have the permission expressly applied and is not a member of a role that has this permission.

21. Right-click SmithB under Users in the AdventureWorks database, and select Properties.

22. On the Securables page, click Add under the Securables list box, select the Specific Objects radio button, and click OK.

23. Click the Objects Type button, select Tables, and click OK.

24. Click Browse, select the HumanResources.Department check box, and click OK.

25. In the Permissions for HumanResources.Department list, select the Deny check box next to Select, and click OK.

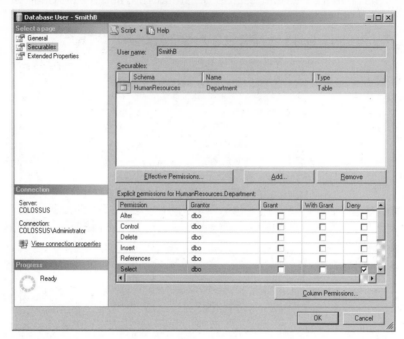

26. Return to the query window, and again run the query from step 11. It fails this time because you've specifically denied SmithB access.

Criteria for Completion

This task is complete when you have successfully assigned the permissions as described in the "Details" section.

Task 1.24: Configuring Encrypted Connections

Thus far, you've seen how to protect your data from intruders by granting access and applying permissions to objects. But when someone legitimately accesses the server and starts transferring data, it travels over the network. If you need really robust security, you can go so far as to encrypt the data as it travels between the client and the server over the network. That way, if anyone is reading your network traffic, they will not be able to interpret the data.

Just like a secure web page, SQL Server uses Secure Sockets Layer (SSL) encryption. This means that to encrypt your connections to SQL Server, you first need to get a certificate, which you can get from one of the major vendors such as VeriSign or can install Windows Certificate services and supply your own.

> If you want to test encryption but do not have a certificate, SQL Server can generate a self-signed certificate for you to use.

> Do not use a self-signed certificate in production; they do not provide strong security and are susceptible to attack. They are for testing and development only.

Although using encryption can help protect your data in a highly secured environment, using encryption has a few drawbacks:

- An extra network round-trip is required at connect time.
- Packets sent from the application to the instance of SQL Server must be encrypted by the client Net-Library and decrypted by the server Net-Library.
- Packets sent from the SQL Server instance to the application must be encrypted by the server Net-Library and decrypted by the client Net-Library.

This means encryption can negatively impact SQL Server's performance, so use encryption only when necessary.

In this task, you'll configure SQL Server to use encryption using a self-signed certificate.

Scenario

You have just installed a new SQL Server for your company and created a database that holds e-commerce data. For your customers' convenience, your company has decided to store credit card information so users do not have to enter it every time they place an order on your site. You know you need to use the highest level of security possible, so you have decided to configure SQL Server to require encrypted connections.

Scope of Task

Duration

This task should take approximately 30 minutes.

Setup

For this task, you need access to the machine you installed SQL Server 2005 on in Task 1.1.

Caveat

In production, you should not use a self-signed certificate. You are using one in this task for simplicity's sake.

Procedure

In this task, you will configure SQL Server to use encrypted connections using a self-signed certificate.

Equipment Used

For this task, you need access to the machine you installed SQL Server 2005 on in Task 1.1.

Details

To configure the server to force clients to use encrypted connections, follow these steps:

1.   In SQL Server Configuration Manager, expand SQL Server 2005 Network Configuration, right-click Protocols for <server instance>, and then select Properties.

2.   In the Protocols for <instance name> Properties dialog box, on the Flags tab, change ForceEncryption to Yes.

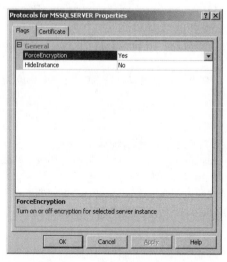

3.   Click OK twice to close the warning dialog box that opens.

4.   Restart the SQL Server service.

5.   Again, right-click Protocols for <server instance>, and then select Properties.

6.   In the Protocols for <instance name> Properties dialog box, on the Certificate tab, select the desired certificate (in this case the self-signed certificate) from the Certificate drop-down list, and then click OK.

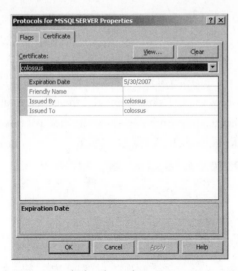

7. Click OK to close the warning dialog box that opens.

8. Restart the SQL Server service.

Next, you need to configure the clients to request encrypted connections to the server. Here's how:

1. In SQL Server Configuration Manager, right-click SQL Native Client Configuration, and select Properties.

2. On the Flags tab, in the Force Protocol Encryption box, select Yes, and then click OK to close the dialog box.

3. Restart the SQL Server service.

Criteria for Completion

This task is complete when you can connect to SQL Server using an encrypted connection. To verify this, follow these steps:

1. Open a new SQL Server query in SQL Server Management Studio.

2. On the Query menu, hover over Connection, and then click Change Connection.

3. Select Windows Authentication from the Authentication list box.

4. Click the Options button, and check the Encrypt Connection box.

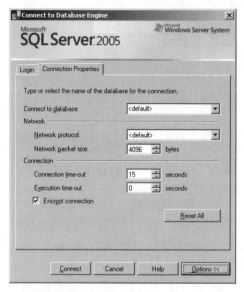

5. Click Connect to make the connection.

Phase 2

Implementing High Availability and Disaster Recovery

After you get SQL Server installed and configured, your users will come to depend on it to perform their daily tasks. In fact, if SQL Server goes down, your users may not be able to do their jobs. This results in lost revenue, lost customers, and lost productivity. As a database administrator (DBA), it is up to you to make sure this does not happen to your company. In other words, you need to make sure SQL Server is available with minimal or no downtime. Of course, disasters will happen, and when they do, it is up to you to get SQL Server back up and running as fast as possible.

That makes the topics discussed in Phase 2 very important. I will present a series of tasks that will cover what you need to do to keep SQL Server available as much as possible and how to recover in the event of a disaster.

I will discuss how to back up databases and transaction logs and, correspondingly, how to restore from those backups. I will also present some tasks that can help you keep SQL Server available as much as possible. This includes tasks such as log shipping, database mirroring, and snapshots. Finally, you will learn how to configure replication, including transactional, snapshot, and merge replication.

I'll start with one of the most basic, and important, steps you can take to ensure that you can recover your databases in the event of a disaster: selecting a recovery model.

Task 2.1: Selecting and Setting a Recovery Model

Before you can start backing up your databases and transaction logs, you need to configure the database to use the right recovery model. You need to know which model to choose because it affects how fast your backups are and how effectively you can restore data after a crash. You can choose from three recovery models:

Simple The transaction log is used for very little in this recovery model. In fact, almost nothing is recorded in the log. This means any database set to use this model can be recovered only up to the last backup. Any changes made to your database after the last backup was performed will be lost because they are not recorded in the transaction log. This model is a good choice for development databases where most data is test data that does not need to be restored after a crash. It is also a good choice for databases that are not changed often, such as an online analytical processing (OLAP) database.

Bulk-Logged   This model records much more information in the transaction log than the Simple model. The only information not recorded is bulk operations such as SELECT INTO, BCP, BULK INSERT, CREATE INDEX, and text and ntext operations. This means you can recover most of the data in the event of a crash; only bulk operations may be lost. You can set this option just before performing a bulk insert operation to speed up the bulk insert. You need to back up your database immediately after performing bulk operations if you select this option because everything that is inserted during this time is not in the transaction log, so it will all be lost if the database crashes before the next backup.

Full   This is the default option, which records every operation against the database in the transaction log. Using this model, you will be able to recover your database up to the minute of a crash. This is a good option for most production databases because it offers the highest level of protection.

In this task, you'll set the recovery model for the AdventureWorks database.

Scenario

You have created a new database on your SQL Server, and you need to make sure it is being backed up as quickly and efficiently as possible. You know that, to ensure this, you need to configure the database to use the correct recovery model, so you decide to set the recovery model for the new database.

Scope of Task

Duration

This task should take approximately 15 minutes.

Setup

For this task, you need access to the machine you installed SQL Server 2005 on in Task 1.1 and the AdventureWorks database installed with the sample data.

Caveat

This task doesn't have any caveats.

Procedure

In this task, you will configure the AdventureWorks database to use the Full recovery model.

Equipment Used

For this task, you need access to the machine you installed SQL Server 2005 on in Task 1.1 and the AdventureWorks database installed with the sample data.

Details

To set the recovery model for the AdventureWorks database, follow these steps:

1. Open SQL Server Management Studio, and in Object Explorer, expand Databases under your server.

2. Right-click AdventureWorks, and click Properties.

3. On the Options page, select Full from the Recovery Model drop-down list.

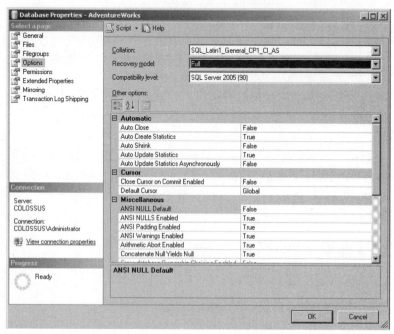

4. Click OK to configure the model.

Criteria for Completion

This task is complete when the AdventureWorks database is configured to use the Full recovery model as outlined in the details of this task.

Task 2.2: Creating a Backup Device

A *backup* is a copy of your data that is stored somewhere other than on the hard drive of your computer, usually on some type of tape (a lot like the kind you listen to); but you can also store a backup on a hard drive on another computer connected over a local area network (LAN).

Why would you want to keep a copy of your data in two places? The following are some reasons:

- The possibility of hardware failure
- The potential for natural disaster
- Disgruntled employees who destroy or maliciously update sensitive data

One of the nicest features of SQL Server backups is that they are all online backups, which means your users can access the database while you're backing it up. This is possible because SQL Server uses transaction logs, which are a lot like a diary for the database. In a diary, you put a date next to everything that happens to you. It might look as follows:

3-21-06	Bought a car
3-22-06	Drove new car to show off
3-23-06	Drove car into tree
3-24-06	Started looking for new car

Much like a diary, a transaction log puts a *log sequence number* (LSN) next to each line of the log. Every time SQL Server writes the data from the transaction log into the database, it creates a *checkpoint* in the log. SQL Server uses the checkpoint like a bookmark, so it will remember where it left off next time it copies from the log to the database. A transaction log would look as follows:

147	Begin Tran 1
148	Update Tran 1
149	Begin Tran 2
150	Update Tran 2
151	Commit Tran 1
152	Checkpoint
153	Update Tran 2
154	Commit Tran 2

When a backup is started, SQL Server records the current LSN. Once the backup is complete, SQL Server backs up all the entries in the transaction log from the LSN it recorded at the start of the backup to the current LSN. Here's an example of how it works:

1. SQL Server checkpoints the data and records the LSN of the oldest open transaction (in this case, 149 Begin Tran 2, because it wasn't committed before the checkpoint).

2. SQL Server backs up all the pages of the database that contain data (no need to back up the empty ones).

3.   SQL Server grabs all the parts of the transaction log that were recorded during the backup process—that is, all the lines of the transaction log with an LSN greater than the LSN recorded at the start of the backup session (in this case, 149 and greater). This way, your users can still do whatever they want with the database while it's being backed up.

Backups are stored on a physical backup media, which can be a tape drive or a hard disk (local or over a network connection). SQL Server isn't aware of the various forms of media attached to your server, so you must inform SQL Server where to store the backups. That is what a backup device is for; it's a representation of the backup media. You can create two types of backup devices: permanent and temporary.

SQL Server creates temporary backup devices on the fly when you perform the backup. They're useful for making a copy of a database to send to another office so that office has a complete copy of your data. Or, you may want to consider using a temporary backup device to make a copy of your database for permanent offsite storage (usually for archiving).

You can use permanent backup devices over and over again; you can even append data to them, making them the perfect device for regularly scheduled backups. Permanent backup devices are created before the backup is performed and, like temporary devices, can be created on a local hard disk, on a remote hard disk over a LAN, or on a local tape drive.

 If you're using a tape drive as a backup medium, it must be physically attached to the SQL Server machine. The only way around this requirement is to use a third-party backup solution.

In this task, you'll create a permanent backup device.

Scenario

You need to start backing up the databases you have created on your new SQL Server. Before you can start backing them up, though, you realize you need a place to store the backups, so you decide to create a backup device for storing backups.

Scope of Task

Duration

This task should take approximately 15 minutes.

Setup

For this task, you need access to the machine you installed SQL Server 2005 on in Task 1.1.

Caveat

This task doesn't have any caveats.

Procedure

In this task, you will create a backup device.

Equipment Used

For this task, you need access to the machine you installed SQL Server 2005 on in Task 1.1.

Details

To create a backup device, follow these steps:

1. Open SQL Server Management Studio by selecting it from the SQL Server 2005 group under Programs on the Start menu. Expand your server, and then expand Server Objects.

2. Right-click Backup Devices in Object Explorer, and select New Backup Device.

3. In the Device Name box of the Backup Device dialog box, enter **AdvWorks**. Notice that the filename and path are filled in for you; make sure you have enough free space on the drive SQL Server has selected.

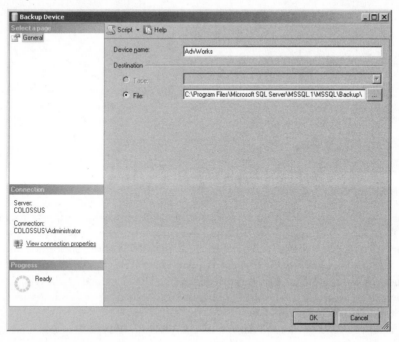

4. Click OK to create the device.

Criteria for Completion

This task is complete when you have created a new backup device. The new device will show up in Object Explorer, as shown in Figure 2.1.

FIGURE 2.1   The new backup device shows up in Object Explorer under Backup Devices.

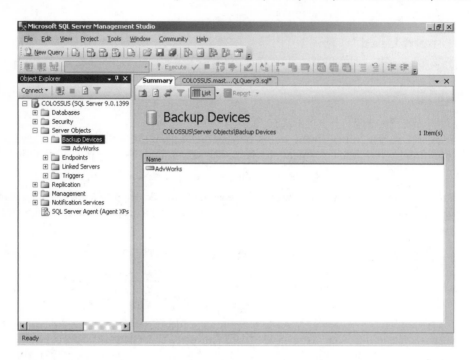

Task 2.3: Performing a Full Backup

Just as the name implies, a *full* backup is a backup of the entire database. It backs up the database files, the locations of those files, and the portions of the transaction log (from the LSN recorded at the start of the backup to the LSN at the end of the backup). This is called a *baseline* backup because it is the first type of backup you need to perform in any backup strategy because all the other backup types depend on the existence of a full backup. This means you can't perform a differential or transaction log backup if you have never performed a full backup.

In this task, you'll perform a full backup of the AdventureWorks database.

Scenario

You need to start backing up the databases you have created on your new SQL Server. You know you need a full backup before you can start using differential or transaction log backups, so you decide to create a baseline by performing a full backup.

Scope of Task

Duration

This task should take approximately 15 minutes.

Setup

For this task, you need access to the machine you installed SQL Server 2005 on in Task 1.1, the AdventureWorks database installed with the sample data, and the AdvWorks backup device you created in Task 2.2.

Caveat

This task doesn't have any caveats.

Procedure

In this task, you will perform a full backup on the AdventureWorks database.

Equipment Used

For this task, you need access to the machine you installed SQL Server 2005 on in Task 1.1, the AdventureWorks database installed with the sample data, and the AdvWorks backup device you created in Task 2.2.

Details

To perform a full backup of the AdventureWorks database, follow these steps:

1. Open SQL Server Management Studio, expand Databases, right-click AdventureWorks, point to Tasks, and click Back Up.

2. In the Backup dialog box, make sure AdventureWorks is the selected database to back up and make sure Backup Type is Full.

3. Leave the default name in the Name box. In the Description box, enter **Full Backup of AdventureWorks.**

4. Under Destination, a disk device may already be listed. If so, select the device, and click Remove.

5. Under Destination, click Add.

6. In the Select Backup Destination box, click Backup Device, select AdvWorks, and click OK.

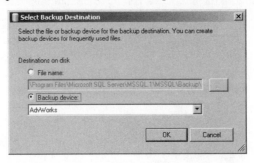

7. You should now have a backup device listed under Destination.

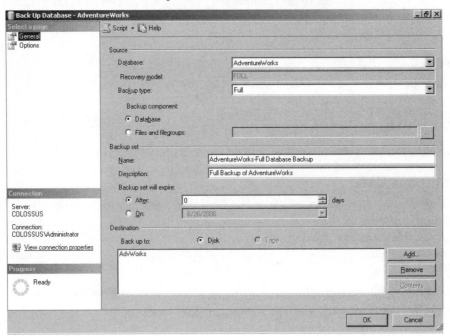

8. Switch to the Options page. On the Options page, select Overwrite All Existing Backup Sets. This option initializes a new device or overwrites an existing one.

9. Select Verify Backup When Finished to check the actual database against the backup copy, and be sure they match after the backup is complete.

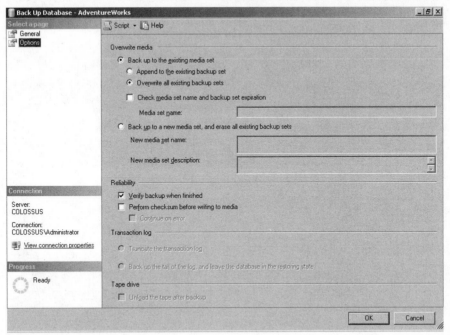

10. Click OK to start the backup.

11. When the backup is complete, you will get a notification; click OK to close it.

Criteria for Completion

This task is complete when you have a full backup of the AdventureWorks database stored in the AdvWorks backup device. Follow these steps to verify:

1. To verify the backup, you can look at the contents of the backup device, so expand Backup Devices under Server Objects in Object Explorer.

2. Right-click AdvWorks, and select Properties.

3. On the Media Contents page, you should see the full backup of AdventureWorks.

4.   Click OK to return to SQL Server Management Studio.

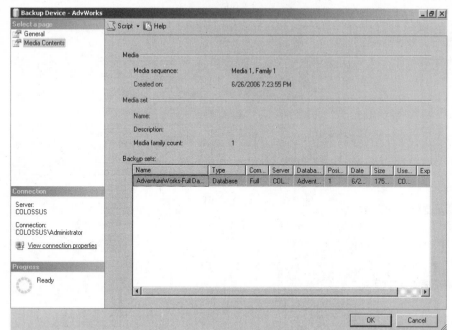

Task 2.4: Performing a Differential Backup

Differential backups are designed to record all the changes made to a database since the last full backup was performed. Thus, if you perform a full backup on Monday and a differential backup on Tuesday, the differential will record all the changes to the database since the full backup on Monday. Another differential backup on Wednesday would record all the changes made since the full backup on Monday. The differential backup gets a little bigger each time it's performed, but it's still a great deal smaller than the full backup; so, a differential is faster than a full backup.

SQL Server figures out which pages in the backup have changed by reading the last LSN of the last full backup and comparing it to the data pages in the database. If SQL Server finds any updated data pages, it backs up the entire extent (eight contiguous pages) of data, rather than just the page that changed.

Performing a differential backup follows almost the same process as a full backup. In this task, you'll perform a differential backup on the AdventureWorks database to the permanent backup device you created in Task 2.2.

Scenario

You have started performing full backups of your databases on a regular basis, and you have noticed that, as the database grows, the backup get slower. You know you need to speed up the backup process, so you decide to incorporate differential backups into your backup scheme.

Scope of Task

Duration

This task should take approximately 15 minutes.

Setup

For this task, you need access to the machine you installed SQL Server 2005 on in Task 1.1, the AdventureWorks database installed with the sample data, and the AdvWorks backup device you created in Task 2.2.

Caveat

This task doesn't have any caveats.

Procedure

In this task, you will perform a differential backup on the AdventureWorks database.

Equipment Used

For this task, you need access to the machine you installed SQL Server 2005 on in Task 1.1, the AdventureWorks database installed with the sample data, and the AdvWorks backup device you created in Task 2.2.

Details

To perform a differential backup of the AdventureWorks database, follow these steps:

1. Open SQL Server Management Studio. Expand your server, and then expand Databases.

2. Right-click AdventureWorks, point to Tasks, and select Back Up.

3. In the Backup dialog box, make sure AdventureWorks is the selected database to back up and Backup Type is Differential.

4. Leave the default name in the Name box. In the Description box, enter **Differential Backup of AdventureWorks**.

5. Under Destination, make sure the AdvWorks device is listed.

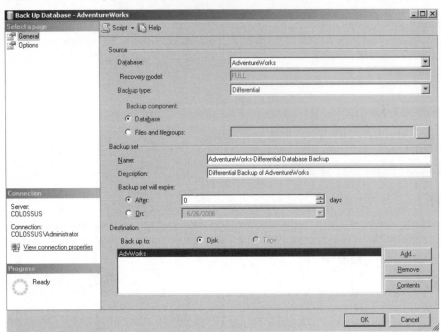

6. On the Options page, make sure Append to the Existing Backup Set is selected so you don't overwrite your existing full backup.

7. On the Options tab, select Verify Backup When Finished.

8. Click OK to start the backup.

Criteria for Completion

This task is complete when you have a differential backup of the AdventureWorks database stored in the AdvWorks backup device. Follow these steps to verify:

1. To verify the backup, you can look at the contents of the backup device, so expand Backup Devices under Server Objects in Object Explorer.

2. Right-click AdvWorks, and select Properties.

3. On the Media Contents page, you should see the differential backup of AdventureWorks.

4. Click OK to return to SQL Server Management Studio.

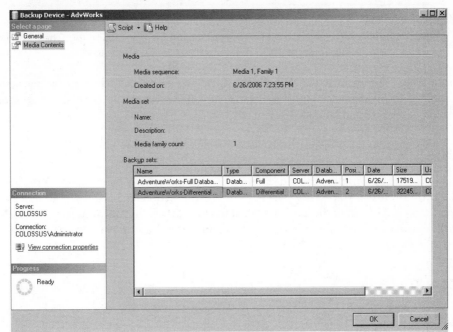

Task 2.5: Performing a Transaction Log Backup

Although they rely on the existence of a full backup, transaction log backups don't back up the database itself. This type of backup records only sections of the transaction log, specifically since the last transaction log backup. It's easier to understand the role of the transaction log backup if you think of the transaction log the way SQL Server does: as a separate object. Then it makes sense that SQL Server requires a backup of the database as well as the log.

In addition to the fact that a transaction log is an entity unto itself, there is another important reason to back it up. When a database is configured to use the Full or Bulk-Logged recovery model, a transaction log backup is the only type of backup that clears old transactions from the transaction log; full and differential backups can clear the log only when the database being backed up is configured to use the Simple recovery model. Therefore, if you were to perform only full and differential backups on most production databases, the transaction log would eventually fill to 100 percent capacity, and your users would be locked out of the database.

WARNING When a transaction log becomes 100 percent full, users are denied access to the database until an administrator clears the transaction log. The best way around this is to perform regular transaction log backups.

Performing a transaction log backup doesn't involve a lot of steps, so let's go through them. In this task, you'll perform a transaction log backup on the AdventureWorks database using the backup device created in Task 2.2.

Scenario

You have started performing full and differential backups of your databases on a regular basis. You know that if you do not start performing transaction log backups, your users will eventually get locked out of the database when the transaction log fills to capacity. You also want the extra safety measure of having transaction log backups in place, so you decide to start performing transaction log backups.

Scope of Task

Duration

This task should take approximately 15 minutes.

Setup

For this task, you need access to the machine you installed SQL Server 2005 on in Task 1.1, the AdventureWorks database installed with the sample data, and the AdvWorks backup device you created in Task 2.2. Also, the AdventureWorks database must be set to use the Full recovery model as outlined in Task 2.1.

Caveat

This task doesn't have any caveats.

Procedure

In this task, you will perform a transaction log backup on the AdventureWorks database.

Equipment Used

For this task, you need access to the machine you installed SQL Server 2005 on in Task 1.1, the AdventureWorks database installed with the sample data, and the AdvWorks backup device you created in Task 2.2.

Details

To perform a transaction log backup of the AdventureWorks database, follow these steps:

1. Open SQL Server Management Studio. Expand your server, and then expand Databases.

2. Right-click AdventureWorks, point to Tasks, and select Back Up.

3. In the Backup dialog box, make sure AdventureWorks is the selected database to back up and Backup Type is Transaction Log.

4. Leave the default name in the Name box. In the Description box, enter **Transaction Log Backup of AdventureWorks**.

5. Under Destination, make sure the AdvWorks device is listed.

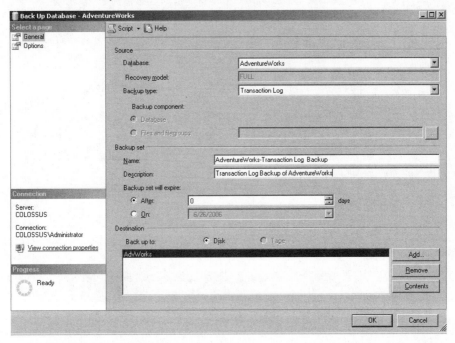

6. On the Options page, make sure Append to the Existing Backup Set is selected so you don't overwrite your existing full backup.

7. On the Options page, select Verify Backup When Finished.

8. Click OK to start the backup.

9. When the backup is complete, you will get a notification; click OK to close it.

Criteria for Completion

This task is complete when you have a transaction log backup of the AdventureWorks database stored in the AdvWorks backup device. Follow these steps to verify:

1. To verify the backup, you can look at the contents of the backup device, so expand Backup Devices under Server Objects in Object Explorer.

2. Right-click AdvWorks, and select Properties.

3. On the Media Contents page, you should see the transaction log backup of AdventureWorks.

4. Click OK to return to SQL Server Management Studio.

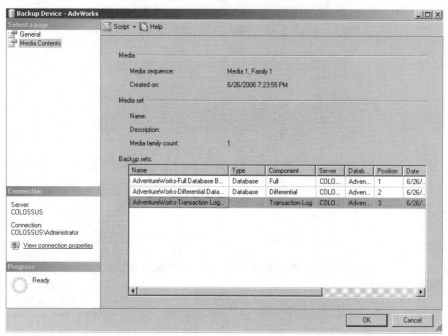

Task 2.6: Performing a Filegroup Backup

A growing number of companies have databases that are reaching the terabyte range. For good reason, these are known as *very large databases* (VLDBs). Imagine trying to perform a backup of a 2TB database on a nightly, or even weekly, basis. Even if you have purchased the latest, greatest hardware, you're looking at a very long backup time. Microsoft knows you don't want to wait that long for a backup to finish, so it gives you a way to back up small sections of the database at a time: a *filegroup backup*. Before you can perform a filegroup backup, you need to know what a filegroup is.

Simply put, a *filegroup* is a logical grouping of database files. Using filegroups, you can explicitly place database objects onto a particular set of database files. For example, you can separate tables and their nonclustered indexes onto separate filegroups. This way, a database isn't limited to being contained on one hard disk; it can be spread out across many hard disks and thus can grow quite large. This can also improve performance, because modifications to the table can be written to both the table and the index at the same time. Another advantage is the ability to mark the filegroup and all data on the files that are part of it as either READONLY or READWRITE. The advantage you are most concerned with here, though, is that filegroups give you the ability to back up only a single filegroup at a time. This can be extremely useful for a VLDB, because the sheer size of the database could make backing up an extremely time-consuming process.

However, you need to be aware of a caveat when using filegroup backups to accelerate the backup process for VLDBs. You can use filegroups to expedite data access by placing tables on one file and the corresponding indexes on another file. Although this speeds up data access, it can slow the backup process because you must back up tables and indexes as a single unit, as shown in Figure 2.2. This means that if the tables and indexes are stored on separate files, you must back up the files as a single unit; you can't back up the tables one night and the associated indexes the next.

In this task, you will add a filegroup to the Sales database and perform a filegroup backup of Sales.

FIGURE 2.2   Tables and indexes must be backed up as a single unit if they're stored on separate files.

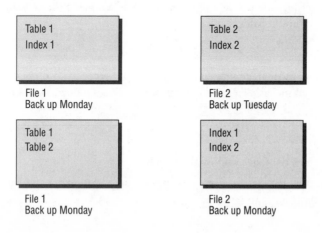

Scenario

The database you created for your sales department has grown very large—so large that it does not fit on a single disk anymore. To accommodate this growth and enhance performance, you have decided to spread the Sales database across multiple disks using a filegroup. You know that performing a filegroup backup is the fastest backup method for large databases, so you have decided to start performing filegroup backups on Sales after you create the filegroup.

Scope of Task

Duration

This task should take approximately 30 minutes.

Setup

For this task, you need access to the machine you installed SQL Server 2005 on in Task 1.1, the Sales database you created in Task 1.3, and the AdvWorks backup device you created in Task 2.2.

Caveat

In a production environment, you would not ordinarily add a new data file to a filegroup on the same disk as the Primary filegroup. The new filegroup would be on a separate disk.

Procedure

In this task, you will create a filegroup for the Sales database, add a table to the new filegroup, and perform a filegroup backup on Sales.

Equipment Used

For this task, you need access to the machine you installed SQL Server 2005 on in Task 1.1, the Sales database you created in Task 1.3, and the AdvWorks backup device you created in Task 2.2.

Details

To add a filegroup to the Sales database, follow these steps:

1. Open SQL Server Management Studio. Expand your server, and then expand Databases.
2. Right-click the Sales database, and select Properties.

3. On the Filegroups page, click the Add button. In the Name text box, enter **Secondary**.

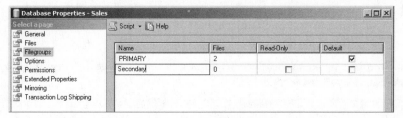

4. On the Files page, click the Add button, and enter this information:

   - Name: **Sales_Data3**
   - File Type: **Data**
   - Filegroup: **Secondary**
   - Initial Size: **3**

5. Click OK to create the new file on the Secondary filegroup.

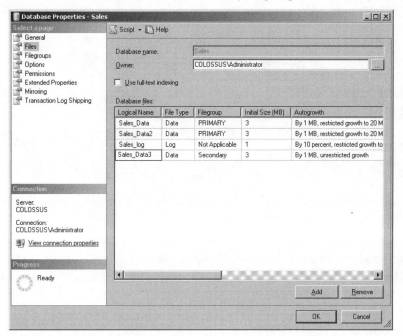

6. Now, to add a table to the new filegroup, expand Sales in Object Explorer, right-click Tables, and select New Table.

7. Under Column Name in the first row, enter **Emp_Name**.

8. Next to Emp_Name, select varchar as the datatype. Leave the default length of 50.

9. Just below Emp_Name in the second row, enter **Emp_Number** as the column name with a type of varchar. Leave the default length of 50.

10. Select View ➢ Properties Window.

11. Expand the Regular Data Space Specification section, and change the Filegroup or Partition Scheme Name setting to Secondary.

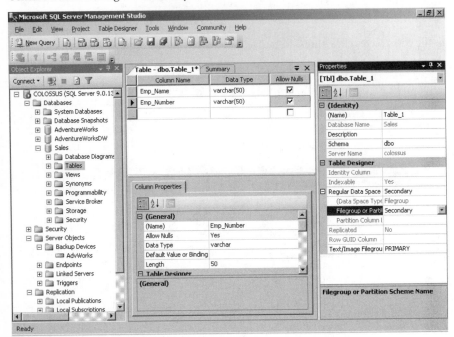

12. Click the Save button (it looks like a floppy disk on the toolbar) to create the new table, and enter **Employees** for the table name.

13. Close the table designer by clicking the *X* in the upper-right corner of the window.

14. Now, to add some data to the new table, open a new query, and execute the following code (note that the second value is arbitrary):

```
USE Sales
INSERT Employees
VALUES('Tim Hsu', 'VA1765FR')
INSERT Employees
VALUES('Sue Hernandez', 'FQ9187GL')
```

15. Close the query window.

With a second filegroup in place that contains data, you can perform a filegroup backup:

1. Right-click the Sales database in Object Explorer, point to Tasks, and select Back Up.

2. In the Backup dialog box, make sure Sales is the selected database to back up and Backup Type is Full.

3. Under Backup component, select Files and Filegroups.

4. In the Select Files and Filegroups dialog box, check the box next to Secondary, and click OK (notice that the box next to Sales_Data3 is automatically checked).

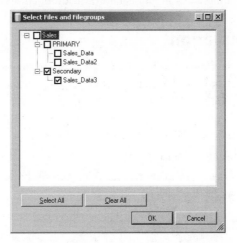

5. Leave the default name in the Name box. In the Description box, enter **Filegroup Backup of Sales**.

6. Under Destination, make sure the AdvWorks device is the only one listed.

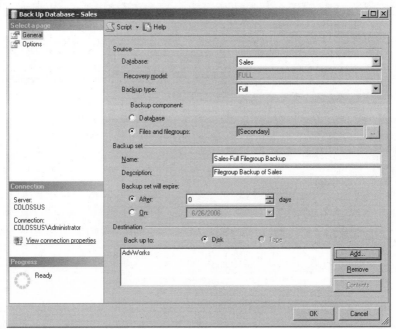

7. On the Options page, make sure Append to the Existing Backup Set is selected so you don't overwrite your existing backups.

8. On the Options page, select Verify Backup When Finished.

9. Click OK to start the backup.

10. When the backup is complete, you will get a notification; click OK to close it.

Criteria for Completion

This task is complete when you have added a new filegroup to the Sales database, added a table named Employees to the new filegroup, and performed a filegroup backup stored in the AdvWorks backup device. Follow these steps to verify:

1. To verify the backup, you can look at the contents of the backup device, so expand Backup Devices under Server Objects in Object Explorer.

2. Right-click AdvWorks, and select Properties.

3. On the Media Contents page, you should see the filegroup backup of Sales.

4. Click OK to return to SQL Server Management Studio.

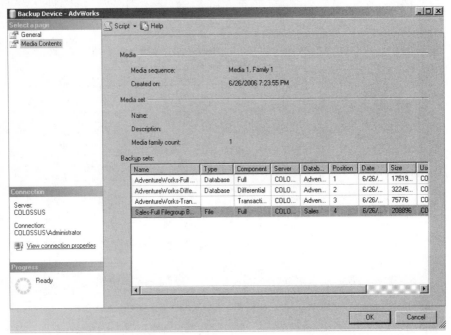

Task 2.7: Restoring a Database

Restoring a database doesn't involve a lot of steps, but you need to understand one important setting before undertaking the task. The RECOVERY option, when set incorrectly, can thwart all your efforts to restore a database. The RECOVERY option tells SQL Server you're finished restoring the database and users should be allowed back in. You should use this option only on the last file of the restore process.

For example, if you performed a full backup, then a differential backup, and then a transaction log backup, you would need to restore all three of them to bring the database back to a consistent state. If you specify the RECOVERY option when restoring the differential backup, SQL Server won't allow you to restore any other backups; you have told SQL Server in effect that you're done restoring and it should let everyone start using the database again. If you have more than one file to restore, you need to specify NORECOVERY on all restores except the last one.

SQL Server also remembers where the original files were located when you backed them up. So, if you backed up files from the D drive, SQL Server will restore them to the D drive. This is great unless your D drive has failed and you need to move your database to the E drive. You'll also run into this problem if you have backed up a database on a server at the home office and need to restore the database to a server at a child office. In this instance, you need to use the MOVE...TO option, which lets you back up a database in one location and move it to another location.

Finally, before SQL Server will allow you to restore a database, it performs a safety check to make sure you aren't accidentally restoring the wrong database. The first action SQL Server takes is to compare the database name that is being restored with the name of the database recorded in the backup device. If the two are different, SQL Server won't perform the restore. Thus, if you have a database on the server named Accounting and you're trying to restore from a backup device that has a backup of a database named Acctg, SQL Server won't perform the restore. This is a lifesaver, unless you're trying to overwrite the existing database with the database from the backup. If that is the case, you need to specify the REPLACE option, which is designed to override the safety check.

With all that said, you're ready to restore a database. In this task, you will make one of the databases suspect so you can see exactly what SQL Server does to restore it, and then you'll restore the database.

Scenario

You have been performing full, differential, and transaction log backups on your databases for some time. Everything was working just fine until this morning; when you came in this morning, the users are complaining that they can't access the database. You try to open the database in SQL Server Management Studio but can't; it just won't expand. You know instantly that the database is down and needs to be restored, so you have decided to start the restore process.

Scope of Task

Duration

This task should take approximately 30 minutes.

Setup

For this task, you need access to the machine you installed SQL Server 2005 on in Task 1.1, the AdventureWorks database installed with the sample data, the AdvWorks backup device you created in Task 2.2, the full backup you created in Task 2.3, the differential backup you created in Task 2.4, and the transaction log backup you created in Task 2.5.

Caveat

This task doesn't have any caveats.

Procedure

In this task, you will simulate a downed database by renaming critical files for the Adventure-Works database, and then you will restore the database.

> You will need to stop all the SQL Server services because while they're running, all the databases are considered open files—you will not be able to work with them outside SQL Server.

Equipment Used

For this task, you need access to the machine you installed SQL Server 2005 on in Task 1.1, the AdventureWorks database installed with the sample data, the AdvWorks backup device you created in Task 2.2, the full backup you created in Task 2.3, the differential backup you created in Task 2.4, and the transaction log backup you created in Task 2.5.

Details

To simulate a downed database, follow these steps:

1. Open SQL Server Configuration Manager from the Start menu.
2. In the left pane, select SQL Server 2005 Services.

3. Right-click SQL Server (MSSQLSERVER) in the right pane, and click Stop. You'll be asked whether you want to stop the SQLServerAgent service as well; click Yes.

4. Find the file `AdventureWorks_Data.mdf` (usually in `C:\Program Files\Microsoft SQL Server\MSSQL.1\MSSQL\Data\`).

5. Rename the file `AdventureWorks_Data.old`.

6. Find the file `AdventureWorks_Log.ldf`, and rename it `AdventureWorks_Log.old`.

7. From the Computer Manager, restart the SQL Agent and SQL Server services.

8. Open SQL Server Management Studio, and expand Databases under your server name. AdventureWorks cannot be expanded and has no summary; it is now inaccessible.

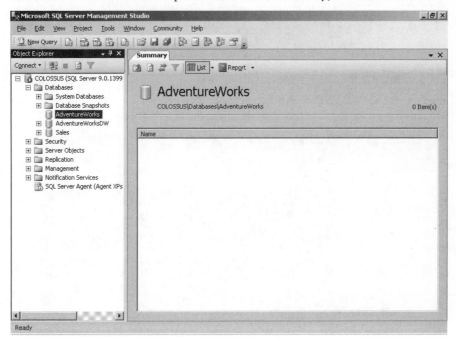

Now you are ready to restore the database:

1. Right-click Databases, and select Restore Database.

2. In the Restore Database dialog box, select AdventureWorks from the To Database drop-down list box.

3. Under Source for Restore, select From Device. Click the ellipsis (…) button next to the text box to select a device.

4. In the Specify Backup dialog box, select Backup Device from the Backup Media drop-down list box, and click Add.

5. In the Specify Backup dialog, select AdvWorks, and click OK.

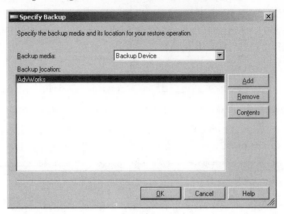

6. Click OK to close the Specify Backup dialog box.

7. Under Select the Backup Sets to Restore, check all three backups (full, differential, and transaction log). Doing so returns the database to the most recent state.

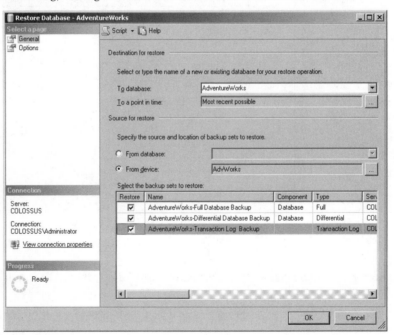

8. On the Options page, make sure the RESTORE WITH RECOVERY option is selected, because you have no more backups to restore.

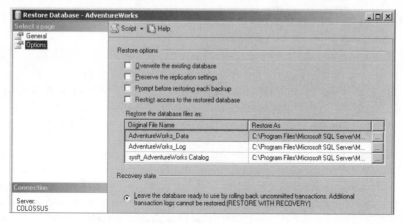

9. Click OK to begin the restore process.

10. Click OK in the dialog box that opens after the restore is complete.

Criteria for Completion

This task is complete when you have taken the AdventureWorks database down and restored it from backup, bringing it back to a usable state. Follow these steps to verify:

1. In SQL Server Management Studio, right-click Databases, and click Refresh.

2. Expand Databases, and you should see AdventureWorks is back to normal.

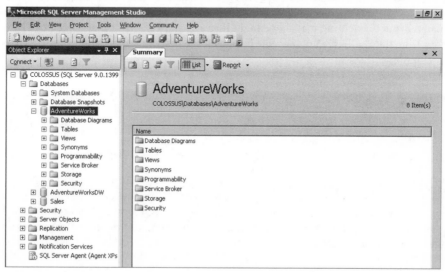

Task 2.8: Performing a Point-in-Time Restore

You do not always need to restore a database to its most current state; sometimes you need to restore it to a previous state. The two most common reasons for this are accidental and malicious updates of data. If this happens to you and if you're performing transaction log backups, then you can perform a *point-in-time* restore.

In addition to stamping each transaction in the transaction log with an LSN, SQL Server stamps them all with a time. That time, combined with the STOPAT clause of the `restore` statement, makes it possible for you to return the data to a previous state. You need to keep two facts in mind while using this process. First, this doesn't work with full or differential backups, only with transaction log backups. Second, you'll lose any changes that were made to your entire database after the STOPAT time. For instance, if you restore your database to the state it was in yesterday at 2 P.M., everything that changed from yesterday at 2 P.M. until the time you restore the database will be lost and must be reinserted. Other than that, the point-in-time restore is a useful and powerful tool.

In this task, you will perform a point-in-time restore on the AdventureWorks database.

Scenario

It is the end of the month, which is the time when your accounting department performs all its month-end transactions to close the books and bring everything into balance. This has been an especially busy month for your company, so your accounting department has brought in some contract workers to assist with the month-end closeout. One of the contract workers is not familiar with your systems and accidentally enters some incorrect data into the system. Fortunately, your accounting manager caught it early and needs your help to remove the corrupt data from the database. You have decided that the best way to accomplish this task is to perform a point-in-time restore.

Scope of Task

Duration

This task should take approximately 30 minutes.

Setup

For this task, you need access to the machine you installed SQL Server 2005 on in Task 1.1, the AdventureWorks database installed with the sample data, and the AdvWorks backup device you created in Task 2.2.

Caveat

This task doesn't have any caveats.

Procedure

In this task, you will update the HumanResources.Shift table of the AdventureWorks database, wait for two minutes, and update it again. You will then perform a transaction log backup of the database and a subsequent point-in-time restore.

Equipment Used

For this task, you need access to the machine you installed SQL Server 2005 on in Task 1.1, the AdventureWorks database installed with the sample data, and the AdvWorks backup device you created in Task 2.2.

Details

First you need to prepare the database for the point-in-time restore by adding some records to the database:

1. You need to add a record that will survive the restore. Open a new SQL Server query in SQL Server Management Studio by clicking the New Query button on the toolbar.

2. To create a new record, enter and execute the following code:

```
USE AdventureWorks
INSERT HumanResources.Shift(Name, StartTime, EndTime, ModifiedDate)
VALUES('Test Shift 1',getdate()+1,getdate()+2,getdate())
```

3. Note the time right now.

4. Wait two minutes, clear the query window, and then enter a new record using the following code:

```
USE AdventureWorks
INSERT HumanResources.Shift(Name, StartTime, EndTime, ModifiedDate)
VALUES('Test Shift 2',getdate()+1,getdate()+2,getdate())
```

5. To see both records, clear the query window, and enter and execute the following code:

```
USE AdventureWorks
SELECT * FROM HumanResources.Shift
```

6. Close all open queries.

7. To perform a point-in-time restore, you must perform a transaction log backup. In Object Explorer, right-click AdventureWorks, point to Tasks, and select Back Up.

8. In the Backup dialog box, make sure AdventureWorks is the selected database to back up and Backup Type is Transaction Log.

9. Leave the default name in the Name box. In the Description box, enter **Point-in-time Backup of AdventureWorks.**

10. Under Destination, make sure the AdvWorks device is listed.

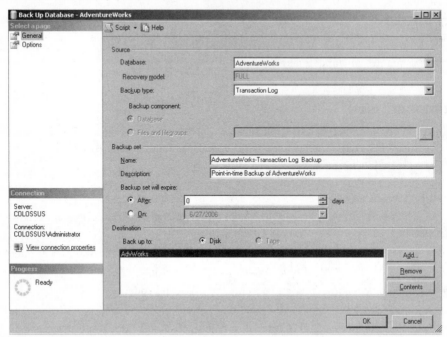

11. On the Options page, make sure Append to the Existing Backup Set is selected so you don't overwrite your existing full backup.

12. On the Options page, select Verify Backup When Finished.

13. Click OK to start the backup.

14. Click OK to close the dialog box that opens when the backup is complete.

15. Now you have to back up the tail of the log, which is all the transactions in the log that have not been backed up or recorded to the data file yet. In Object Explorer, right-click AdventureWorks, point to Tasks, and select Back Up.

16. In the Backup dialog box, make sure AdventureWorks is the selected database to back up and Backup Type is Transaction Log.

17. Leave the default name in the Name box. In the Description box, enter **Tail Backup of AdventureWorks.**

18. Under Destination, make sure the AdvWorks device is listed.

19. On the Options page, make sure Append to the Existing Backup Set is selected so you don't overwrite your existing full backup.

20. On the Options page, select Verify Backup When Finished.

21. On the Options page, back up the tail of the log.

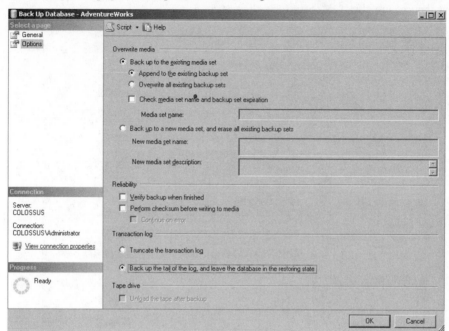

22. Click OK to start the backup.

23. Click OK to close the dialog box that opens when the backup is complete.

Now you are ready to perform a point-in-time restore to eliminate the most recent update to the database:

1. Open SQL Server Management Studio. Expand your server, and then expand Databases.

2. Right-click AdventureWorks, point to Tasks, move to Restore, and select Database.

3. Click the ellipsis button next to the To a Point in Time text box.

4. In the Point in Time Restore dialog box, enter the time from step 3 of the previous series of steps, and click OK.

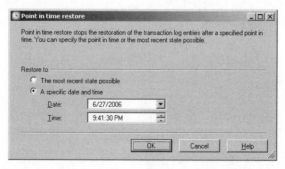

5. Make sure you're restoring from the AdvWorks device, select all the available backups in the device, and click OK to perform the restore.

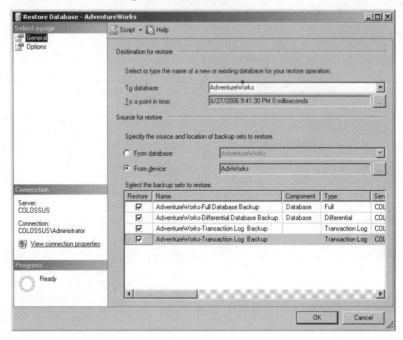

6. Click OK to close the dialog box that opens when the restore is complete.

Criteria for Completion

This task is complete when you have created two new records in the HumanResources.Shift table of the AdventureWorks database and performed a point-in-time restore to eliminate the most recent update. Follow these steps to verify:

1. Open a new SQL Server Query in SQL Server Management Studio, and enter and execute the following code:

```
USE AdventureWorks
SELECT * FROM HumanResources.Shift
```

2. Notice that Test Shift 2 is no longer there, but Test Shift 1 remains.

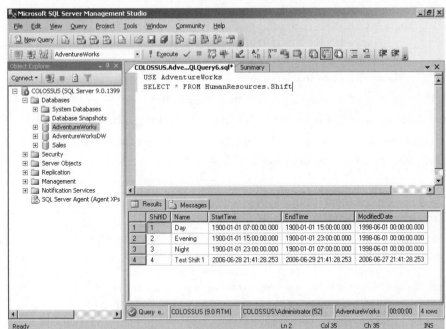

Task 2.9: Implementing Database Mirroring

When a user makes a change to a database, that change is not written to the database immediately; a few steps are involved:

1. A user makes a change to the database.

2. SQL Server stores the change in the database's *log buffer*, a special location in memory.

3. As quickly as possible, the log buffer is written to the transaction log on disk, a process called *hardening*.

4. The changes in the transaction log are then written, or *flushed*, to the database.

This process changes when you implement database mirroring. In database mirroring, two servers keep a copy of the database. These two servers are called partners. The server with the original database is called the principal, and the server with the copy is called the mirror.

When a user makes a change to a mirrored database, the steps to harden the log change slightly:

1. A user makes a change to the database

2. SQL Server stores the change in the database's log buffer.

3. As quickly as possible, the log buffer is written to the transaction log on disk.

4. Simultaneously, the principal server copies the log buffer to the mirror server.

5. As quickly as possible, the mirror server hardens the transaction log.

6. The changes in the transaction log on the principal server are then flushed to the database.

7. The changes recorded in the transaction log on the mirror server are replayed against the mirrored database, making it a copy of the principal.

When only the two servers are in place and the principal server fails, you must manually force the mirror server to start serving the database. To have the server fail over automatically, you need a witness server, which provides automatic failover when the principal server fails.

When you implement a witness server, both of the partners in the database-mirroring session communicate with the witness. When one of the servers fails, the witness provides confirmation to the surviving server, and that server automatically takes over serving the mirrored database.

The automatic failover makes a witness server sound attractive, but you have a good reason not to use one: performance. To fully understand this statement, you need to know how to configure database mirroring.

You can configure database mirroring in one of three operating modes:

- High availability

- High protection

- High performance

The high-availability and high-protection modes both have the transaction safety set to Full. When the transaction safety is set to Full, the principal server hardens its log to disk, sends the log buffer to the mirror server, and then waits for a response from the mirror server before moving forward with the process. This ensures the databases are always in sync, but it degrades performance on the principal server.

High-performance mode leaves the transaction safety set to Off, which means the principal server does not wait for a response from the mirror server after sending the log buffer. This keeps the principal server running nice and fast, but you could lose data on the mirror server.

High-availability mode is the only mode that uses a witness server; the other two modes do not.

You should keep a few other points to keep in mind if you want to implement database mirroring:

- The principal database must be in the Full recovery model.
- The mirror database must be initialized from a restore of the principal database with NORECOVERY, followed by restores in a sequence of principal transaction log backups.
- The mirror database must have the same name as the principal database.
- Because the mirror database is in a recovering state, you can't access it directly, though you can access it through a database snapshot.

In this task, you will implement a high-safety database mirror.

Scenario

You created a database for your sales department several months ago, and your sales staff has started to rely on it quite heavily. In fact, if the database were to go down, your sales managers have told you that their staff would not be able to get their work done. This means lost sales, lost productivity, and possibly even lost customers. This is not something you can let happen; you know that the database must be available to your sales staff at all times because the sales representatives make sales calls at all hours of the day and night. To ensure that the database is always available, you decide to implement a high-safety database mirror.

Scope of Task

Duration

This task should take approximately 60 minutes.

Setup

For this task, you need access to the machine you installed SQL Server 2005 on in Task 1.1, the Second instance of SQL Server 2005 you installed in Task 1.2, and the Sales database you created in Task 1.3. You will also need to make sure you install SQL Server 2005 Service Pack 1 before performing this task.

Caveat

You must have SQL Server 2005 Service Pack 1 installed to use database mirroring.

Procedure

In this task, you will make a backup of the Sales database and then restore it to the Second instance of SQL Server in the RECOVERY state. You will then create a high-safety database mirror of the Sales database on the Second instance.

Equipment Used

For this task, you need access to the machine you installed SQL Server 2005 on in Task 1.1, the Second instance of SQL Server 2005 you installed in Task 1.2, and the Sales database you created in Task 1.3.

Details

First, you need a backup of the Sales database from the default instance:

1. Open SQL Server Management Studio, expand Databases, right-click Sales, point to Tasks, and click Back Up.

2. In the Backup dialog box, make sure Sales is the selected database to back up and Backup Type is Full.

3. Leave the default name in the Name box. In the Description box, enter **Full Backup of Sales**.

4. Under Destination, a disk device may already be listed. If so, select the device, and click Remove.

5. Under Destination, click Add.

6. In the Select Backup Destination box, click File Name, and in the text box enter *x*:\temp\Sales.bak (make sure the temp directory exists on the selected drive). Click OK.

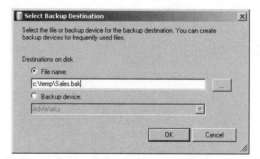

7. Click OK to start the backup.

8. When the backup is complete, you will get a notification; click OK to close it.

Next, you need to back up the transaction log of the Sales database on the default instance:

1. Open SQL Server Management Studio, expand Databases, right-click Sales, point to Tasks, and click Back Up.

2. In the Backup dialog box, make sure Sales is the selected database to back up and Backup Type is Transaction Log.

3. Leave the default name in the Name box. In the Description box, enter **Transaction Log Backup of Sales**.

4. Make sure *x*:\temp\Sales.bak is the only device listed, and click OK.

5. Click OK to start the backup.

6. When the backup is complete, you will get a notification; click OK to close it.

Now you are ready to restore the database to the Second instance:

1. Open SQL Server Management Studio, and connect to the Second instance by selecting *Server*\SECOND from the Server Name drop-down list.

2. Right-click Databases, and select Restore Database.

3. Enter **Sales** in the To Database box.

4. Under Source for Restore, select From Device. Click the ellipsis (…) button next to the text box to select a device.

5. In the Specify Backup dialog box, select File from the Backup Media drop-down list box, and click Add.

6. In the Locate Backup File dialog box, find the `Sales.bak` file, and click OK.

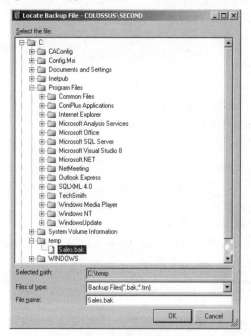

7. Click OK to close the Specify Backup dialog box.

8. Under Select the Backup Sets to Restore, check the boxes for both backups of Sales.

9. On the Options page, in the Restore the Database Files As grid, under the Restore As column, make these changes:

   - Change `Sales_data.mdf` to `Sales_data_mir.mdf`.
   - Change `Sales_data2.ndf` to `Sales_data_mir2.ndf`.
   - Change `Sales_data3.ndf` to `Sales_data_mir3.ndf`.
   - Change `Sales_log.ldf` to `Sales_log_mir.ldf`.

10. Also on the Options page, make sure the RESTORE WITH NORECOVERY option is selected.

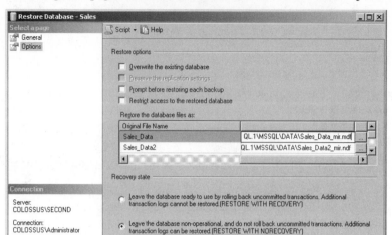

11. Click OK to begin the restore process.

12. Click OK in the dialog box that opens after the restore is complete.

Now you can configure database mirroring:

1. Open SQL Server Management Studio, and connect to the default instance.

2. Expand Databases, right-click Sales, point to Tasks, and click Mirror.

3. Click the Configure Security button to start the Configure Database Mirroring Security Wizard, which will create the endpoints required for mirroring.

4. On the welcome screen, click Next.

5. Select No on the Include Witness Server screen, and then click Next.

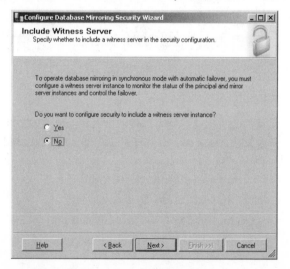

6. On the Choose Servers to Configure screen, click Next.

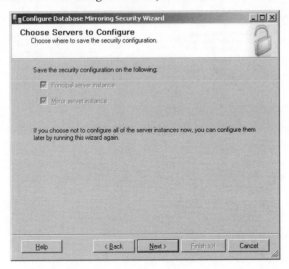

7. On the Principal Server Instance screen, accept the defaults, and click Next.

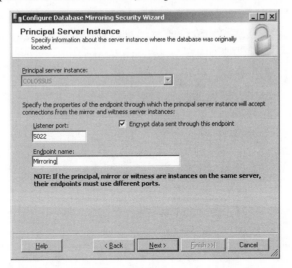

8. On the Mirror Server Instance screen, select the Second instance of SQL Server, and click the Connect button. Then click Connect.

9. Accept the defaults that are filled in for you, and click Next.

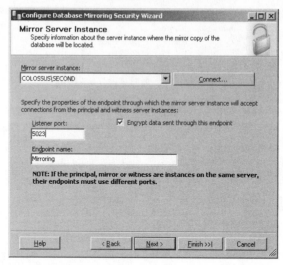

10. On the Service Accounts screen, leave both account names blank because you configured the services to use the same accounts. Click Next.

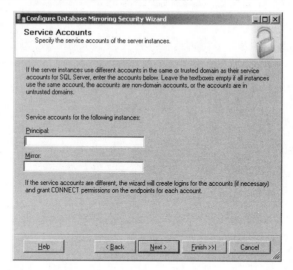

11. On the Complete the Wizard screen, click Finish.

12. Click Close when the wizard is complete.

13. In the Database Properties dialog box that opens, click Start Mirroring.

14. Click OK to close the Database Properties dialog box.

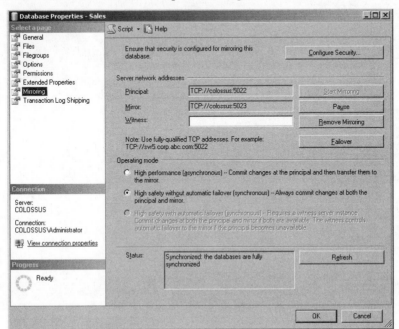

Criteria for Completion

This task is complete when you have successfully mirrored the Sales database from the default instance on your machine to the Second instance. You can tell whether you are successful by connecting to both instances and looking at the Sales database in Object Explorer. On the default instance, you should see (Principal, Synchronized) next to the Sales database, and on the Second instance you should see (Mirror, Synchronized/Restoring) next to Sales (as shown in Figure 2.3).

FIGURE 2.3 The label for the Sales database will show you what role it plays in the database-mirroring session.

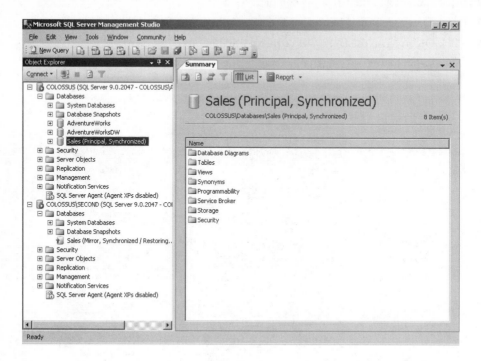

Task 2.10: Implementing Log Shipping

To achieve high availability, *log shipping* copies transactions from a primary server to one or more secondary servers. This may sound a lot like database mirroring, but the process is quite different. In database mirroring, the database log buffer is copied from one server to another and then replayed. In log shipping, transaction log backups are sent to one or more secondary servers and then restored on each of the destination servers individually.

A server can play three possible roles in a log-shipping scenario:

Primary   This is your production server; it holds the original copy of the database. All log shipping administration should take place on this machine.

Secondary   The secondary servers hold the standby copy of the database. You must initialize the database on a secondary server by restoring a backup of the database from the primary server using either the NORECOVERY option or the STANDBY option. The STANDBY option allows you to continue restoring backups to the database and gives users read-only access to it; NORECOVERY does not allow users to access the database.

Monitor   This is an optional server that tracks all the details about log shipping such as the following:

- When the transaction log on the primary server was last backed up
- When the secondary servers last copied and restored the backups from the primary server
- Backup failure alert information, if any

You can accomplish all of this with four jobs that run on any of the three servers:

Backup   The backup job is created on the primary server and runs every two minutes by default (though you can change this). This job performs the backup operation, logs history to the local server and the monitor server, and deletes old backup files and history information.

Copy   A copy job is created on each secondary server instance and should run just after the backup job completes. This job copies the backup files from the primary server to a configurable destination on the secondary server and logs history on the secondary server and the monitor server.

Restore   Also created on the secondary servers, the restore job restores the copied backup files to the secondary databases. It also logs history on the local server and the monitor server and deletes old files and old history information. You can schedule this to run as frequently as the copy job, or you can delay the restore job:

- Scheduling the restore and copy jobs with the same frequency keeps the secondary database as closely aligned with the primary database as possible to create a warm standby database that you can fail over to in an emergency.

- Delaying restore jobs can be useful in the event of a serious user error, such as when a user accidentally deletes the wrong data from a table. If you know the time of the error, you can move the secondary database forward to a time just before the error. Then you can export the lost data and import it back into the primary database.

Alert   An alert job is created on the monitor server, if you choose to use one. If not, then alert jobs are created on the primary server and each secondary server in the log-shipping scenario. This job raises alerts (for which you must specify alert numbers) for primary and secondary databases when the backup and restore operations have not completed successfully within specified thresholds. You must configure these alerts to have an operator receive notification of the log-shipping failure. This alert job is shared by the primary and secondary databases of all log-shipping configurations using this monitor server instance. So if you change this job in any way, all primary and secondary servers that use the monitor server are affected.

Because they work in similar ways, you may be wondering which technology to use—database mirroring or log shipping. Two specific instances call for log shipping:

- If you need a copy of the original database on more than one backup server, you should use log shipping. Mirroring allows for only one copy.

- If you need to delay the restore on the secondary server to avoid logical errors, you should consider log shipping.

In this task, you will configure log shipping between the default instance and the Second instance on your server.

Scenario

Your accounting department has come to rely on SQL Server to get their work done. They need it to be up and running at all times during the day, so you know you need to implement some form of high availability. In the past, some contract workers, who were not familiar with your systems, accidentally updated the data incorrectly, and you do not want future mistakes to be propagated to the standby server right away. Bearing this in mind, you decide to implement log shipping so you can control the delay of the restore on the secondary server.

Scope of Task

Duration

This task should take approximately 60 minutes.

Setup

For this task, you need access to the machine you installed SQL Server 2005 on in Task 1.1, the Second instance of SQL Server 2005 you installed in Task 1.2, and the AdventureWorks database installed with the sample data.

Caveat

This task doesn't have any caveats.

Procedure

In this task, you will make a backup of the AdventureWorks database and restore it to the Second instance of SQL Server in the RECOVERY state. You will then ship the AdventureWorks database logs to the Second instance.

Equipment Used

For this task, you need access to the machine you installed SQL Server 2005 on in Task 1.1, the Second instance of SQL Server 2005 you installed in Task 1.2, and the AdventureWorks database installed with the sample data.

Details

First, you need a backup of the AdventureWorks database from the default instance:

1. Open SQL Server Management Studio, expand Databases, right-click AdventureWorks, point to Tasks, and click Back Up.

2. In the Backup dialog box, make sure AdventureWorks is the selected database to back up and Backup Type is Full.

3. Leave the default name in the Name box. In the Description box, enter **Full Backup of AdventureWorks**.

4. Under Destination, a disk device may already be listed. If so, select the device, and click Remove.

5. Under Destination, click Add.

6. In the Select Backup Destination box, click File Name, and in the text box enter *x*:\temp\AdvWorks.bak (make sure the temp directory exists on the selected drive). Click OK.

7. Click OK to start the backup.

8. When the backup is complete, you will get a notification; click OK to close it.

Next, you need to back up the transaction log of the AdventureWorks database on the default instance:

1. Open SQL Server Management Studio, expand Databases, right-click AdventureWorks, point to Tasks, and click Back Up.

2. In the Backup dialog box, make sure AdventureWorks is the selected database to back up and Backup Type is Transaction Log.

3. Leave the default name in the Name box. In the Description box, enter **Transaction Log Backup of AdventureWorks**.

4. Make sure *x*:\temp\AdventureWorks.bak (the same device used in step 6 in the previous set of steps) is the only device listed, and click OK.

5. Click OK to start the backup.

6. When the backup is complete, you will get a notification; click OK to close it.

Now you are ready to restore the database to the Second instance:

1. Open SQL Server Management Studio, and connect to the Second instance by selecting *Server*\SECOND from the Server Name drop-down list.

2. Right-click Databases, and select Restore Database.

3. Enter **AdventureWorks** in the To Database box.

4. Under Source for Restore, select From Device. Click the ellipsis (…) button next to the text box to select a device.

5. In the Specify Backup dialog box, select File from the Backup Media drop-down list box, and click Add.

6. In the Locate Backup File dialog box, find the AdventureWorks.bak file, and click OK.

7. Click OK to close the Specify Backup dialog box.

8. Under Select the Backup Sets to Restore, check the boxes for both backups of AdventureWorks.

9. On the Options page, in the Restore the Database Files As grid, under the Restore As column, make these changes so you do not accidentally overwrite the original AdventureWorks data and log files:

   - Change `AdventureWorks_data.mdf` to `AdventureWorks_data_ls.mdf`.
   - Change `AdventureWorks_log.ldf` to `AdventureWorks_log_ls.ldf`.
   - Change AdventureWorks Catalog to AdventureWorks Catalog LS (if it exists).

10. Also on the Options page, make sure the `RESTORE WITH STANDBY` option is selected.

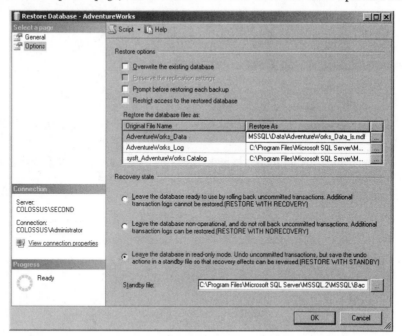

11. Click OK to begin the restore process.

12. Click OK in the dialog box that opens after the restore is complete.

Now you can configure log shipping:

1. Open SQL Server Management Studio, and connect to the default instance.

2. Expand Databases, right-click AdventureWorks, point to Tasks, and click Ship Transaction Logs.

3. Check the box next to Enable This As a Primary Database in a Log Shipping Configuration.

4. Click the Backup Settings button.

5. Enter a network path for the backup folder by typing *server_name*\c$\temp in the first text box.

6. Enter a local path for the backup folder by typing *x*:\temp in the second text box.

7. Select the defaults for the job schedules and file deletion, and click OK to return to the Database Properties dialog box.

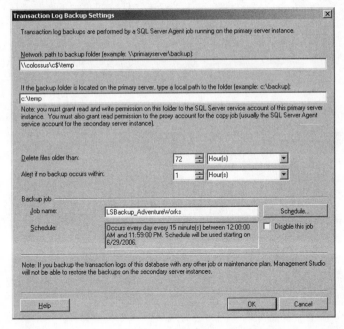

8. Click the Add button under the Secondary Server Instances and Databases grid.

9. Click the Connect button next to the Secondary Server Instance text box, and connect to the Second instance.

10. On the Initialize Secondary Database tab, make sure the No, the Secondary Database Is Initialized option is selected.

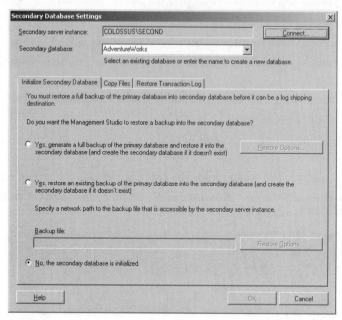

11. On the Copy Files tab, enter *x*:\temp\copy (make sure this subdirectory exists in temp).

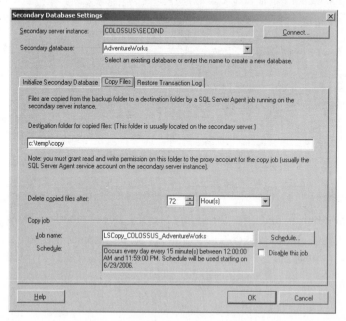

12. On the Restore Transaction Log tab, select the standby mode option to allow users read-only access to the standby database.

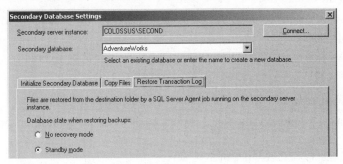

13. Click OK to return to the Database Properties dialog box.

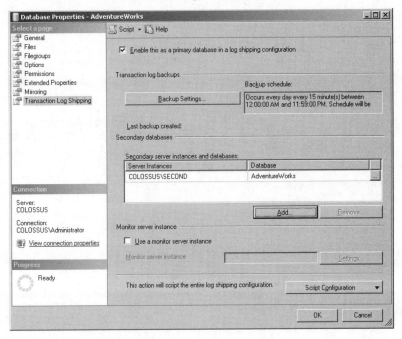

14. Click OK again to finish configuring log shipping.

15. Close the Configuration dialog box when it is complete.

Criteria for Completion

This task is complete when you have successfully configured log shipping for the Adventure-Works database from the default instance on your machine to the Second instance. You can tell whether you are successful by following these steps:

1. Open a new query in SQL Server Management Studio.

2. From the Query menu, hover over Connection, and click Change Connection.

3. Connect to the default instance of SQL Server.

4. To create a new record to ship to the Second instance, enter and execute the following code:

```
USE AdventureWorks
INSERT HumanResources.Shift(Name, StartTime, EndTime, ModifiedDate)
VALUES('Test Shift 3',getdate()+1,getdate()+2,getdate())
```

5. Wait approximately 15 minutes for the log-shipping jobs to run.

6. Clear the query window. From the Query menu, hover over Connection, and click Change Connection.

7. Connect to the Second instance of SQL Server.

8. Run this query to see whether the log was successfully shipped:

```
USE AdventureWorks
SELECT * FROM HumanResources.Shift
```

9. You should see the new Test Shift 3 record after the logs are shipped.

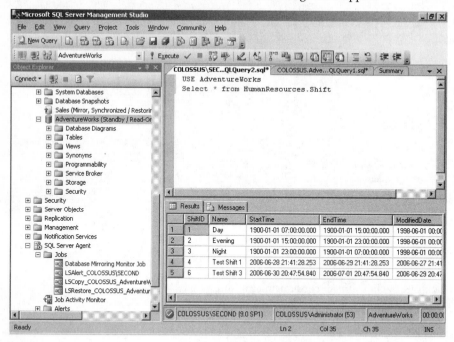

If the logs do not ship, make sure the SQL Server Agent is running on both instances.

Task 2.11: Creating a Database Snapshot

You have probably taken snapshots with a camera before, so you know that a photographic snapshot is an image of something as it existed when you took the picture. A database snapshot works much the same way; it is an image of a database as it existed at the point in time that the snapshot was taken.

When first created, a database snapshot is just an empty shell that contains only pointers to the original database pages. This means when someone reads data from a new snapshot, they are actually reading data from the original database. Things get interesting when modifications are made to the original database, though. Just before a modification is written to the original data page, the page is copied to the snapshot file. That way, the original page still exists so when users query a snapshot, they will see the data as it existed before the modification. Figure 2.4 will help you visualize the process.

You can use snapshots for a variety of reasons:

- These are an excellent choice for archiving historical data to which you still need access. For example, you may create a snapshot of a financial database every quarter, and then at the end of the year you can still access the quarterly snapshots to generate a year-end report.

- You can use snapshots to revert to an older copy of a database in the event of a user error or lost data.

- Snapshots can increase performance when used to generate reports because while you are reading from the snapshot, your users can continue writing to the original database with less impact.

In this task, you will create a new test database and make a snapshot of the new database.

FIGURE 2.4   Data pages are copied from the original database file to the snapshot file before modifications are written to disk.

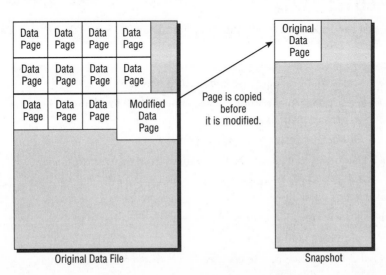

Scenario

You have created a new database for your engineering department to store their data, some of which is important test results for new products. Your chief engineer is naturally concerned about keeping the database available, but he does not want the database copied to another server for security reasons. You decide that the best way to protect against disaster, and get the data back as fast as possible, is to create a database snapshot.

Scope of Task

Duration

This task should take approximately 30 minutes.

Setup

For this task, you need access to the machine you installed SQL Server 2005 on in Task 1.1.

Caveat

In production, you should give the snapshot a more descriptive name, using the date and time of the snapshot, because you can create more than one per day. A good example is `Test_Snapshot_20060629_1130AM.mdf`. I'm using a short name to keep the task simple.

Procedure

In this task, you will create a new database named Test, create a new table in the database, and then create a snapshot of the new database.

Equipment Used

For this task, you need access to the machine you installed SQL Server 2005 on in Task 1.1.

Details

First you need to create the Test database and insert a new table:

1. Start SQL Server Management Studio by selecting Start ➤ Programs ➤ Microsoft SQL Server 2005 ➤ Management Studio.
2. Connect to your default instance of SQL Server.
3. Right-click Databases, and choose New Database from the context menu.
4. On the General page of the Database properties sheet, enter the database name **Test,** and leave the owner as <default>.
5. Accept the all the defaults, and click OK to create the Test database.
6. In Object Explorer, expand the Test database.
7. Right-click the Tables icon, and select New Table to open the table designer.

8. In the first row, under Column Name, enter **ProdID** with a datatype of int, and uncheck Allow Nulls.

9. In the second row under Column Name, enter **Results** with a datatype of **nvarchar(100)**, and uncheck Allow Nulls.

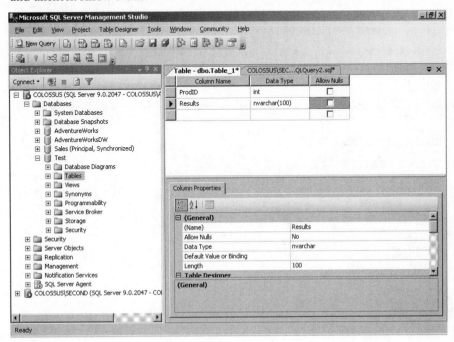

10. Click the Save button (it looks like a floppy disk) on the left side of the toolbar.

11. In the Choose Name box that opens, enter **TestResults**.

12. Close the table designer screen by clicking the *X* in the upper-right corner of the window.

13. To create a new record in the TestResults table, enter and execute the following code:

```
USE Test
INSERT dbo.TestResults(ProdID,Results)
VALUES(1,'Success')
```

Now you are ready to create a snapshot of the Test database:

1. Open a new query in SQL Server Management Studio.

2. To create a snapshot of Test on the C drive, execute the following code (note that you should replace the C:\ with the drive on which you installed SQL Server):

```
CREATE DATABASE Test_Snapshot
ON
(
    NAME = Test,
```

```
    FILENAME = 'c:\Program Files\Microsoft SQL
Server\MSSQL.1\MSSQL\data\Test_shapshot.mdf'
)
AS SNAPSHOT OF Test
```

3. In the results pane (on the bottom) in the query window, you should see a message stating that the command completed successfully.

4. To verify that the snapshot has been created, expand your server in Object Explorer, and then expand Database Snapshots. You should see Test_Snapshot in the list of available snapshots.

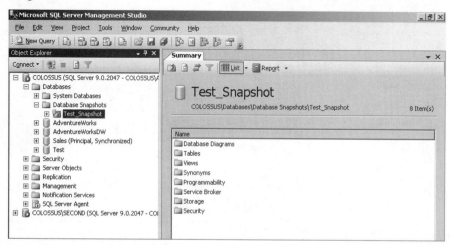

Criteria for Completion

This task is complete when you have created a new database named Test, created a new table named TestResults in that database, and created a snapshot of the new Test database. You can tell whether you are successful by following these steps:

1. Open a new query in SQL Server Management Studio.

2. To create a new record in the TestResults table, enter and execute the following code:

```
USE Test
INSERT dbo.TestResults(ProdID,Results)
VALUES(2,'Fail')
```

3. Clear the query window, and run this query to see whether the update was applied to the snapshot:

```
USE Test_snapshot
SELECT * FROM dbo.TestResults
```

4. You should see only the record that existed before that snapshot was taken, which is the ProdID: 1, Results: Success record.

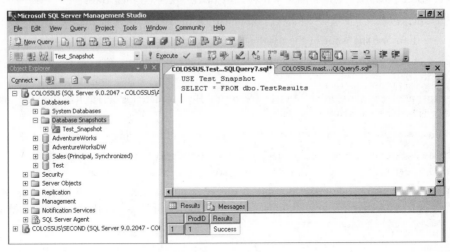

Task 2.12: Reverting from a Database Snapshot

Have you ever looked at a snapshot you took of yourself on vacation, thought about how much fun it was, and wished you could relive that moment? All of us probably have, but we realize that it is not possible, at least not with a photographic snapshot.

With a database snapshot, you can revert your database to the time you created the snapshot. It will look exactly like it did when the snapshot was created; it will have all the same tables, the same schema, the same data...everything will be the same.

You accomplish this feat by reversing the process for creating a snapshot. When you have a snapshot in place for a database, pages that are being modified are copied to the snapshot before they are updated in the original database so the snapshot contains the unmodified page and the original database holds the modified page. When you revert from a snapshot, the unmodified pages that are held in the snapshot are simply copied to the original database file. The transaction log is also overwritten and rebuilt during the process to return it to the proper state.

You need to remember that a snapshot is an incomplete copy of a database, so it is not meant to replace regular database backups. Why use it? Think of this as a high-speed point-in-time restore, which you learned about in Task 2.8. If you know when a data input error occurred and if you have been performing transaction log backups, you can restore a database to a point in time just before the error occurred. It can take quite a while to get all the tapes together and loaded, so reverting from a recent snapshot can be much faster. It may be the only way to revert to a point in time before the error if you do not use transaction log backups.

Bear in mind that you cannot revert from a snapshot if any of the following is true:

- The source database contains any read-only or compressed filegroups.

- Any filegroups are offline that were online when the snapshot was created.

- More than one snapshot of the database exists at the time of reverting.

You should keep the following points in mind about reverting from a snapshot if you ever need to do so:

- Snapshots are not intended for media recovery. If your media is corrupted, then the snapshot is probably corrupted as well.

- Both the original and snapshot databases are unavailable during the revert operation.

- If you are using transaction log backups, reverting breaks the log backup chain, so you need to perform a full database backup as soon as you have finished reverting.

- You should also back up the log of the original database before reverting. You cannot restore this log to the original database, but you can restore it to another database and use it to recover lost data.

WARNING   When you revert to a database snapshot, you must delete all other snapshots from that database.

In this task, you will revert to a snapshot of the Test database.

Scenario

Your chief engineer recently asked you to help protect his database and keep it available, so you decided to create regular snapshots of the database. Today, one of the engineers accidentally updated several records in the database, indicating that several products had passed safety tests when in fact they had failed, and the engineer doesn't remember which records were updated in error. You need to get the database back to the point before the errors were introduced, so you decide that the fastest method is to revert from the most recent snapshot.

Scope of Task

Duration

This task should take approximately 15 minutes.

Setup

For this task, you need access to the machine you installed SQL Server 2005 on in Task 1.1 and the Test database and Test_Snapshot database snapshot you created in Task 2.11.

Caveat

In a production environment, you should perform a full backup of your database after reverting from a snapshot. I will now show how to do so here for simplicity's sake.

Procedure

In this task, you will revert the Test database from the Test_Snapshot database snapshot.

Equipment Used

For this task, you need access to the machine you installed SQL Server 2005 on in Task 1.1 and the Test database and the Test_Snapshot database snapshot you created in Task 2.11.

Details

First you need to create the Test database, and then you need to insert a new table:

1. Start SQL Server Management Studio by selecting Start ➢ Programs ➢ Microsoft SQL Server 2005 ➢ Management Studio.

2. To view all the records in the TestResults table of the original database, run the following query (you should see two records):

```
USE Test
SELECT * FROM TestResults
```

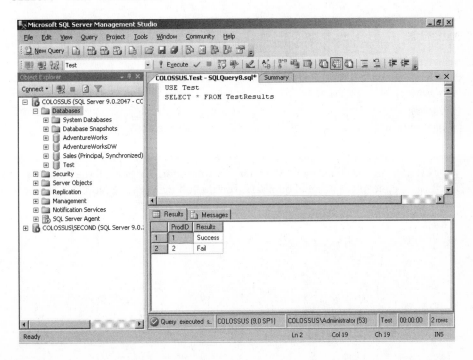

3. To view all the records in the TestResults table of the snapshot, run the following query (you should see one record):

```
USE Test_Snapshot
SELECT * FROM TestResults
```

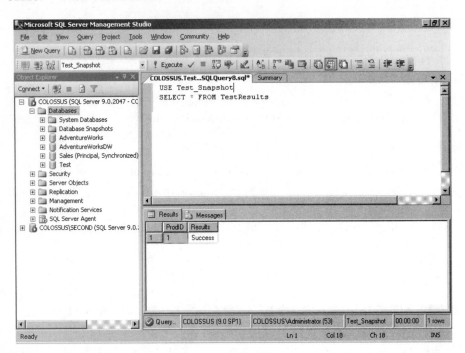

4. To revert from the snapshot, clear the query window, and enter and execute the following code:

```
USE Master
RESTORE DATABASE Test
FROM DATABASE_SNAPSHOT = 'Test_Snapshot'
```

5. Your original database should now match your snapshot. To view all the records in the TestResults table of the original database, run the following query (you should now see one record):

```
USE Test
SELECT * FROM TestResults
```

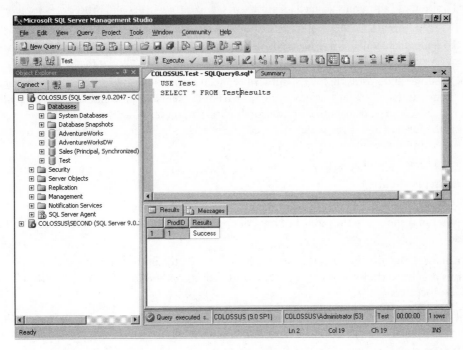

6. To remove the now defunct snapshot, expand Database Snapshots in Object Explorer, right-click Test_Snapshot, and click Delete.

7. Click OK in the Delete an Object dialog box.

Criteria for Completion

This task is complete when you have reverted from the Test_Snapshot database snapshot. You will have only one surviving record in the original TestResults table of the Test database.

Task 2.13: Choosing a Replication Type

You use *replication* to put copies of the same data at different locations throughout the enterprise. You might want to replicate your data for several reasons, but the following are the most common:

- To move data closer to the user

- To reduce locking conflicts when multiple sites want to work with the same data

- To allow site autonomy so each location can set up its own rules and procedures for working with its copy of the data

- To remove the impact of read-intensive operations such as report generation and ad hoc query processing from the online transaction processing (OLTP) database

SQL Server 2005 uses a publisher/subscriber metaphor to describe and implement replication. Your database can play different roles as part of the replication scenario: it can be a publisher, a subscriber, a distributor, or any combination of these. When you publish data, you do it in the form of an article, which is stored in a publication. Here are the key terms used as part of the publisher/subscriber metaphor:

Publisher   The publisher is the source database where replication begins. It makes data available for replication.

Subscriber   The subscriber is the destination database where replication ends. It either receives a snapshot of all the published data or applies transactions that have been replicated to itself.

Distributor   The distributor is the intermediary between the publisher and subscriber. It receives published transactions or snapshots and then stores and forwards these publications to the subscribers.

Publication   The publication is the storage container for different articles. A subscriber will subscribe to an entire publication, but subscribers can read individual articles in the publication.

Article   An article is the actual information that is going to be replicated. You do not have to replicate an entire table; you can select a subset of columns in a table (called *vertical partitioning*) and/or a subset of records in a table (called *horizontal portioning*).

Two-phase commit   *Two-phase commit* (sometimes referred to as 2PC) is a form of replication in which modifications made to the publishing database are made at the subscription database at the same time. This is handled through the use of distributed transactions. As with any transaction, either all statements commit successfully or all modifications are rolled back. Two-phase commit uses the Microsoft Distributed Transaction Coordinator (DTC) to accomplish its tasks. The DTC implements the functionality of a portion of the Microsoft Transaction Server. In this phase, I will focus on replication as opposed to two-phase commits.

Before you can choose a distribution type, you should understand the factors that influence your decision. The three main items to consider are autonomy, latency, and transactional consistency:

Autonomy   This refers to how much independence you want to give each subscriber with regard to the replicated data. Will the replicated data be considered read-only? How long will the data at a subscriber be valid? How often do you need to connect to the distributor to download more data?

Latency   This refers to how often your data will be updated. Does it need to be in synchronization at all times? Is every minute enough? What if you are a salesperson on the road who dials in to the office once a day to update your data? Is this good enough?

Transactional consistency   Although several types of replication exist, the most common method is to move transactions from the publisher through the distributor and onto the subscriber. Transactional consistency comes into play here. Do all the transactions that are stored need to be applied at the same time and in order? What happens if there is a delay in the processing?

Once you understand these factors, you need to start asking yourself the following questions, after which you can decide on a distribution type:

- What am I going to publish? Will it be all the data in a table, or will I partition information?
- Who has access to my publications? Are these subscribers connected, or are they dial-up users?
- Will subscribers be able to update my data, or is their information considered read-only?
- How often should I synchronize my publishers and subscribers?
- How fast is my network? Can subscribers be connected at all times? How much traffic is there on my network?

Each of the several types of distribution you can use has different levels of autonomy, transactional consistency, and latency involved. You can choose from three basic types: snapshot replication, transactional replication, and merge replication. When you factor in latency, autonomy, and consistency, you end up with seven different distribution types:

- Distributed transactions
- Transactional replication
- Transactional replication with immediate updating subscribers
- Snapshot replication
- Snapshot replication with immediate updating subscribers
- Merge replication
- Queued updating

As shown in Figure 2.5, distributed transactions have the least amount of latency and autonomy, but they have the highest level of consistency. Merge replication has the highest amount of latency and autonomy and a lower level of consistency.

FIGURE 2.5   Distribution types

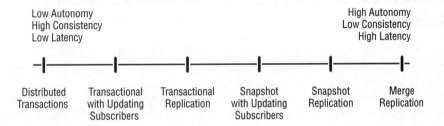

Using Distributed Transactions

When you use distributed transactions (also called *two-phase commit*, or 2PC) to replicate your data, you have almost no autonomy or latency, but you do have guaranteed transactional consistency. With 2PC, either all changes are made at the same time or no changes are made. Remember that all the affected subscribers must be in contact with the publisher at all times. This type of distribution is most useful when subscribers must have real-time data, such as in a reservation system.

For example, think of a cruise line that has only so many rooms of a particular type available. If someone in Dallas wants the captain's suite and someone in California also wants the captain's suite, the first one to book the room will get it. The other booking won't be allowed because that location will immediately show that the room is already booked.

Using Transactional Replication

When you use the transactional replication distribution method, transactions are gathered from the publishers and stored in the distribution database. Subscribers then receive these transactions and must work with the data as if it were read-only. This is because any changes made to their local copy of the data might prohibit new transactions from being applied properly, which would destroy the transactional consistency.

Each site, however, has some limited autonomy. You can introduce some latency because the subscribers don't have to be in contact at all times. Transactional consistency can be maintained as long as the subscribed data remains unchanged by the subscribers.

An advantage to this approach is that transactions are relatively small items to move through the system (unlike snapshot replication, which you will look at shortly). The main disadvantage of using transactional replication is that subscribers must treat the data as read-only.

Use this distribution method when subscribers can treat their data as read-only and need the updated information with a minimal amount of latency.

This type of replication would be useful in an order-processing/distribution system with several locations where orders are taken. Each of the order locations would be a publisher, and the published orders could then be replicated to a subscription database at your central warehouse. The central warehouse could then accept the orders, fill them, and ship them.

Using Transactional Replication with Immediate Updating Subscribers

When you use transactional replication with immediate updating subscribers, you are gaining site autonomy, minimizing latency, and keeping transactional consistency. This (in most cases) would be considered the best possible solution.

When you implement transactional replication with immediate updating subscribers, you are essentially working with all the tenets of transactional replication. The major difference is that when you change the subscription data, 2PC changes the publishing database as well. In this fashion, your local subscriber is updated at the same time as the publisher. Other subscribers will have your changes downloaded to them at their next synchronization.

This scenario can be useful for a reservation system that needs to be updated frequently but does not need total synchronization. Let's use a library as an example here. You want to reserve a book about SQL Server 2005. You go to the computer, look up the book you want to reserve, and find that one copy is currently available at the library. When you try to reserve the book, however, you might find that the data isn't 100 percent up-to-date and the book has already been checked out. In this example, when you try to reserve your book, the subscriber automatically runs a 2PC transaction to the publisher. At the publisher, someone has already checked out the last copy, and therefore the update fails. At the next synchronization, your subscriber will be updated with the news that the last copy has been checked out.

Using Snapshot Replication

When you use snapshot replication as your distribution method, you are actually moving an entire copy of the published items through the distributor and onto the subscribers. This type of replication allows for a high level of both site autonomy and transactional consistency because all records are going to be copied from the publisher and because the local copy of the data will be overwritten at the next synchronization. Latency may be a bit higher because you probably will not move an entire snapshot every few minutes.

Online analytical processing (OLAP) servers are prime candidates for this type of replication. The data at each subscriber is considered read-only and doesn't have to be 100 percent in synchronization all the time. This allows your information technology (IT) departments to run their reporting and ad hoc queries on reasonably fresh data without affecting the OLTP server (which is doing all of the order-processing work).

Keep in mind that most people who run ad hoc queries generally don't modify the data. They are looking for historical information such as how many widgets they sold, so the data that is a few hours or even a few days old will generally not make a difference to the results returned by the queries.

Using Snapshot Replication with Immediate Updating Subscribers

The initial portion of this distribution style works just as in snapshot replication, and in addition, it gives the subscriber the ability to update the publisher with new information. The updates use the 2PC protocol as described previously.

This maintains a high level of site autonomy, a high level of transactional consistency, and a moderate level of latency. The data may be downloaded to the subscriber only once a day, but the publisher must first approve any updates the subscriber tries to make to the data.

This type of distribution is useful when you have read-only data that needs to be updated infrequently. If your data needs to be updated often, I suggest you use transactional replication with immediate updating subscribers.

Snapshot replication might be useful when auditing your database, downloading portions of the data, and then double-checking that everything is being updated properly. You could then quickly fix the occasional mistake, and auditing could continue.

Using Merge Replication

Merge replication provides the highest amount of site autonomy, the highest latency, and the lowest level of transactional consistency. Merge replication allows each subscriber to make changes to their local copy of the data. At some point, these changes are merged with those made by other subscribers as well as changes made at the publisher. Ultimately, all sites receive the updates from all other sites. This is known as *convergence*; that is, all changes from all sites converge and are redistributed so that all sites have the same changes.

Transactional consistency is nearly nonexistent here because different sites may all be making changes to the same data, resulting in conflicts. SQL Server 2005 will automatically choose a particular change over another change and then converge that data. To simplify, sooner or later, all sites will have the same copy of the data, but that data may not necessarily be what you want. For example, subscriber A makes changes to record 100. Subscriber B also makes changes to record 100. Although this doesn't sound too bad, suppose the changes that subscriber A made to record 100 are because of changes that were made to record 50. If subscriber B doesn't have the same data in record 50, then subscriber B will make a different decision. Obviously, this can be incredibly complex.

You might wonder why anyone would want to use merge replication. Many reasons exist for using it, and with some careful planning, you can make merge replication work to your advantage. You can modify triggers to determine which record is the correct record to use. The default rule when records are changed at multiple sites is to take the changes based on a site priority, converge the results, and then send them. The exception to this general rule occurs when the main database and all the user databases are changed. In this case, the user changes are applied first, and then the main database changes are applied. For example, say you have a central server that you call Main and you have 20 salespeople who are using merge replication. If one of your salespeople modifies record 25 and you modify record 25 at the Main server, when the records are converged, the user changes will first be placed in the Main server, and then the Main server changes will overwrite them.

If you design your publishers and subscribers to minimize conflicts, merge replication can be advantageous. Look at the highway patrol, for example. A patrol car might pull over a car and write the driver a ticket for speeding. At the end of the day, that data is merged with data from other officers who have also written tickets. The data is then converged back to all the different squad cars' computers, and now all the police know who to watch for on the roads.

Using Queued Updating

With transactional and snapshot replication, you can also configure queued updating. Like the immediate updating subscribers option, this gives your users the ability to make changes to the subscription database, but unlike immediate updating subscribers, queued updating will store changes until the publisher can be contacted.

This can be extremely useful in networks where you have subscribers who are not always connected or the connection is unreliable. Here is how it works:

1. Updates made on the subscribers are captured by triggers on the subscribing tables and stored in the storage queue.

2. The updates are stored in a table named MSreplication_queue in the subscription database. These messages are automatically sent to the distributor when it becomes available.

3. The queue reader agent applies the changes to the publication.

4. Any conflicts are detected and resolved according to a conflict resolution policy that is defined when the publication is created.

5. Changes made at the publisher are applied to all remaining subscribers.

Here are some points to keep in mind if you plan to use queued updating:

- INSERT statements must include a column list.

- Subscribers using immediate or queued updating cannot republish at the subscriber.

- Once a publication is configured to use queued updating, the option cannot be removed (though subscribers do not need to use it). To remove the option, you must delete and re-create the publication.

- You cannot use transformable subscriptions with queued updating. The Transform Published Data screen of the Create Publication Wizard will not be displayed.

- Only SQL Server 2000 (and newer) servers can subscribe using queued updating.

Understanding how the transactions or snapshots are handled is essential to a full understanding of how SQL Server 2005 implements replication.

When you set up your subscribers, you can create either pull or push subscriptions. Push subscriptions help centralize your administrative duties because the subscription itself is stored on the distribution server. This allows the publisher to determine what data is in the subscription and when that subscription will be synchronized. In other words, the data can be pushed to the subscribers based on the publisher's schedule. Push subscriptions are most useful if a subscriber needs to be updated whenever a change occurs at the publisher. The publisher knows when the modification takes place, so it can immediately push those changes to the subscribers.

Pull subscriptions are configured and maintained at each subscriber. The subscribers will administer the synchronization schedules and can pull changes whenever they consider it necessary. This type of subscriber also relieves the distribution server of some of the overhead of processing. Pull subscriptions are also useful in situations in which security is not a primary issue. In fact, you can set up pull subscriptions to allow anonymous connections, including pull subscribers residing on the Internet.

In either a push environment or a pull environment, five replication agents handle the tasks of moving data from the publisher to the distributor and then onto the subscribers. The location of the particular agent depends upon the type of replication (push or pull) you are using:

Logreader agent   Located on the distribution server, the logreader's job is to monitor the transaction logs of published databases that are using this distributor. When the logreader agent finds a transaction, it moves the transaction to the distribution database on the distributor; transactions are stored and then forwarded to the subscribers by the distribution agent for transactional and snapshot replication or by the merge agent for merge replication.

Distribution agent   The distribution agent is responsible for moving the stored transactions from the distributor to the subscribers.

Snapshot agent   This agent, which is also used for snapshot replication, is responsible for copying the schema and data from the publisher to the subscriber. Before any type of replication can begin, a copy of the data must reside on each subscriber. With this baseline established, transactions can then be applied at each subscriber, and transactional consistency can be maintained.

Merge agent   The merge agent is responsible for converging records from multiple sites and then redistributing the converged records back to the subscribers.

Queue reader agent   The queue reader agent runs on the distributor and is responsible for reading messages from the queue on the subscribers and applying them to the appropriate publication. It is used only with queued updating publications and subscribers.

You do not have to choose a single type of distribution for all your subscribers. Each subscriber can implement a different type of data distribution.

In this task, you decide on a replication type to use for a given scenario.

Scenario

You work for a medium-sized company that has offices throughout the world. Many of the users in these offices need access to the data stored on SQL Server, and they need it as fast as possible. You know that the best way to get this data to the users is via replication; however, before you can configure replication, you need to figure out which type of replication to use.

Scope of Task

Duration

This task should take approximately 15 minutes.

Setup

You don't need to perform any setup for this task because it is all takes place on paper.

Caveat

This task doesn't have any caveats.

Procedure

In this task, you will read each scenario and decide on the proper replication type.

Equipment Used

The only equipment you need for this task is some paper and a pencil or pen.

Details

For each scenario presented, choose the correct replication type:

1. One of your servers, located in New York City, contains a Sales database that needs to be replicated to your satellite offices in Berlin, London, and Moscow, which are connected via a partial T1 connection that consistently runs at 80 percent capacity. Your sales associates make changes to the database regularly throughout the day, but the users in the satellite offices do not need to see the changes immediately. Which type of replication should you use?

    a. Merge

    b. Transactional

    c. Snapshot

    d. Transactional with updating subscribers

    e. Snapshot with updating subscribers

2. Each branch office of your company has its own accounting department. The network connections between the branch offices are reliable, but they are consistently at 80 percent usage during the day. Each of your branch office accounting departments needs a copy of the main accounting database that they can update locally, and they need it to be as current as possible. Which replication type best suits your needs?

    a. Merge

    b. Transactional

    c. Snapshot

    d. Transactional with immediate updating subscribers

    e. Snapshot with updating subscribers

3. Several of your company's sales offices are located throughout the country. Headquarters needs an up-to-date copy of the sales offices' databases. When headquarters sends new inventory to the sales offices, they want to update the database at headquarters and have the new data replicated to the respective sales offices. Which replication type should you use?

    a. Merge

    b. Transactional

    c. Snapshot

    d. Transactional with immediate updating subscribers

    e. Snapshot with updating subscribers

4. The retail division of your company manages shops in various cities. Each shop maintains its own inventory database. The retail manager in Phoenix wants each of her four shops to be able to share inventory with each other so employees can pick up a part from another nearby store rather than waiting for a shipment from the manufacturer. To do this, employees at each shop should be able to update their local copy of the inventory database, decrement the other store's inventory, and then go pick up the part. This way, the other store won't sell its part because the part will have already been taken out of stock. Which replication type should you use to accomplish this?

   a. Merge

   b. Transactional

   c. Snapshot

   d. Transactional with updating subscribers

   e. Snapshot with updating subscribers

Criteria for Completion

This task is complete when you have chosen the correct replication type for each of the scenarios presented. The correct answers are as follows:

Scenario 1   The answer is B. Because the entire database does not change every day, you do not need to use the snapshot type. Also, the snapshot type would use a great deal more bandwidth than the transactional type. Because the subscribers do not need to update their copy of the data, you do not need the added complexity of merging or updating subscribers. Also, you do not have much network bandwidth to play with, and transactional replication uses the least amount of bandwidth.

Scenario 2   The answer is D. Because the network is running close to capacity most of the time, it would not support snapshot replication. Because the users would be updating only their own data, merge replication would be overkill. Transactional with updating subscribers fits your needs because the network usage is lower than snapshot and still allows users to update local copies of the data.

Scenario 3   The answer is D. Because each office needs to be able to update their own inventory databases each time they make a sale and headquarters needs to be able to update the main database, you need to give the sales offices the capability to update. Merge replication would be overkill here because each sales office does not need to update other sales offices' data.

Scenario 4   The answer is A. In this scenario, you do not have a central "main" database that each subscriber will update. All the stores must be able to update data for the other stores' data. The best way to accomplish this is through merge replication.

Task 2.14: Designing a Replication Topology

After you have chosen a replication topology, you need to decide on a replication type. You can use one of several topologies when you implement replication:

- Central publisher/central distributor
- Remote distribution
- Central subscriber/multiple publishers
- Multiple publishers/multiple subscribers

Central Publisher/Central Distributor

As shown in Figure 2.6, both the publishing database and the distribution database are on the same SQL Server system. This configuration is useful when modeling replication strategies for the following business scenarios:

- Asynchronous order processing during communication outages
- Distribution of price lists, customer lists, vendor lists, and so on
- Removal of administrative activities from the OLTP environment
- Establishment of executive information systems

FIGURE 2.6   The central publisher model

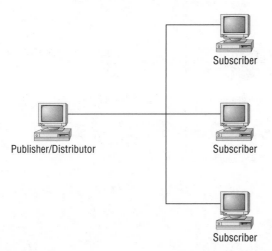

One of the most important aspects of the central publisher model is the ability to move data to a separate SQL Server system. This allows the publishing server to continue handling online transaction processing duties without having to absorb the impact of the ad hoc queries generally found in information technology (IT) departments.

You can use any type of replication here—transactional, merge, or snapshot. If you do not have to update BLOB objects such as text, ntext, and image datatypes, I suggest you use transactional replication. IT departments generally don't need to make changes to the subscribed data.

Remote Distribution

In this model, you remove the impact of the distribution process from your OLTP server, which gives you the best possible speed on the OLTP server. This model is useful in situations in which you need the optimal performance from your OLTP server. A single distribution server can work with multiple distributors and multiple subscribers. Figure 2.7 shows a representation of this strategy.

This calls for transactional replication and minimizing the impact of replication on the publishing database. By moving just transactions rather than moving snapshots or attempting to merge data at the publisher, you can gain the most possible speed and have the lowest impact on the publisher.

FIGURE 2.7   The remote distribution model

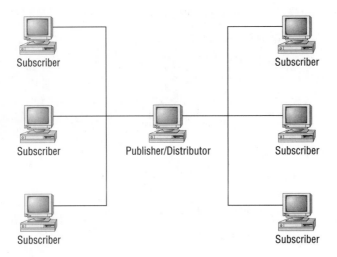

Central Subscriber/Multiple Publishers

The central subscriber model shown in Figure 2.8 is useful in the following situations:

- Roll-up reporting
- Local warehouse inventory management
- Local customer order processing

You need to keep several issues in mind when you attempt to use this model. Because multiple publishers are writing to a single table in the database, you must take some precautions to ensure that referential integrity is maintained. If your New York office sent an order with a key of 1000 and your Milwaukee office also sent an order with a key of 1000, you would have two records with the same primary key. You could get bad data in your database because the primary key is designed to guarantee the uniqueness of each record. In this situation, only one of those records would post.

To make sure this doesn't become a problem, implement a composite primary key using the original order ID number along with a location-specific code. You could, for example, give New York a location code of NY and the Milwaukee branch a location code of MW. This way, the new composite keys would be NY1000 and MW1000. There would be no more conflicting records, and both orders would be filled from the Denver offices.

This scenario is especially suited to transactional replication because the data at the Denver site is really read-only. Snapshot replication wouldn't work here because that would overwrite everyone else's data. You could use merge replication if the other locations needed to be able to see all the orders placed.

FIGURE 2.8   The central subscriber model

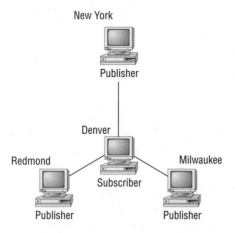

Multiple Publishers/Multiple Subscribers

Use this model when you need to maintain a single table on multiple servers. Each server subscribes to the table and also publishes the table to other servers. This model can be particularly useful in the following business situations:

- Reservations systems

- Regional order-processing systems

- Multiple warehouse implementations

Think of a regional order-processing system, as shown in Figure 2.9. Suppose you place an order on Monday and want to check on that order on Tuesday. When you call the company, you may be routed to any of several regional order-processing centers. Each of these centers should have a copy of your order so you can go over the order with a salesperson.

I suggest you use transactional replication for this scenario, using some type of region code (as described in the central subscriber/multiple publishers scenario). Each order-processing center should publish only its own data, but it should subscribe to data being published by the other publishers. In addition, each location should update only the data it owns. This scenario is also a good candidate for the transactional replication with an updating subscriber model. In this case, each center could update data owned by another center; however, this update would take place at both servers and therefore maintain transactional consistency.

 You can also replicate from SQL Server 2005 to Oracle or IBM databases that conform to the IBM Distributed Relational Database Architecture (DRDA) data protocol.

In this task, you will decide on a replication type to use for a given scenario.

FIGURE 2.9 Multiple publishers of one table model

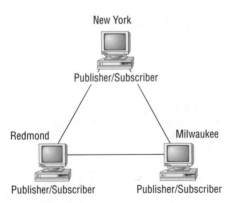

Scenario

You work for a medium-sized company that has offices throughout the world. Many of the users in these offices need access to the data stored on SQL Server, and they need it as fast as possible. You know that the best way to get this data to the users is via replication; however, before you can configure replication, you need to decide on a replication topology.

Scope of Task

Duration

This task should take approximately 15 minutes.

Setup

You don't need to perform any setup for this task because it is all takes place on paper.

Caveat

This task doesn't have any caveats.

Procedure

In this task, you will read each scenario and decide on the proper replication topology.

Equipment Used

The only equipment you need for this task is some paper and a pencil or pen.

Details

For each scenario presented, choose the correct replication topology:

1. One of your servers, located in New York City, contains a Sales database that needs to be replicated to your satellite offices in Berlin, London, and Moscow, which are connected via a partial T1 connection that consistently runs at 80 percent capacity. Your sales associates make changes to the database regularly throughout the day, but the users in the satellite offices do not need to see the changes immediately. You have decided to use transactional replication. Which replication topology should you use?

    a. Central subscriber/multiple publishers

    b. Multiple publishers/multiple subscribers

    c. Central publisher/central distributor

    d. Remote distribution

2. Each branch office of your company has its own accounting department. The network connections between the branch offices are reliable, but they are consistently at 80 percent usage during the day. Each of your branch office accounting departments needs a copy of

the main accounting database that they can update locally, and they need it to be as current as possible. You have decided to use transactional replication with immediate updating subscribers. Which replication topology best suits your needs?

    a. Central subscriber/multiple publishers

    b. Multiple publishers/multiple subscribers

    c. Central publisher/central distributor

    d. Remote distribution

3. Several of your company's sales offices are located throughout the country. Headquarters needs an up-to-date copy of the sales offices' databases. When headquarters sends new inventory to the sales offices, they want to update the database at headquarters and have the new data replicated to the respective sales offices. You have decided to use transactional replication with immediate updating subscribers. Which replication topology should you use?

    a. Central subscriber/multiple publishers

    b. Multiple publishers/multiple subscribers

    c. Central publisher/central distributor

    d. Remote distribution

4. The retail division of your company manages shops in various cities. Each shop maintains its own inventory database. The retail manager in Phoenix wants each of her four shops to be able to share inventory with each other so employees can pick up a part from another nearby store rather than waiting for a shipment from the manufacturer. To do this, employees at each shop should be able to update their local copy of the inventory database, decrement the other store's inventory, and then go pick up the part. This way, the other store won't sell its part because the part will have already been taken out of stock. You have decided to use merge replication. Which replication topology should you use?

    a. Central subscriber/multiple publishers

    b. Multiple publishers/multiple subscribers

    c. Central publisher/central distributor

    d. Remote distribution

Criteria for Completion

This task is complete when you have chosen the correct replication type for each of the scenarios presented. The correct answers are as follows:

Scenario 1 The answer is D. The models that involve multiple publishers obviously won't work here because you have only one publisher. The remote distributor option can save long-distance charges because instead of making several long-distance calls from New York to the satellites, you can place a distributor in London and let the distributor make less-expensive calls to the remaining satellites.

Scenario 2   Either answer C or answer D is acceptable here. Because you are using transactional replication with updating subscribers, you can use a central publisher at headquarters with each sales office being a subscriber.

Scenario 3   As with scenario 2, either answer C or answer D is acceptable. Because you are using transactional replication with updating subscribers, you can use a central publisher at headquarters with each sales office being a subscriber.

Scenario 4   The answer is B. Each store will publish its inventory database and subscribe to the other stores' inventory databases. This makes it the perfect scenario for a multiple publishers/multiple subscribers model.

Task 2.15: Configuring Replication

Before you can configure your SQL Server for replication, the computer itself must meet the following requirements:

- All servers involved with replication must be registered in SQL Server Management Studio.
- If the servers are from different domains, you must establish trust relationships before replication can occur.
- Any account you use must have access rights to the Distribution working folder on the distribution server.
- You must enable access to the Distribution working folder on the distribution server. For a Windows server, this is the *ServerName*\C$\Program Files\Microsoft SQL Server\MSSQL\REPLDATA folder. On Windows XP and earlier computers, you must create the C$ share because it exists by default only on Windows Server–family operating systems.

I suggest you use a single Windows domain account for all your SQL Server Agents. Do not use a LocalSystem account because this account has no network capabilities and will therefore not allow replication. Also, you need to make the account a member of the Domain Admins group because only administrators have access to the administrative shares.

Before you can enable a publication database, you must be a member of the sysadmin fixed server role. Once you have enabled publishing, any member of that database's db_owner role can create and manage publications.

Before you can start replicating data, you need to install a distribution server. In this task, you will install a distribution server on the default instance of SQL Server.

Scenario

You work for a medium-sized company that has offices throughout the world. Many of the users in these offices need access to the data stored on SQL Server, and they need it as fast as possible. You know that the best way to get this data to the users is via replication; however, before you can create publications and subscriptions, you must configure a distribution server.

Scope of Task

Duration

This task should take approximately 30 minutes.

Setup

For this task, you need access to the machine you installed SQL Server 2005 on in Task 1.1.

Caveat

Make sure the SQL Server Agent is set to start automatically before starting this task.

Procedure

In this task, you will configure the default instance of SQL Server on your machine as a distribution server.

Equipment Used

For this task, you need access to the machine you installed SQL Server 2005 on in Task 1.1.

Details

Follow these steps to configure your default instance as a distribution server:

1. Open SQL Server Management Studio, and connect to your server.
2. Right-click Replication, and click Configure Distribution.
3. You are presented with a welcome screen; click Next to continue.

4. The Distributor screen appears. Select the server that will act as its own distributor option, and click Next.

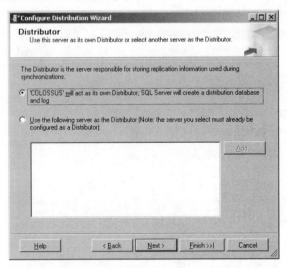

5. If your SQL Server agent is not configured to start automatically, you may be presented with a screen asking you to configure the agent. Set it to start automatically, and click Next.

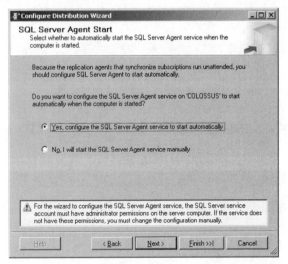

6. You are now asked to specify the snapshot folder. A good reason to change this is if you are replicating over the Internet and need to specify a folder that is accessible via FTP. Accept the defaults, and click Next.

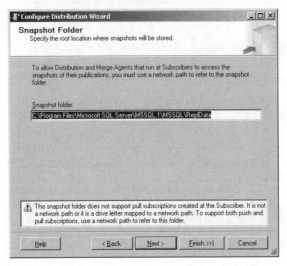

7. The Distribution Database screen appears next. You can supply a name for the distribution database as well as location information for its database file and transaction log. Keep the defaults, and click Next to continue.

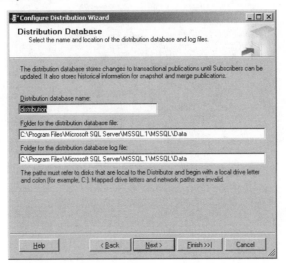

8. Now you are on the Publishers screen where you can choose which servers you want to configure as publishers. Clicking the ellipsis (...) button allows you to specify security credentials
such as login ID and password, as well as the location of the snapshot folder. Be sure to place
a check mark next to your local SQL Server system, and then click Next to continue.

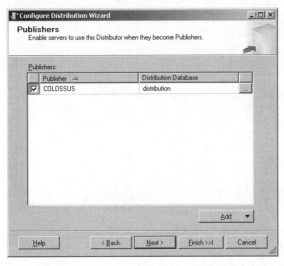

9. On the Wizard Actions screen, you can have the wizard configure distribution, write a
script to configure distribution that you can run later, or do both. Leave the Configure
Distribution box checked, and click Next to continue.

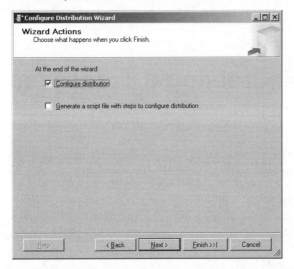

10. On the Complete the Wizard screen, review your selections, and click Finish.

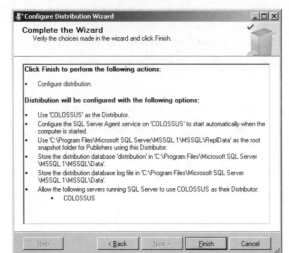

11. When the wizard is finished, click Close.

Criteria for Completion

This task is complete when you have configured your default instance of SQL Server to act as a distributor. To verify this, right-click Replication in Object Explorer; you should see an option labeled Distributor Properties. When you click that option, you should see the dialog box shown in Figure 2.10.

Task 2.16: Creating a Transactional Publication

When you use transactional replication, only the changes (transactions) made to the data are moved. Before these transactions can be applied at a subscriber, however, the subscriber must have a copy of the data as a base. Because of its speed and its relatively low overhead on the distribution server, transactional replication is currently the most often used form of replication. Generally, data on the subscriber is treated as read-only, unless you are implementing transactional replication with immediate updating subscribers. Because the transactions are so small, this type of replication is often set up to run continuously. Every time a change is made at the publisher, it is automatically applied to the subscriber, generally within one minute.

FIGURE 2.10   You should see the Distributor Properties dialog box when distribution is configured.

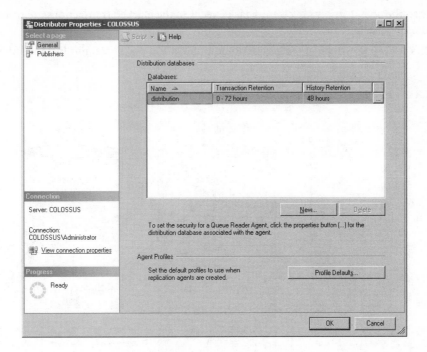

When you use transactional replication, you don't need the merge agent. The snapshot agent must still run at least once; it uses the distribution agent to move the initial snapshot from the publisher to the subscriber. You also use the logreader agent when using transactional replication. The logreader agent looks for transactions in published databases and moves those transactions to the distribution database. The following steps (see Figure 2.11) outline the transactional replication process:

1. The logreader agent reads the published article and then creates the schema on the subscriber and bulk copies the snapshot over to the subscriber. (This happens only when the subscription is created or re-created.)

2. The logreader agent scans the transaction logs of databases marked for publishing. When it finds an appropriate transaction, it copies the transaction to the distribution database. The distribution database will store the transaction for a configurable length of time.

3. The distribution agent will then apply those transactions to the subscribers at the next synchronization. The subscriber then runs the sp_repldone system stored procedure

on the distribution database. This marks the newly replicated transactions stored on the distributor in the MSrepl_commands table as completed.

4. When the next distribution cleanup task executes, the marked transactions are truncated from the distribution server.

In this task, you will create a transactional publication on the default instance of SQL Server.

FIGURE 2.11 The transactional replication process

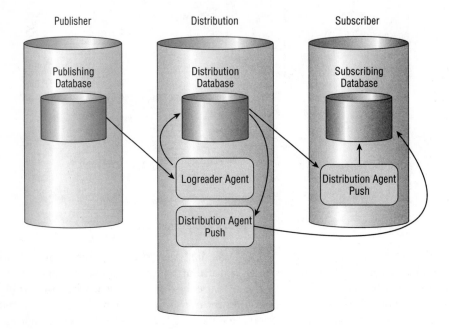

Scenario

You work for a medium-sized company that has offices throughout the world. The sales department in the Fresno branch office needs access to some of the data stored in the main database housed on the SQL Server at the corporate headquarters. They do not need the data immediately, so there is room for some latency; in addition, they are connected by a partial T1 that is at about 80 percent capacity, so there is little room for more traffic. Bearing these factors in mind, you decide the best way to get the data to the users in Fresno is to configure a transactional publication.

Scope of Task

Duration

This task should take approximately 30 minutes.

Setup

For this task, you need access to the machine you installed SQL Server 2005 on in Task 1.1, the AdventureWorks database installed with the sample data, and the default instance of SQL Server you configured as a distributor in Task 2.15.

Caveat

If you still have log shipping enabled on the AdventureWorks database (from Task 2.10), you will need to disable it. Here's how:

1. Open SQL Server Management Studio, and connect to the default instance.
2. Expand Databases, right-click AdventureWorks, point to Tasks, and click Ship Transaction Logs.
3. Uncheck the box next to Enable This as a Primary Database in a Log Shipping Configuration.
4. Click Yes on the subsequent dialog box, and then click OK.
5. Click Close when the configuration is complete.

Procedure

In this task, you will create a transactional publication on your default instance of SQL Server on the Production.ProductCategory table in the AdventureWorks database.

Equipment Used

For this task, you need access to the machine you installed SQL Server 2005 on in Task 1.1, the AdventureWorks database installed with the sample data, and the default instance of SQL Server you configured as a distributor in Task 2.15.

Details

Follow these steps to create a transactional publication on the Production.ProductCategory table:

1. Open SQL Server Management Studio, and connect to your SQL Server.
2. Expand Replication, right-click Local Publications, and click New Publication. This brings you to the New Publication Wizard welcome screen.

3. Click Next to continue.

4. On the Publication Database screen, highlight AdventureWorks, and click Next to continue.

5. On the Publication Type screen, you can choose what type of publication to create. For this task, choose Transactional Publication, and click Next to continue.

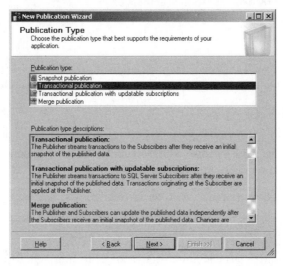

6. On the Articles screen, you can select what data and objects you want to replicate. Expand Tables, and check the ProductCategory box.

7.   You can also set the properties for an article from this screen. Make sure ProductCategory is highlighted, click Article Properties, and then click Set Properties of Highlighted Table Article.

8.   In the Destination Object section, change the destination object name to **ReplicatedCategory,** change the destination object owner to **dbo,** and click OK.

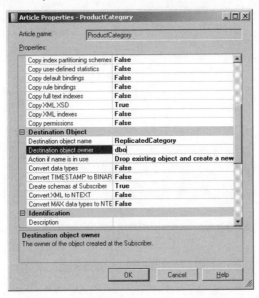

9.   Back at the Articles screen, click Next to continue.

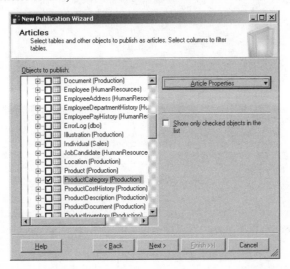

10. On the next screen, you can filter the data that is replicated. You do not want to filter the data in this case, so click Next to continue.

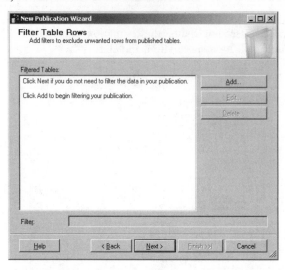

11. On the Snapshot Agent screen, check the box to create a snapshot immediately, and click Next.

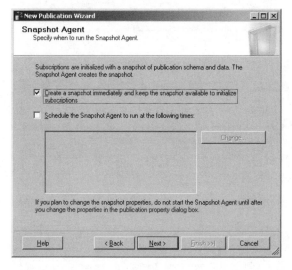

12. On the Agent Security screen, you are asked how the agents should log in and access data. To set this for the snapshot agent, click the Security Settings button next to Snapshot Agent.

13. Ordinarily you would create an account for the agent to run under, but to make the task simpler, you will run the agent using the SQL Server Agent account, so select the radio button for that option, and click OK.

14. Back at the Agent Security screen, click Next to continue.

15. On the Wizard Actions screen, you can have the wizard create the publication, write a script to create the publication that you can run later, or do both. Leave the Create the Publication box checked, and click Next to continue.

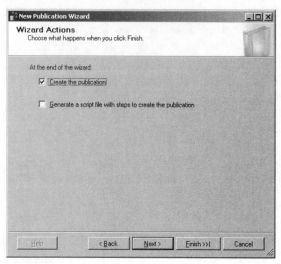

16. On the Complete the Wizard screen, you need to enter a name for the new publication, so enter **CategoryPub**, and click Finish.

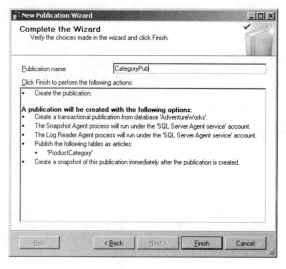

17. When the wizard is finished, click Close.

Criteria for Completion

This task is complete when you have created a transactional publication based on the Production.ProductCategory table in the AdventureWorks database on the default instance of SQL Server. To verify this, follow these steps:

1. Open SQL Server Management Studio, connect to your SQL Server, and expand Replication. You should see the CategoryPub publication listed.

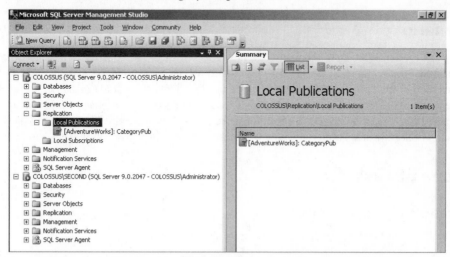

2. Right-click CategoryPub, and click Properties. The type should be Transactional.

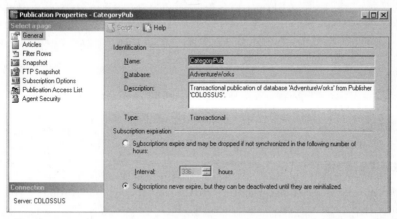

3. Click OK.

Task 2.17: Subscribing to a Transactional Publication

After you have created a publication, you can configure one or more servers as subscribers. In this task, you will subscribe to a transactional publication.

Scenario

You work for a medium-sized company that has offices throughout the world. The sales department in the Fresno branch office needs access to some of the data stored in the main database housed on the SQL Server at the corporate headquarters. They do not need the data immediately, so there is room for some latency; in addition, they are connected by a partial T1 that is at about 80 percent capacity, so there is little room for more traffic. You have already configured a transactional publication at headquarters; now you must create a subscription on the server in Fresno.

Scope of Task

Duration

This task should take approximately 30 minutes.

Setup

For this task, you need access to the machine you installed SQL Server 2005 on in Task 1.1, the Second instance of SQL Server installed in Task 1.2, the AdventureWorks database installed with the sample data, the default instance of SQL Server configured as a distributor in Task 2.15, and the transactional publication configured in Task 2.16.

Caveat

Make sure the SQL Agent service for the Second instance is set to start automatically before starting this task.

Procedure

In this task, you will create a pull subscription to the transactional publication on your default instance of SQL Server.

Equipment Used

For this task, you need access to the machine you installed SQL Server 2005 on in Task 1.1, the Second instance of SQL Server installed in Task 1.2, the AdventureWorks database installed with the sample data, the default instance of SQL Server you configured as a distributor in Task 2.15, and the transactional publication you configured in Task 2.16.

Details

Follow these steps to create a pull subscription to the transactional publication on the default instance of SQL Server:

1. Open SQL Server Management Studio, and connect to the Second instance by selecting it from the Server Name drop-down list.

2. Expand Replication, right-click Local Subscriptions, and click New Subscription. This brings you to the New Subscription Wizard welcome screen. Click Next to continue.

3. On the Publication screen, select the default instance of your server from the Publisher drop-down list (if it is not listed, select Find SQL Server Publisher), select CategoryPub from the Databases and Publications list, and click Next to continue.

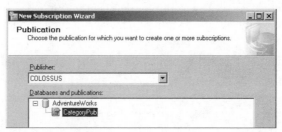

4. On the Distribution Agent Location screen, you are asked which machine should run the replication agents—at the distributor or at the subscriber. Because you want to create a pull subscription, select the Run Each Agent at Its Subscriber option, and click Next.

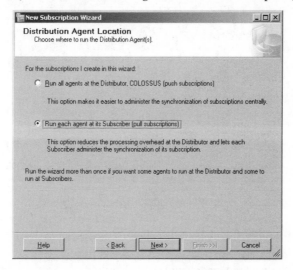

5. On the Subscribers screen, you can choose a subscriber for the publication. Check the box next to the Second instance of your server.

6. Then the drop-down list is populated with all the available databases on the subscriber. Select New Database from the list to open the New Database dialog box.

7. Enter **TR_Test** in the Database name box, and click OK. Then click Next.

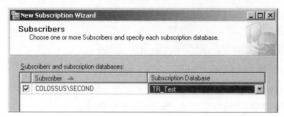

8. On the next screen you need to set the distribution agent security. To do so, click the ellipsis (…) button in the Subscription Properties list.

9. Ordinarily you would create an account for the agent to run under, but to make the task simpler, you will run the agent using the SQL Server Agent account, so select the radio button for that option, and click OK.

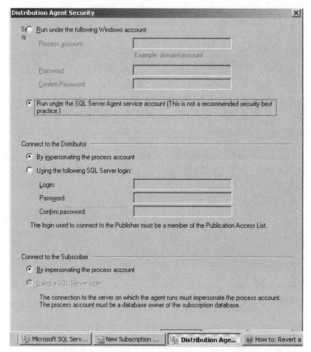

10. Back at the Distribution Agent Security screen, click Next to continue.

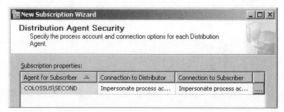

11. The next step is to set the synchronization schedule. Because you are using transactional replication, select Run Continuously, and click Next to continue.

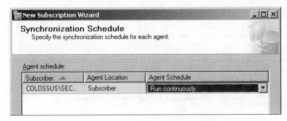

12. On the next screen, you can tell SQL Server when to initialize the subscription, if at all. If you have already created the schema on the subscriber, then you do not need to initialize the subscription. In this case, you should select Immediately from the drop-down list, make sure the Initialize box is checked, and click Next to continue.

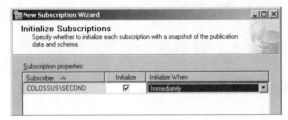

13. On the Wizard Actions screen, you can have the wizard create the subscription, write a script to create the subscription that you can run later, or do both. Leave the Create the Subscription box checked, and click Next to continue.

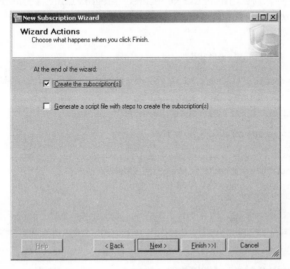

14. On the Complete the Wizard screen, review your options, and click Finish to create the subscription.

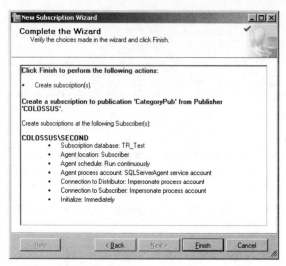

15. When the wizard is finished, click Close.

Criteria for Completion

This task is complete when replication is running properly. Follow these steps to verify:

1. You should have four records in the ReplicatedCategory table. To verify that, open a new query, connect to the Second instance, and execute the following code:

```
USE TR_Test
SELECT * FROM ReplicatedCategory
```

2. Now add a new record to the ProductCategory table in the AdventureWorks database on the default instance. Open a new query, and from the Query menu, select Connection and Change Connection. Then connect to the default instance.

3. Run the following code to add a new record:

```
USE AdventureWorks
INSERT INTO Production.ProductCategory (Name)
VALUES('Tools')
```

4. You should get the message that one row was added. Give the server about a minute to replicate the transaction; then run the following query against the Second instance:

```
USE TR_Test
SELECT * FROM ReplicatedCategory
```

5.   You should get five records. The last record should be the new Tools record.

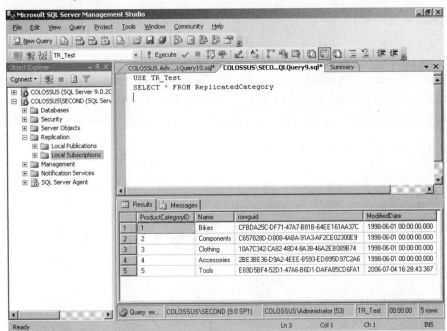

Task 2.18: Creating a Snapshot Publication

When you use snapshot replication, an entire copy of the publication is moved from the publisher to the subscriber. Everything on the subscriber database is overwritten, allowing for autonomy as well as transactional consistency because all changes are made at once. Latency can be high for this type of replication if you want it to be. You can schedule your refreshes when and as often as you want. (I have found that this normally occurs once a day, at off-peak hours.) Keep in mind that snapshot replication occurs on demand. This means no data is transferred from the publisher to the distributor until a subscriber is ready to receive it. The snapshot then moves straight through. Status information is stored in the distribution database; however, the snapshot agent and the distribution agent do all their work at the time the snapshot is initiated.

When you use snapshot replication, there is no merge agent. Snapshot replication uses the distribution agent. If you are using a pull replication, the distribution agent resides on the subscription server. If you are doing a push replication, the agent resides on the distributor. When used in a push scenario, snapshot replication consumes a large amount of overhead on the distribution server. I suggest that most snapshot subscribers use a pull scenario at regularly scheduled intervals. The following steps (see Figure 2.12) outline the snapshot replication process:

1. The snapshot agent reads the published article and then creates the table schema and data in the Distribution working folder.

2. The distribution agent creates the schema on the subscriber.

3. The distribution agent moves the data into the newly created tables on the subscriber.

4. Any indexes that were used are re-created on the newly synchronized subscription database.

FIGURE 2.12   The snapshot replication process

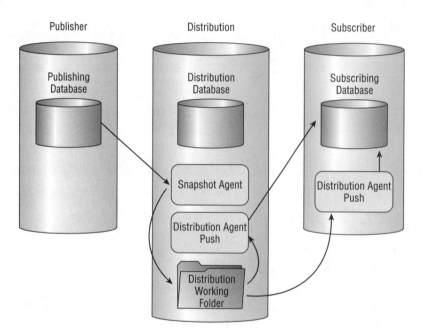

This works in the same fashion when you are using snapshot replication with immediate updating subscribers. The only difference is that the subscriber will use a two-phase commit to update both the subscription database and the publishing database at the same time. During the next refresh, all subscribers will receive a copy of the modified data.

In this task, you will create a snapshot publication on the default instance of SQL Server.

Scenario

You work for a medium-sized company that has offices throughout the world. The sales department in the Tucson branch office needs access one of the databases housed on the SQL Server at the corporate headquarters. They will use the data only for reporting purposes, so they will not be making updates to their local copy of the data. They need the data to be refreshed only once a day, so you can allow for a full day of latency. They are connected by a partial T1 that is at about 75 percent capacity during peak hours, but off-hours it is at about 30 percent capacity, so the network has plenty of room during off-hours. Bearing these factors in mind, you decide that the best way to get the data to the users in Tucson is to configure a snapshot publication.

Scope of Task

Duration

This task should take approximately 30 minutes.

Setup

For this task, you need access to the machine you installed SQL Server 2005 on in Task 1.1, the AdventureWorks database installed with the sample data, and the default instance of SQL Server you configured as a distributor in Task 2.15.

Caveat

If you still have log shipping enabled on the AdventureWorks database (from Task 2.10), you will need to disable it. Here's how:

1. Open SQL Server Management Studio, and connect to the default instance.
2. Expand Databases, right-click AdventureWorks, point to Tasks, and click Ship Transaction Logs.
3. Uncheck the box next to Enable This as a Primary Database in a Log Shipping configuration.
4. Click Yes in the subsequent dialog box, then click OK.
5. Click Close when the configuration is complete.

Procedure

In this task, you will create a snapshot publication on your default instance of SQL Server on the Person.AddressType table in the AdventureWorks database.

Equipment Used

For this task, you need access to the machine you installed SQL Server 2005 on in Task 1.1, the AdventureWorks database installed with the sample data, and the default instance of SQL Server you configured as a distributor in Task 2.15.

Details

Follow these steps to create a snapshot publication on the Person.AddressType table:

1. Open SQL Server Management Studio, and connect to the default instance of SQL Server.

   2.   Expand Replication, right-click Local Publications, and click New Publication. This brings you to the New Publication Wizard welcome screen.

   3.   Click Next to continue.

   4.   On the Publication Database screen, highlight AdventureWorks, and click Next to continue.

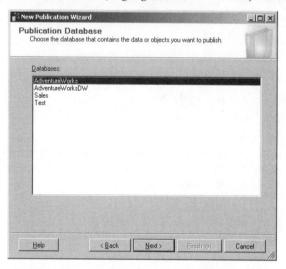

   5.   On the Publication Type screen, you can choose what type of publication to create. For this task, choose Snapshot Publication, and click Next to continue.

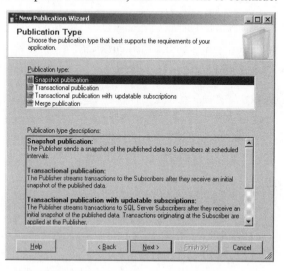

   6.   On the Articles screen, you can select what data and objects you want to replicate. Expand Tables, and check the AddressType box.

7. You can also set the properties for an article from this screen. Make sure AddressType is highlighted, click Article Properties, and then click Set Properties of Highlighted Table Article.

8. In the Destination Object section, change the destination object name to **ReplicatedType**, change the destination object owner to **dbo,** and click OK.

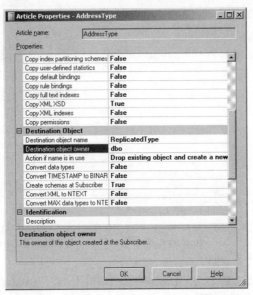

9. Back at the Articles screen, click Next to continue.

10. On the next screen, you can filter the data that is replicated. You do not want to filter the data in this case, so click Next to continue.

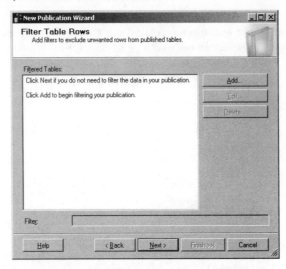

11. On the Snapshot Agent screen, check the box to create a snapshot immediately, and check the Schedule the Snapshot agent to run at the following times. Leave the default schedule of one hour, and click Next.

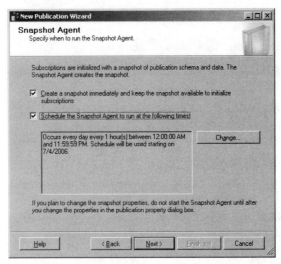

12. On the Agent Security screen, you are asked how the agents should log in and access data. To set this for the snapshot agent, click the Security Settings button next to Snapshot Agent.

13. Ordinarily you would create an account for the agent to run under, but to make the task simpler, you will run the agent using the SQL Server Agent account, so select the radio button for that option, and click OK.

14. Back at the Agent Security screen, click Next to continue.

15. On the Wizard Actions screen, you can have the wizard create the publication, write a script to create the publication you can run later, or do both. Leave the Create the Publication box checked, and click Next to continue.

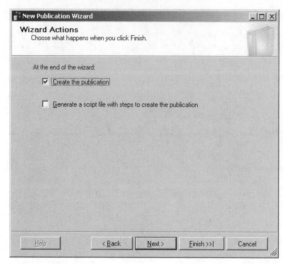

16. On the Complete the Wizard screen, you need to enter a name for the new publication, so enter **AddressTypePub**, and click Finish.

17. When the wizard is finished, click Close.

Criteria for Completion

This task is complete when you have created a snapshot publication based on the Person.AddressType table in the AdventureWorks database on the default instance of SQL Server. To verify this, follow these steps:

1. Open SQL Server Management Studio, connect to your SQL Server, expand Replication, and then expand Local Publications. You should see the AddressTypePub publication listed.

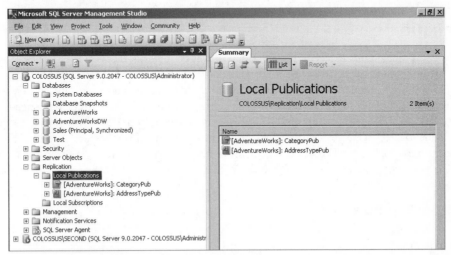

2. Right-click AddressTypePub, and click Properties. The type should be Snapshot.

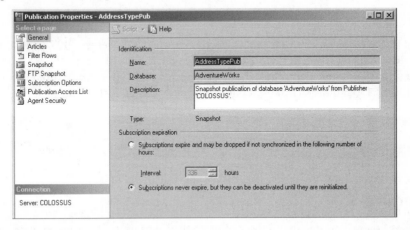

3. Click OK.

Task 2.19: Subscribing to a Snapshot Publication

After you have created a publication, you can configure one or more servers as subscribers. In this task, you will subscribe to a snapshot publication.

Scenario

You work for a medium-sized company that has offices throughout the world. The sales department in the Tucson branch office needs access to one of the databases housed on the SQL Server at the corporate headquarters. They will use the data for reporting purposes only, so they will not be making updates to their local copy of the data. They need the data to be refreshed only once a day, so you can allow for a full day of latency. They are connected by a partial T1 that is at about 75 percent capacity during peak hours, but off-hours it is at about 30 percent capacity, so the network has plenty of room during off-hours. You have already configured a snapshot publication at the headquarters; now you must create a subscription on the server in Tucson.

Scope of Task

Duration

This task should take approximately 30 minutes.

Setup

For this task, you need access to the machine you installed SQL Server 2005 on in Task 1.1, the Second instance of SQL Server installed in Task 1.2, the AdventureWorks database installed with the sample data, the default instance of SQL Server configured as a distributor in Task 2.15, and the snapshot publication configured in Task 2.18.

Caveat

Make sure the SQL Agent service for the Second instance is set to start automatically before starting this task.

Procedure

In this task, you will create a pull subscription to the snapshot publication on your default instance of SQL Server.

Equipment Used

For this task, you need access to the machine you installed SQL Server 2005 on in Task 1.1, the Second instance of SQL Server installed in Task 1.2, the AdventureWorks database installed with the sample data, the default instance of SQL Server configured as a distributor in Task 2.15, and the snapshot publication configured in Task 2.18.

Details

Follow these steps to create a pull subscription to the snapshot publication on the default instance of SQL Server:

1. Open SQL Server Management Studio, and connect to the Second instance by selecting it from the Server Name drop-down list.

2. Expand Replication, right-click Local Subscriptions, and click New Subscription. This brings you to the New Subscription Wizard welcome screen. Click Next to continue.

3. On the Publication screen, select the default instance of your server from the Publisher drop-down list, select AddressTypePub from the Databases and Publications list, and click Next to continue.

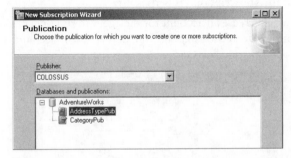

4. On the Distribution Agent Location screen, you are asked which machine should run the replication agents—at the distributor or at the subscriber. Because you want to create a pull subscription, select the Run Each Agent at Its Subscriber option, and click Next.

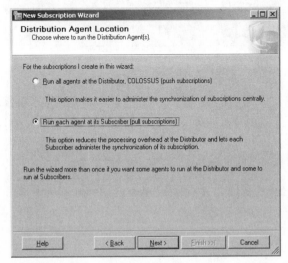

5. On the Subscribers screen, you can choose a subscriber for the publication. Check the box next to the Second instance of your server.

6. Then the drop-down list is populated with all the available databases on the subscriber. Select New Database from the list to open the New Database dialog box.

7. Enter **SR_Test** in the Database Name box, click OK, and then click Next.

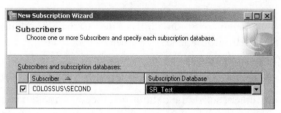

8. On the next screen you need to set the distribution agent security. To do so, click the ellipsis (…) button in the Subscription Properties list.

9. Ordinarily you would create an account for the agent to run under, but to make the task simpler, you will run the agent using the SQL Server Agent account, so select the radio button for that option, and click OK.

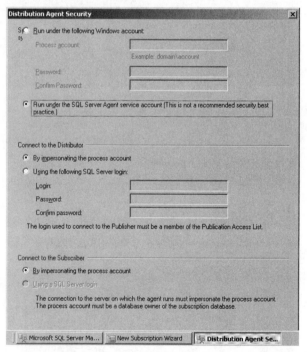

10. Back at the Distribution Agent Security screen, click Next to continue.

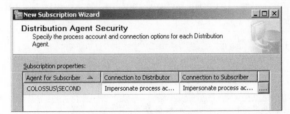

11. The next step is to set the synchronization schedule, so select Define Schedule.

12. In the New Job Schedule dialog box, under Frequency, set Occurs to Daily, and click OK.

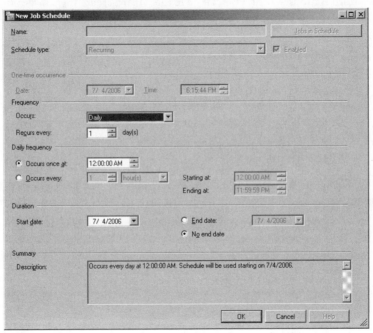

13. Back at the Synchronization Schedule screen, click Next.

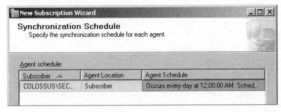

14. On the next screen, you can tell SQL Server when to initialize the subscription, if at all. If you have already created the schema (an empty copy of the database to be replicated)

on the subscriber, then you do not need to initialize the subscription. In this case, you should select Immediately from the drop-down list, make sure the Initialize box is checked, and click Next to continue.

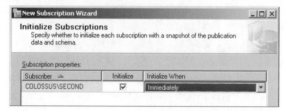

15. On the Wizard Actions screen, you can have the wizard create the subscription, write a script to create the subscription that you can run later, or do both. Leave the Create the Subscription box checked, and click Next to continue.

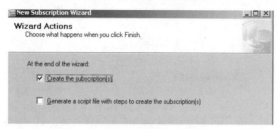

16. On the Complete the Wizard screen, review your options, and click Finish to create the subscription.

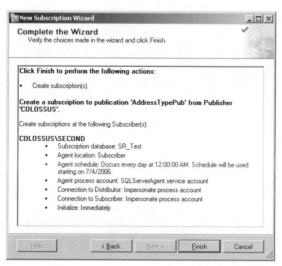

17. When the wizard is finished, click Close.

Criteria for Completion

This task is complete when replication is running properly. Follow these steps to verify:

1. You should have several records in the ReplicatedType table. To verify that, open a new query, connect to the Second instance, and execute the following code:

    ```
    USE SR_Test
    SELECT * FROM dbo.ReplicatedType
    ```

2. Now add a new record to the Person.AddressType table in the AdventureWorks database on the default instance. Open a new query, and from the Query menu, select Connection and Change Connection. Then connect to the default instance.

3. Run the following code to add a new record:

    ```
    USE AdventureWorks
    INSERT INTO Person.AddressType (Name)
    VALUES('Tucson Office')
    ```

4. Now you could wait for 24 hours or so for this to replicate, but that is a bit too long, so you need to run replication manually. To start, expand your default instance server in Object Explorer.

5. Expand SQL Agent, and then expand Jobs.

6. Right-click the job whose name starts with *Servername*-AdventureWorks-AddressType-Pub-2, click Start Job at Step, and select step 1.

7. Click Close when the job is complete.

8. Next, expand your Second instance in Object Explorer.

9. Expand SQL Agent, and then expand Jobs.

10. Right-click the job whose name starts with *Servername*-AdventureWorks-AddressType-Pub-*Servername*\SECOND-SR_Test, and click Start Job at Step.

11. Click Close when the job is complete.

12. Run the following query against the Second instance:

    ```
    USE SR_Test
    SELECT * FROM dbo.ReplicatedType
    ```

13. One of the records in the result set should be the new Tucson Office record.

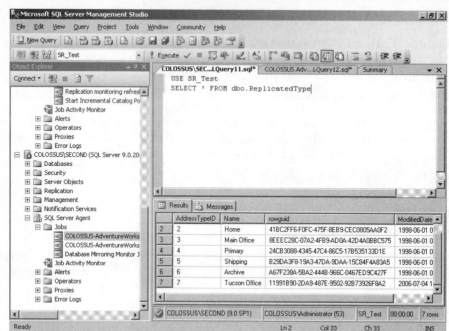

Task 2.20: Creating a Merge Publication

When you use merge replication, the merge agent can be centrally located on the distributor, or it can reside on every subscriber involved in the merge replication process. When you have implemented push replication, the merge agent will reside on the distributor. In a pull scenario, the merge agent is on every subscriber.

The following steps outline the merge process and how each agent interacts with the other agents:

1. As shown in Figure 2.13, the snapshot agent that resides on the distribution server takes an initial snapshot of the data and moves it to the subscribers. This move takes place through the Distribution working folder. The folder is just a holding area for the snapshot data before it is moved to the subscriber. As stated earlier, you must do this first so you can apply later transactions.

Subscribers must have the appropriate permissions to access the Distribution working folder on the distribution server.

FIGURE 2.13   How the merge replication process works

ReCode	EmpID	Q1	Q2	Q3
1	5	40.1	39.8	37.7
1	7	28.7	33.5	38.2
1	8	39.9	42.2	48.1
1	13	28.8	32.8	33.7ReCod

Horizontal Partition

ReCode	EmpID	Q1	Q2	Q3
2	2		44.6	
1	5		39.8	
2	3		41.7	
3	11		28.8	
1	7		33.5	
1	8		42.2	
3	22		45.5	
1	13		32.8	ReCode

Vertical Partition

2. Replication can now begin.

3. The merge agent (wherever it resides) will take modifications from the publishers and apply them to the subscribers.

4. The merge agent will also take modifications from the subscribers and apply them to the publishers.

5. The merge agent will gather any merge conflicts and resolve them by using triggers. Merge information will be stored in tables at the distributor. This allows you to track data lineage.

To track these changes, SQL Server adds some new tables to the publication and subscription databases. The most important of these is the MSmerge_contents table, which is used to track changes to the replicated table as well as possible conflicts. SQL Server also creates triggers on the publishing and subscription servers used for merge replication. These triggers are automatically invoked when changes are made at either of these locations. Information about the changes is stored in the database system tables on the distribution server. With this change information, SQL Server can track the lineage or history of changes made to a particular row of data.

Merge replication is most useful in situations in which there will be few con-flicts. A horizontally partitioned table based on a region code or some other ID is best suited to merge replication.

In this task, you will create a merge publication on the default instance of SQL Server.

Scenario

You work for a medium-sized company that has offices throughout the world. The retail division of your company manages shops in various cities. Each shop maintains its own inventory database. The retail manager in Phoenix wants each of her four shops to be able to share inventory with each other so employees can pick up a part from another nearby store rather than wait for a shipment from the manufacturer. To do this, employees at each shop need to be able to update their local copy of the inventory database, decrement the other store's inventory, and then go pick up the part. This way, the other store won't sell its part because the part will have already been taken out of stock. To accomplish this goal, you have decided to create a merge publication.

Scope of Task

Duration

This task should take approximately 30 minutes.

Setup

For this task, you need access to the machine you installed SQL Server 2005 on in Task 1.1, the AdventureWorks database installed with the sample data, and the default instance of SQL Server configured as a distributor, as shown in Task 2.15.

Caveat

If you still have log shipping enabled on the AdventureWorks database (from Task 2.10), you will need to disable it. Here's how:

1. Open SQL Server Management Studio, and connect to the default instance.

2. Expand Databases, right-click AdventureWorks, point to Tasks, and click Ship Transaction Logs.

3. Uncheck the box next to Enable This as a Primary Database in a Log Shipping Configuration.

4. Click Yes in the subsequent dialog box, and then click OK.

5. Click Close when the configuration is complete.

Procedure

In this task, you will create a merge publication on your default instance of SQL Server on the ProductionCulture table in the AdventureWorks database.

Equipment Used

For this task, you need access to the machine you installed SQL Server 2005 on in Task 1.1, the AdventureWorks database installed with the sample data, and the default instance of SQL Server you configured as a distributor in Task 2.15.

Details

Follow these steps to create a merge publication on the Production.Culture table:

1. Open SQL Server Management Studio, and connect to your SQL Server.

2. Expand Replication, right-click Local Publications, and click New Publication. This brings you to the New Publication Wizard welcome screen.

3. Click Next to continue.

4. On the Publication Database screen, highlight AdventureWorks, and click Next to continue.

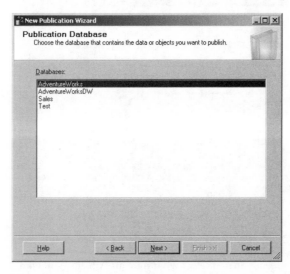

5. On the Publication Type screen, you can choose what type of publication to create. For this task, choose Merge Publication, and click Next to continue.

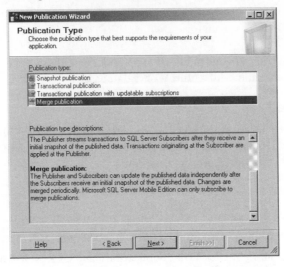

6. On the next screen you are asked what version of SQL Server the subscribers are running. This is because different versions of SQL Server handle merge replication differently. In this case, check only SQL Server 2005, and click Next.

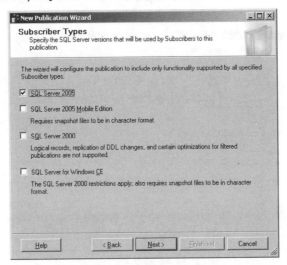

7. On the Articles screen, you can select what data and objects you want to replicate. Expand Tables, and check the Culture box.

8. You can also set the properties for an article from this screen. Make sure Culture is highlighted, click Article Properties, and then click Set Properties of Highlighted Table Article.

9. Notice all of the defaults, but do not make any changes; click OK.

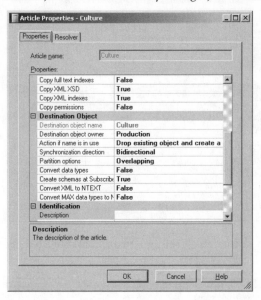

10. Back at the Articles screen, click Next to continue.

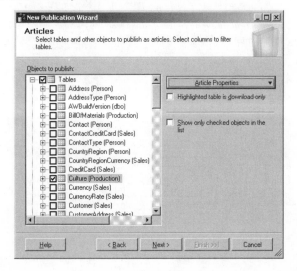

11. On the next screen, you are reminded that a uniqueidentifier column will be added to the replicated table. Click Next to continue.

12. On the next screen, you can filter the data that is replicated. You do not want to filter the data in this case, so click Next to continue.

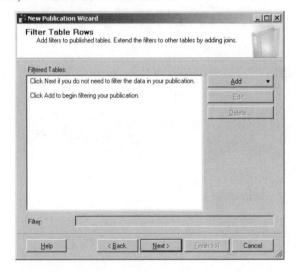

13. On the Snapshot Agent screen, check the box to create a snapshot immediately, and check the Schedule the Snapshot agent to run at the following times. Leave the default schedule, and click Next.

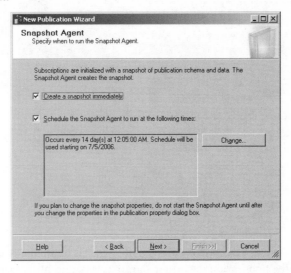

14. On the Agent Security screen, you are asked how the agents should log in and access data. To set this for the snapshot agent, click the Security Settings button next to Snapshot Agent.

15. Ordinarily you would create an account for the agent to run under, but to make the task simpler, you will run the agent using the SQL Server Agent account, so select the radio button for that option, and click OK.

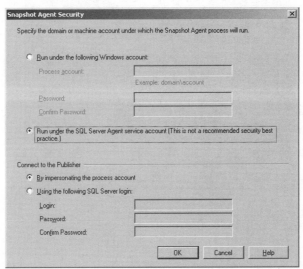

16. Back at the Agent Security screen, click Next to continue.

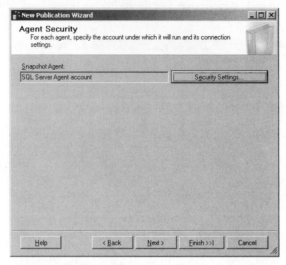

17. On the Wizard Actions screen, you can have the wizard create the publication, write a script to create the publication that you can run later, or do both. Leave the Create the Publication box checked, and click Next to continue.

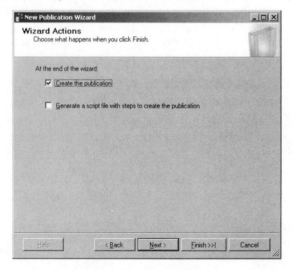

18. On the Complete the Wizard screen, you need to enter a name for the new publication, so enter **CulturePub**, and click Finish.

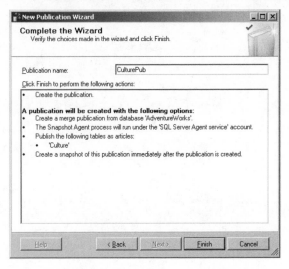

19. When the wizard is finished, click Close.

Criteria for Completion

This task is complete when you have created a merge publication based on the Production.Culture table in the AdventureWorks database on the default instance of SQL Server. To verify this, follow these steps:

1. Open SQL Server Management Studio, connect to your SQL Server, and expand Replication. You should see the CulturePub publication listed.

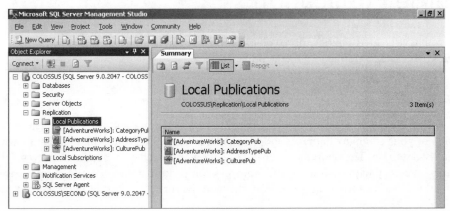

2. Right-click CulturePub, and click Properties. The type should be Merge.

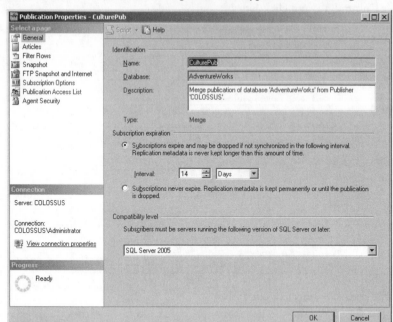

3. Click OK.

Task 2.21: Subscribing to a Merge Publication

After you have created a publication, you can configure one or more servers as subscribers. In this task, you will subscribe to a merge publication.

Scenario

You work for a medium-sized company that has offices throughout the world. The retail division of your company manages shops in various cities. Each shop maintains its own inventory database. The retail manager in Phoenix wants each of her four shops to be able to share inventory with each other so employees can pick up a part from another nearby store rather than wait for a shipment from the manufacturer. To do this, employees at each shop need to be able to update their local copy of the inventory database, decrement the other store's inventory, and then go pick up the part. This way, the other store won't sell its part because the part will have already been taken out of stock. You have already configured a merge publication to which you must now subscribe.

Scope of Task

Duration

This task should take approximately 30 minutes.

Setup

For this task, you need access to the machine you installed SQL Server 2005 on in Task 1.1, the Second instance of SQL Server installed in Task 1.2, the AdventureWorks database installed with the sample data, the default instance of SQL Server you configured as a distributor in Task 2.15, and the merge publication you configured in Task 2.20.

Caveat

Make sure the SQL Agent service for the Second instance is set to start automatically before starting this task.

Procedure

In this task, you will create a pull subscription to the merge publication on your default instance of SQL Server.

Equipment Used

For this task, you need access to the machine you installed SQL Server 2005 on in Task 1.1, the Second instance of SQL Server installed in Task 1.2, the AdventureWorks database installed with the sample data, the default instance of SQL Server you configured as a distributor in Task 2.15, and the merge publication you configured in Task 2.20.

Details

Follow these steps to create a pull subscription to the merge publication on the default instance of SQL Server:

1. Open SQL Server Management Studio, and connect to the Second instance by selecting it from the Server Name drop-down list.

2. Expand Replication, right-click Local Subscriptions, and click New Subscription. Click Next to continue. This brings you to the New Subscription Wizard welcome screen.

3. On the Publication screen, select the default instance of your server from the Publisher drop-down list. Select CulturePub from the Databases and Publications list, and click Next to continue.

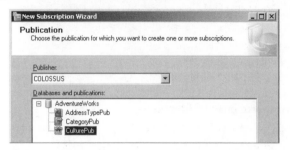

4. On the Merge Agent Location screen, you are asked which machine should run the replication agents—at the distributor or at the subscriber. Because you want to create a pull subscription, select the Run Each Agent at Its Subscriber option, and click Next.

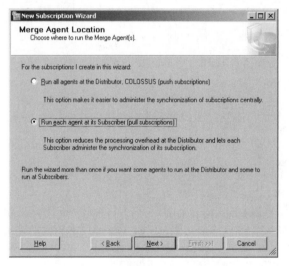

5. On the Subscribers screen, you can choose a subscriber for the publication. Check the box next to your server.

6. Then the drop-down list is populated with all the available databases on the subscriber. Select New Database from the list to open the New Database dialog box.

7. Enter **MR_Test** in the Database Name box, and click OK. Then click Next.

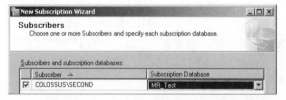

8. On the next screen you need to set the merge agent security. To do so, click the ellipsis (…) button in the Subscription Properties list.

9. Ordinarily you would create an account for the agent to run under, but to make the task simpler, you will run the agent using the SQL Server Agent account, so select the radio button for that option, and click OK.

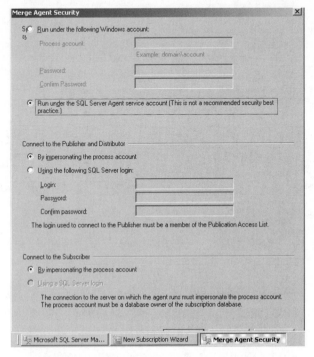

10. Back at the Merge Agent Security screen, click Next to continue.

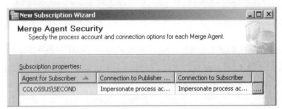

11. The next step is to set the synchronization schedule, so select Define Schedule.

12. In the New Job Schedule dialog box, make these changes:

   ▪ Under Frequency, set Occurs to Daily.

   ▪ Under Daily Frequency, select Occurs Every, and set the interval to 10 minutes.

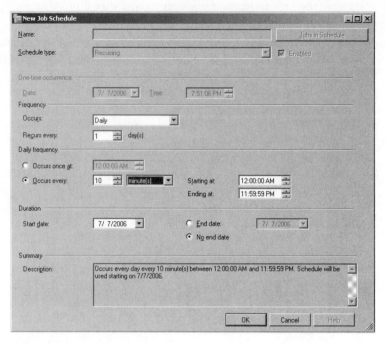

13. Click OK.

14. Back at the Synchronization Schedule screen, click Next.

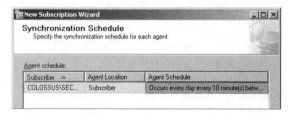

15. On the next screen, you can tell SQL Server when to initialize the subscription, if at all. If you have already created the schema (an empty copy of the database to be replicated) on the subscriber, then you do not need to initialize the subscription. In this case, you should select Immediately from the drop-down list, make sure the Initialize box is checked, and click Next to continue.

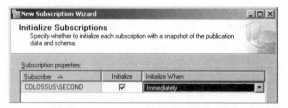

16. The next screen shows you how conflicts will be resolved when they occur. In this case, select the defaults, and click Next.

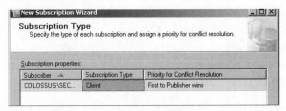

17. On the Wizard Actions screen, you can have the wizard create the subscription, write a script to create the subscription that you can run later, or do both. Leave the Create the Subscription box checked, and click Next to continue.

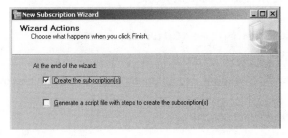

18. On the Complete the Wizard screen, review your options, and click Finish to create the subscription.

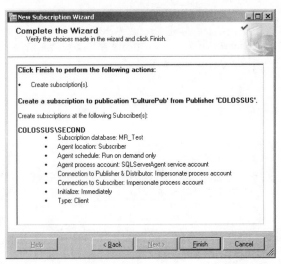

19. When the wizard is finished, click Close.

Criteria for Completion

This task is complete when replication is running properly. Follow these steps to verify:

1. You should have several records in the Culture table. To verify that, open a new query, connect to the Second instance, and execute the following code:

```
USE MR_Test
SELECT * FROM Production.Culture
```

2. Now add a new record to the Production.Culture table in the AdventureWorks database on the default instance. Open a new query, and from the Query menu, select Connection and Change Connection. Then connect to the default instance.

3. Run the following code to add a new record:

```
USE AdventureWorks
INSERT INTO Production.Culture (CultureID, Name)
VALUES('DE', 'German')
```

4. Wait about 10 minutes, and run the following query against the Second instance:

```
USE MR_Test
SELECT * FROM Production.Culture
```

5. One of the records in the result set should be the new DE record.

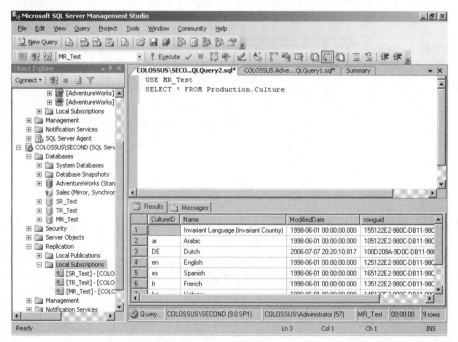

6. Now to test replication from the subscriber back to the publisher, run the following code on the Second instance to add a new record:

```
USE MR_Test
INSERT INTO Production.Culture (CultureID, Name)
VALUES('AL', 'Albanian')
```

7. Wait about 10 minutes, and run the following query against the default instance. You should see the new AL record.

```
USE AdventureWorks
SELECT * FROM Production.Culture
```

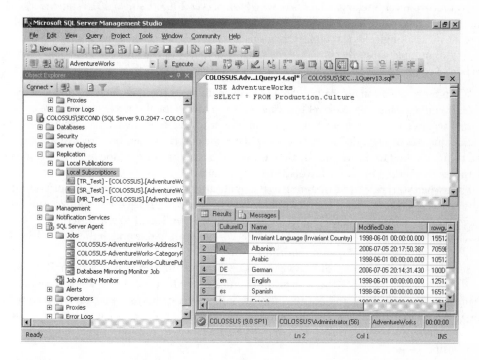

Task 2.22: Resolving Merge Conflicts

Performing updates to the same records at multiple locations causes conflicts. To resolve these conflicts, SQL Server 2005 uses the MSmerge_contents table and some settings from the publication itself.

When you first create a merge publication, you can choose from three levels of conflict resolution tracking in a merge publication:

Row-level tracking   In row-level tracking, any change to an entire row on multiple subscribers is considered a conflict. If one subscriber modifies data in ColA and another modifies data in ColB on the same row, then SQL Server considers this a conflict.

Column-level tracking   In column-level tracking, any change to a single column on multiple subscribers is considered a conflict. If one subscriber modifies data in ColA and another modifies data in ColB on the same row, it is not viewed as a conflict. However, if they both modify ColA on the same row, then SQL Server considers this a conflict.

Logical record-level tracking   This is new to SQL Server 2005. Using a JOIN statement, you can create logical records to replicate. This means you can combine data from multiple tables to replicate as a single, logical table. Using this level of conflict tracking tells SQL Server that if users at multiple subscribers modify the same data in any of the joined tables, then there is a possible conflict.

When the publication is created, changes to the data are tracked in the MSmerge_contents table. If you are using record-level tracking, then the metadata about the changes are stored in the lineage column; if you are using column-level tracking, then the COLV1 column is also used. Using this lineage, the merge agent evaluates the current values for a record or column and the new values to determine whether a conflict exists. If a conflict does exist, SQL Server considers two more important factors before resolving it.

First, when you create a subscription to the publication, you can also set the priority for the subscription. When there is a conflict, subscribers with higher priority win out over subscribers with lower priority, and the higher-priority change is replicated to all subscribers. The lower-priority change is logged to the MSmerge_conflicts_info table and, if there is an INSERT or UPDATE conflict, the conflict_*publication_article* table.

Second, you have a choice of resolvers to use when creating a new publication. If you use the default resolver, then SQL Server will automatically resolve the conflict, apply the winning changes to all subscribers, and notify you of a conflict. If you choose a manual resolver, then you will have to manually choose the winning changes and apply them yourself. The manual option works best only if you have a complex merge replication scenario that requires complex business logic.

When you begin to customize the conflict resolution process, I suggest you store both the record that is converged and the conflicting records that were not converged. This allows you to manually test and optimize your triggers. Note that covering how to create and modify triggers is beyond the scope of this book. For more information, see the SQL Server Books Online or *Mastering SQL Server 2005* (Sybex, 2006).

In this task, you will create and resolve a conflict in a merge subscription.

Scenario

You have created a merge publication and a corresponding subscription so employees at each of the four shops in Phoenix are able to share inventory with each other and automatically affect inventory. This has been working fine for some time, but recently two of the stores tried to get a part from a third store at the same time. This has caused a merge conflict that you need to resolve.

Scope of Task

Duration

This task should take approximately 30 minutes.

Setup

For this task, you need access to the machine you installed SQL Server 2005 on in Task 1.1, the Second instance of SQL Server installed in Task 1.2, the AdventureWorks database installed with the sample data, the default instance of SQL Server you configured as a distributor in Task 2.15, the merge publication you configured in Task 2.20, and a subscription to the merge publication you configured in Task 2.21.

Caveat

This task doesn't have any caveats.

Procedure

In this task, you will create and resolve a merge conflict.

Equipment Used

For this task, you need access to the machine you installed SQL Server 2005 on in Task 1.1, the Second instance of SQL Server installed in Task 1.2, the AdventureWorks database installed with the sample data, the default instance of SQL Server you configured as a distributor in Task 2.15, the merge publication you configured in Task 2.20, and a subscription to the merge publication you configured in Task 2.21.

Details

To create a merge conflict, follow these steps:

1. First you will update a record in the Production.Culture table in the AdventureWorks database on the default instance. Open a new query, and from the Query menu, select Connection and Change Connection. Then connect to the default instance.

2. Run the following code to update an existing record:

```
USE AdventureWorks
UPDATE Production.Culture SET [Name] = 'Dutch' WHERE CultureID = 'DE'
```

3. Now you will update the same record in the Production.Culture table in the MR_Test database on the Second instance. Open a new query, and from the Query menu, and select Connection and Change Connection. Then connect to the Second instance.

4. Run the following code to update an existing record:

```
USE MR_Test
UPDATE Production.Culture SET [Name] = 'Danish' WHERE CultureID = 'DE'
```

5. Wait about 10 minutes for the updates to apply before moving on to conflict resolution.

To view and resolve the conflict, follow these steps:

1. In Object Explorer, expand Replication ➢ Publications, right-click the [AdventureWorks]: CulturePub publication, and click View Conflicts.

2. In the Select Conflict Table dialog box, double-click the Culture(1) listing. The (1) denotes that there is one conflict.

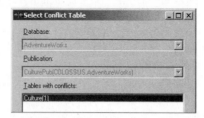

3. In the Replication Conflict Viewer, click the line under Conflict Loser in the top grid. This will change the data on the bottom to show you which record is the winner (currently displayed in all databases) and which is the loser (not shown to anyone).

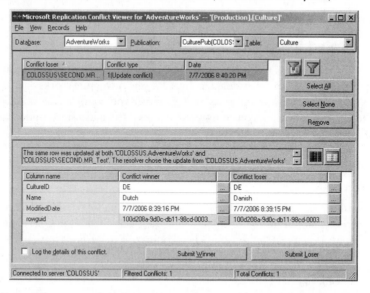

4. Click the Submit Loser button to accept the losing record and discard the winning record (that is, if Dutch is the winner, change it to Danish).

5. Click OK in the subsequent dialog box, and click OK again to exit the Replication Conflict Viewer.

Criteria for Completion

This task is complete when you have successfully created and resolved a conflict in a merge publication as outlined in the preceding steps.

Task 2.23: Monitoring Replication

You can administer your publishers, subscribers, and publications as well as the different replication agents through the Replication Monitor utility. You can also look at agent properties and histories and even set replication alerts with this utility.

The Replication Monitor resides on the computer where the distribution server has been installed and gathers replication information about the different replication agents. This includes the agent history with information about inserts, updates, deletes, and any other transactions that were processed. Through the Replication Monitor, you can also edit the various schedules and properties of the replication agents.

In this task, you will use the Replication Monitor to work with the replication agents.

Scenario

You have created several publications on your server at corporate headquarters, and you have created several subscriptions on servers throughout your enterprise. Many of these servers are scattered geographically, so it is difficult for you to go there in person to work with the subscriptions. To monitor and configure the publications and subscriptions remotely, you have decided to use Replication Monitor.

Scope of Task

Duration

This task should take approximately 15 minutes.

Setup

For this task, you need access to the machine you installed SQL Server 2005 on in Task 1.1, the Second instance of SQL Server installed in Task 1.2, the AdventureWorks database installed with the sample data, the default instance of SQL Server you configured as a distributor in Task 2.15, the transactional publication you configured in Task 2.16, and a subscription to the transactional publication you configured in Task 2.17.

Caveat

This task doesn't have any caveats.

Procedure

In this task, you will use the Replication Monitor to view replication status. You will insert a tracer record to monitor performance and set up a replication alert.

Equipment Used

For this task, you need access to the machine you installed SQL Server 2005 on in Task 1.1, the Second instance of SQL Server installed in Task 1.2, the AdventureWorks database installed with the sample data, the default instance of SQL Server you configured as a distributor in Task 2.15, the transactional publication you configured in Task 2.16, and a subscription to the transactional publication you configured in Task 2.17.

Details

To configure replication properties using the Replication Monitor, follow these steps:

1. Open SQL Server Management Studio on the distribution server, which is the default instance.

2. Right-click Replication, and select Launch Replication Monitor.

3. Expand your server to view the publications available.

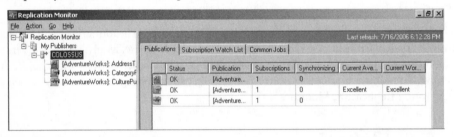

4. Switch to the Subscriptions Watch List tab. From here you can view reports about the performance of all publications and subscriptions that this distributor handles.

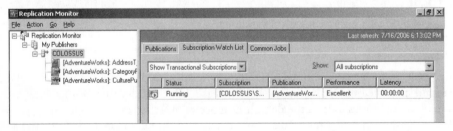

5. Switch to the Common Jobs tab. On this tab, you can view the status of replication jobs that affect all publications and subscriptions handled by this distributor.

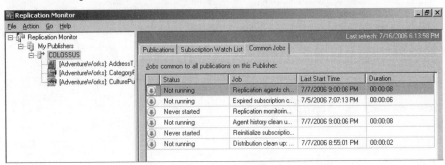

6. Select the CategoryPub publication in the left pane.

7. On the All Subscriptions tab, you can view reports about all the subscriptions for this particular publication.

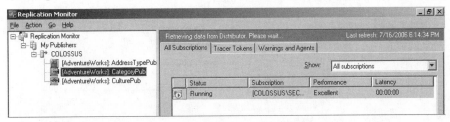

8. Switch to the Tracer Tokens tab. From here you can insert a special record called a *tracer token* that is used to measure performance for this subscription.

9. To test it, click the Insert Tracer button, and wait for the results.

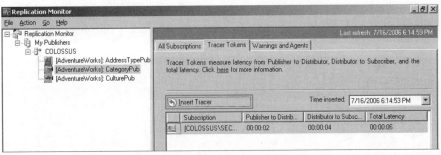

10. Switch to the Warnings and Agents tab. From here you can change settings for agents and configure replication alerts.

11. Click the Configure Alerts button, select Replication: Agent Failure, and click Configure.

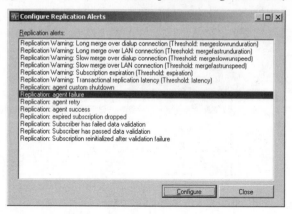

12. Notice that this opens a new alert dialog box (which I will discuss in Phase 3). Check the Enable box, and click OK to enable this alert.

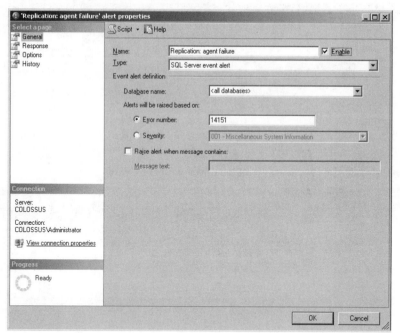

13. Click Close to return to Replication Monitor.

14. Close Replication Monitor.

Criteria for Completion

This task is complete when you have successfully viewed and configured replication properties using the Replication Monitor. Many of these steps are self-explanatory, but you can follow these steps to verify that you have successfully configured the replication alert:

1. Open SQL Server Management Studio on the distribution server, which is the default instance.

2. In Object Explorer, expand your server, and then expand SQL Server Agent.

3. Click Alerts, and you should see the Replication: Agent Failure alert in the right pane.

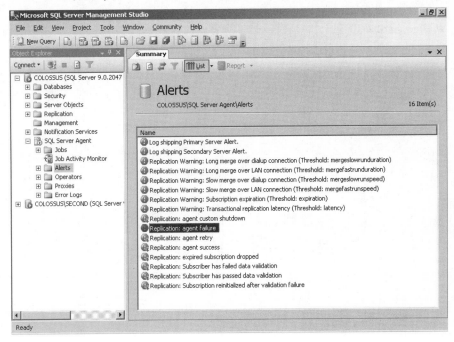

Phase

3

Maintaining and Automating SQL Server

Throughout this book, I have discussed administrative activities that would best be performed during off-hours. These activities include backing up databases, creating large databases, reconstructing indexes—the list goes on. You need to perform most of these activities on a regular basis, not just once. For example, you'll need to back up at frequent intervals. Because most database administrators (DBAs) would rather go home than stay at work to start a maintenance task, SQL Server has the built-in capability to automate tasks.

You can automate nearly any administrative task you can think of through SQL Server:

- Any Transact-SQL code
- Scripting languages such as VBScript and JavaScript
- Operating system commands
- Replication tasks

Some popular tasks to automate using the built-in functionality are as follows:

- Database backups
- Index reconstruction
- Database creation (for very large databases, or VLDBs)
- Report generation

Because these tasks are so powerful, it's easy to see why you need to use SQL Server's automation capabilities. However, before you start to use this functionality, you need to know how it works.

At the heart of SQL Server's automation capability is the SQL Server Agent service (also referred to as the *agent*). Automation and replication are the sole functions of this service. The service uses three subcomponents to accomplish its automation tasks (all of which we will discuss in detail in this phase):

Alerts   An alert is an error message or event that occurs in SQL Server and is recorded in the Windows Application log. SQL Server can sent alerts to users via e-mail, pagers, or Net Send. If an error message isn't written to the Windows Application log, an alert is never fired.

Operators   When an alert is fired, SQL Server can send it to an operator, which basically is a user. You set up operators to configure who receives alerts and when certain users are available to receive these messages.

Jobs   A job is a series of steps that define the task to be automated. It also defines schedules, which dictate when the task will be executed. Such tasks can be run one time or on a recurring basis.

These three components work together to complete the tapestry of automation. Here is an example of what may happen:

1. A user defines a job that is specified to run at a certain time.

2. When the job runs, it fails and thus writes an error message to the Windows event log.

3. When the SQL Server Agent service reads the Windows event log, the agent finds the error message that the failed job wrote and compares it to the sysalerts table in the MSDB database.

4. When the agent finds a match, it fires an alert.

5. The alert, when fired, can send an e-mail, pager message, or Net Send message to an operator.

6. You can also configure the alert to run another job, designed to repair the problem that caused the alert.

For any of this to function, though, you must properly configure the SQL Server Agent service. For starters, the agent must be running for automation to work. You can verify this in three ways. First, you can open SQL Server Management Studio and notice the SQL Server Agent icon—if it's a red circle with an *X*, the service is stopped; if it's a green arrow, the service is running. (You can start the service by right-clicking the icon and selecting Start.) You can also check and change the state of the service by using the SQL Server Configuration Manager or by using the Services applet in Control Panel.

Not only should the agent be running, but it's also best to have it log in with a domain account as opposed to a local system account, because using the local system account won't allow you to work with other SQL Servers on your network. This means you can't perform multiserver jobs, carry out replication, or use SQL Server's e-mail capabilities. To make sure the agent is logging on with a domain account, open the Services applet in Administrative Tools, double-click the SQL Server Agent service, and select a domain account by clicking the ellipsis button next to This Account on the Log On tab.

Once all this is in place, you're nearly ready to begin working with automation. First, you should configure SQL Server to send e-mail using Database Mail.

Task 3.1: Configuring Database Mail

Database Mail is what enables SQL Server to send e-mail using the standard Simple Mail Transfer Protocol (SMTP). It is actually a separate process that runs in the background (called SQLiMail90.exe), so if a problem occurs, SQL Server is unaffected. You can also specify more than one SMTP server, so if one SMTP server goes down, Database Mail can still process mail. Additionally, Database Mail is scalable because it uses the Service Broker queue, which allows the request to be handled asynchronously and even saves the request if the server goes down before it can be handled.

Service Broker is a new component in SQL Server 2005 that provides reliable messaging and queuing.

To top it off, Database Mail provides granular control so you can limit which users are allowed to send mail. You can also specify what file extensions are allowed and disallowed as attachments, as well as the maximum size of those attachments. Everything Database Mail does is logged in the Windows Application log, and sent messages are retained in the *mailhost* database for auditing.

To use Database Mail, you first need access to an SMTP mail server with a mail account configured for the SQL Server Agent service account. The topics of setting up and configuring an SMTP server are beyond the scope of this book, but if you have an e-mail account with your Internet service provider (ISP), you can use that. Then you can configure Database Mail using the configuration wizard.

To send e-mail to operators, the MSDB database must be a mailhost, so in this task, you'll configure MSDB as a mailhost database.

Scenario

You work for a medium-sized company that has SQL Server 2005 installations at major offices throughout the country. You need to make sure the systems are up and running at all times, but it is not always easy for you to check the servers' status because they are geographically scattered. You have decided the best way to keep track of your servers is to have them e-mail you when there is a notable status change, such as an error or a completed job. To make that happen, you need to configure the MSDB database as a mailhost database.

Scope of Task

Duration

This task should take approximately 30 minutes.

Setup

For this task, you need access to the machine you installed SQL Server 2005 on in Task 1.1.

Caveat

This task doesn't have any caveats.

Procedure

In this task, you will configure a mailhost, and then you will configure the SQL Server Agent service to use the mailhost.

Equipment Used

For this task, you need access to the machine you installed SQL Server 2005 on in Task 1.1.

Details

To configure a mailhost, follow these steps:

1. Open SQL Server Management Studio, and connect to your server.

2. Expand Management in Object Explorer, right-click Database Mail, and select Configure Database Mail. On the welcome screen, click Next.

3. On the Select Configuration Task screen, select Set Up Database Mail by Performing the Following Tasks, and click Next.

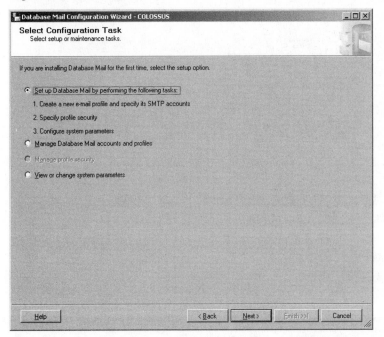

4. If a dialog box opens and asks you whether you would like to enable Database Mail, click Yes.

5. On the New Profile screen, create a mail profile, and associate it with a mail server account:

   a. Enter **SQLAgentProfile** in the Profile Name box.

   b. Under SMTP Accounts, click Add.

   c. In the Account Name box, enter **Mail Provider Account 1**.

   d. In the Description box, enter **Email account information**.

   e. Enter your outgoing mail server information using the information provided by your ISP or network administrator.

f.   If your e-mail server requires you to log in, check the Basic Authentication box, and
     enter your login information.

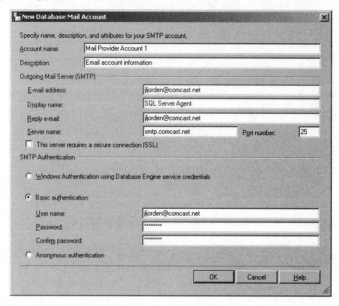

g.   Click OK to return to the wizard. Your account should now be listed under SMTP
     Accounts.

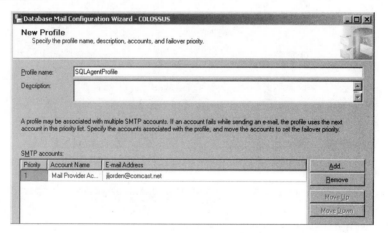

6.   Click Next.

7. On the Manage Profile Security screen, check the Public box next to the mail profile you just created to make it accessible to all users. Set the Default Profile option to Yes, and click Next.

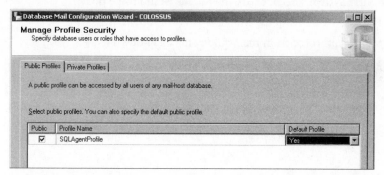

8. On the Configure System Parameters screen, accept the defaults, and click Next.

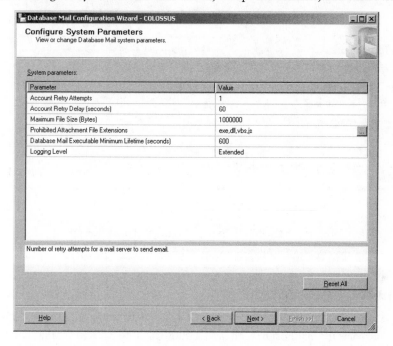

9. On the Complete the Wizard screen, review all your settings, and click Finish.

10. When the system is finished setting up Database Mail, click Close.

Now you will configure the SQL Server Agent to use the mail profile you just created:

1. In Object Explorer, right-click SQL Server Agent, and select Properties.

2. On the Alert System screen, check the Enable Mail Profile box.

3. Select Database Mail from the Mail System drop-down list.

4. Select SQLAgentProfile from the Mail Profile drop-down list.

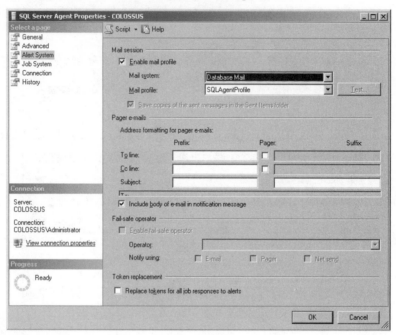

5. Click OK.

6. In Object Explorer, right-click SQL Server Agent, and click Restart.

7. Click Yes in the subsequent dialog box that opens.

Criteria for Completion

This task is complete when you have configured a mailhost and configured the SQL Server Agent service to use the mailhost to send mail. Follow these steps to verify that you have properly configured Database Mail:

1. Expand Management in Object Explorer, right-click Database Mail, and select Send Test E-mail.

2. Enter your e-mail address in the To text box, and click Send Test E-mail.

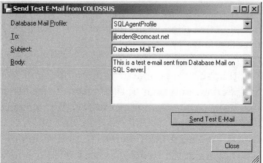

3. Wait for the e-mail to arrive in your inbox. When it arrives, click OK in the dialog box that opens.

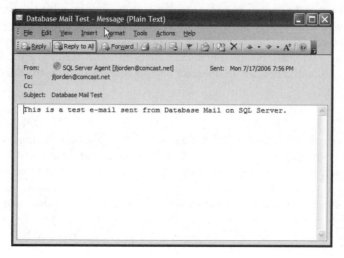

Task 3.2: Creating an Operator

You need to configure several settings for SQL Server to be able to contact you when problems occur. Such settings include the person to contact, when the people are available, how those people should be contacted (via e-mail, pager, or Net Send), and what problems they should be alerted about. An *operator* is the object used in SQL Server to configure all these settings.

> Net Send messages are messages sent from a source machine to a destina-
> tion machine that open on the user's screen in a dialog box in front of all the
> open applications.

Suppose, for example, that several people in your company need to be alerted when a problem occurs with SQL Server, and each of them needs to be alerted for different problems and in various ways. Your database administrator (DBA) may need to be alerted about any administration issues (for example, a failed backup or a full transaction log) via e-mail and pager. Your developers may need to be alerted to programming issues (for example, deadlocks) via e-mail. Managers in your company may need to know about other issues, such as a user deleting a customer from a customer database, via a Net Send message. You can handle these types of users by creating separate operators for each and then configuring the desired settings.

Because you can make operators active at different times, it's possible to accidentally leave a small period of time uncovered. If an error occurs during that window of time, no operator will receive the alert, because no one is on duty. To avoid such a problem, you should create a fail-safe operator who will receive alerts when no one is scheduled to be on duty.

In this task, you will configure an operator and set that operator as the fail-safe operator.

Scenario

You work for a medium-sized company that has SQL Server 2005 installations at major offices throughout the country. You are the lead DBA, and you have several assistant DBA working for you at the remote offices. You need to make sure you are alerted to problems on the servers when they arise and you want to make sure the appropriate assistant DBA is alerted as well, so you have decided to create operators for yourself and your assistants. You also want to make sure coverage exists 24/7, so you have decided to configure yourself as the fail-safe operator.

Scope of Task

Duration

This task should take approximately 15 minutes.

Setup

For this task, you need access to the machine you installed SQL Server 2005 on in Task 1.1.

Caveat

Make sure the Messenger service is running, or you will not receive Net Send messages.

Procedure

In this task, you will create an operator and configure that operator as the fail-safe operator.

Equipment Used

For this task, you need access to the machine you installed SQL Server 2005 on in Task 1.1.

Details

Follow these steps to create an operator:

1. Open SQL Server Management Studio.
2. In Object Explorer, expand your server, and then expand SQL Server Agent.
3. Right-click Operators, and select New Operator.
4. In the Name box, enter **Administrator**.
5. If you configured your system to use Database Mail, enter your e-mail address as the e-mail name. If you didn't configure your system to use e-mail, skip this step.
6. Enter the name of your machine in the Net Send Address box. You can find the name by right-clicking the My Computer icon on the Desktop, selecting Properties, and then clicking the Network Identification tab. The computer name is the first section of the full computer name (before the first period). For instance, if the full computer name is `instructor.domain.com`, the computer name is `instructor`.
7. If you carry a pager that is capable of receiving e-mail and you've configured Database Mail, you can enter your pager's e-mail address in the Pager E-mail Name box.
8. At the bottom of the page, you can select the days and times this operator is available for notification. If a day is checked, the operator will be notified on that day between the start and end times noted under Start Time and End Time. Check the box for each day, and leave the default workday times of 8 A.M. to 6 P.M.

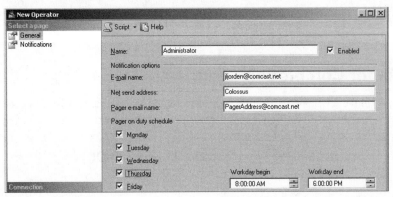

9. I'll discuss the Notifications tab later in this phase; for now, click OK to create the operator.

Now you will configure the SQL Server Agent to use the new operator as the fail-safe operator:

1. In SQL Server Management Studio, right-click the SQL Server Agent icon in Object Explorer, and select Properties.

2. On the Alert System screen, check the Enable Fail-Safe Operator box.

3. Select Administrator in the Operator drop-down list.

4. Check the box next to Net Send so you'll receive Net Send messages as a fail-safe operator.

5. Click OK to apply the changes.

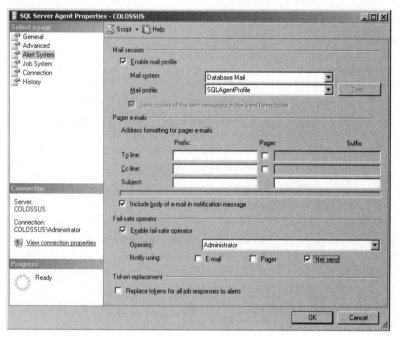

Criteria for Completion

This task is complete when you have successfully created an operator and configured the SQL Server Agent to use that operator as the fail-safe operator. Follow these steps to make sure you have successfully configured the operator:

1. In Object Explorer, expand your server, and then expand SQL Server Agent.

2. Expand Operators; you should see the Administrator operator listed.

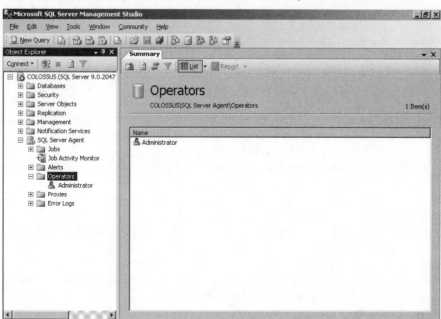

Task 3.3: Creating a Job

A *job* is a series of tasks that you can automate to run whenever you need them to run. It may be easier to think of them as like cleaning your house. Most of us think of cleaning our house as one big job that needs to be done, but it's really a series of smaller tasks such as dusting the furniture, vacuuming the carpet, doing the dishes, and so on. Some of these steps need to take place in succession (for example, dusting before vacuuming); others can happen at any time (for example, the dishes don't need to be done before you can wash the windows).

A job for SQL Server works in much the same way. Take, for example, a job that creates a database. This isn't just one big job with one step to accomplish before you're finished; several steps need to take place. The first step creates the database. The next step backs up the newly created database, because it's in a vulnerable state until it's backed up. After you've backed up the database, you can create tables in it and then perhaps import data into those tables from text files. Each of these tasks is a separate step that needs to be completed before the next can start, but not all jobs are that way.

By controlling the flow of the steps, you can build error correction into your jobs. For example, in the create-database job, each step has simple logic that states, "On success, go to the next step; on failure, quit the job." If the hard disk turns out to be full, the job stops. If you create a step at the end of the job that is designed to clear up hard disk space, you can create logic that states, "If step 1 fails, go to step 5; if step 5 succeeds, return to step 1." With the steps in place, you're ready to tell SQL Server when to start the job.

To tell SQL Server when to run a job, you need to create schedules, and you have a lot of flexibility there. If a job creates a database, it wouldn't make much sense to run the job more than once, so you need to create a single schedule that activates the job after-hours. If you're creating a job that is designed to perform transaction log backups, you want a different schedule; you may want to perform these backups every two hours during the day (from 9 A.M. to 6 P.M.) and then every three hours at night (from 6 P.M. to 9 A.M.). In this instance, you need to create two schedules: one that is active from 9 A.M. to 6 P.M. and activates the job every two hours and another that is active from 6 P.M. to 9 A.M. and activates the job every three hours. If you think that's fancy, you'll love the next part.

Not only can you schedule jobs to activate at certain times of the day, you can also schedule them to activate on certain days of the week (for example, every Tuesday); or, you can schedule them to run on certain days of the month (for example, every third Monday). You can schedule jobs to run every time the SQL Server Agent service starts, and you can even schedule them to run every time the processor becomes idle.

You can set schedules to expire after a certain amount of time, so if you know you're going to be done with a job after a few weeks, you can set it to expire—it will automatically be disabled (not deleted, just shut off).

You also have the capacity to be notified about the outcome of a job. When you create a job, you can add an operator to the job that's notified on success, on failure, or on completion (regardless of whether the job failed or succeeded). This comes in handy when the job you're running is critical to your server or application.

With the ability to change the logical flow of steps, schedule jobs to run whenever you want, and have jobs notify you on completion, you can see how complex jobs can become. With this complexity in mind, it's always a good idea to sit down with a pencil and paper and plan your jobs before creating them; doing so will make your work easier in the long run.

And you can do more than just run Transact-SQL statements. You can schedule any active scripting language: VBScript, JavaScript, Perl, and so forth. This frees you from the boundaries of Transact-SQL, because scripting languages have features that Transact-SQL doesn't implement. For example, you can't directly access the file structure on the hard disk using Transact-SQL (to create a new text file, for example), but you can do so with a scripting language.

You can also create jobs that run on more than one server, which are called *multiserver jobs*. A *multiserver job* is a job that is created once, on one server, and downloaded to other servers over the network where the job is run. To create multiserver jobs, you must first designate two types of servers: a master and targets. The master server (or MSX) is where the multiserver jobs are created and managed. The target servers poll the master server at regular intervals for jobs, download those jobs, and then run them at the scheduled time.

For a more detailed discussion of multiserver and scripting jobs, see *Mastering SQL Server 2005* (Sybex, 2006).

In this task, you'll create a job that builds a new database and then backs it up.

Scenario

You work for a medium-sized company that has SQL Server 2005 installations at major offices throughout the country. As the lead DBA, it is up to you to make sure maintenance takes place regularly on the databases. You know that the best way to guarantee this is to create jobs to automate the maintenance tasks.

Scope of Task

Duration

This task should take approximately 30 minutes.

Setup

For this task, you need access to the machine you installed SQL Server 2005 on in Task 1.1 and the operator you created in Task 3.2.

Caveat

This task doesn't have any caveats.

Procedure

In this task, you'll create a job that builds a new database named JobTest and then backs it up.

Equipment Used

For this task, you need access to the machine you installed SQL Server 2005 on in Task 1.1 and the operator you created in Task 3.2.

Details

Follow these steps to create a job that builds and backs up a new database:

1. Open SQL Server Management Studio by selecting it from the SQL Server 2005 group under Programs on the Start menu.

2. Expand your server in Object Explorer, and then expand SQL Server Agent.

3. Right-click Jobs, and select New Job.

4. In the Name box, enter **Create JobTest Database** (leave the rest of the boxes on this screen with the default settings).

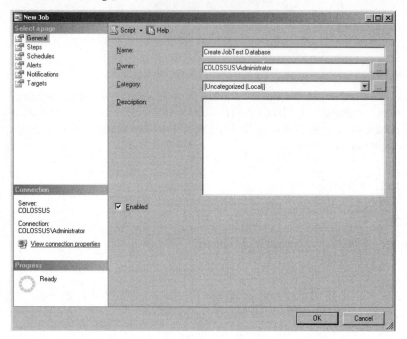

5. Go to the Steps page, and click the New button to create a new step.

6. In the Step Name box, enter **Create Database**.

7. Leave Type as Transact-SQL, and enter the following code in the Command text box to create a database named JobTest on the C drive:

```
CREATE DATABASE JOBTEST ON
PRIMARY (NAME=jobtest_dat,
FILENAME='c:\jobtest.mdf',
SIZE=10MB,
MAXSIZE=15,
FILEGROWTH=10%)
```

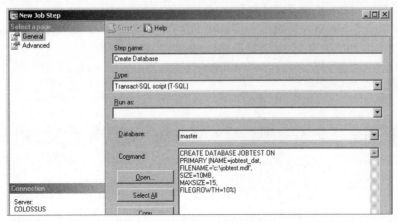

8. Click the Parse button to verify you entered the code correctly, and then move to the Advanced page.

9. On the Advanced page, verify that On Success Action is set to Go to the Next Step and that On Failure Action is set to Quit the Job Reporting Failure. Click OK.

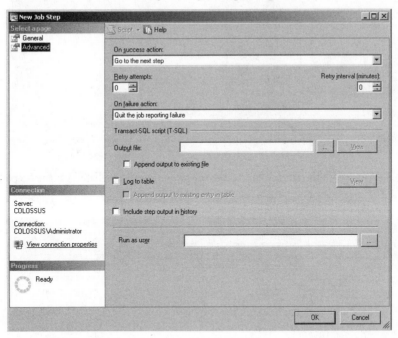

10. To create the second step of the job, click the New button.

11. In the Name box, enter **Back Up Test**.

12. Leave Type as Transact-SQL Script, and enter the following code in the Command text box to back up the database once it has been created:

```
EXEC sp_addumpdevice 'disk', 'JobTest_Backup',
'c:\JobTest_Backup.dat'
BACKUP DATABASE JOBTEST TO JobTest_Backup
```

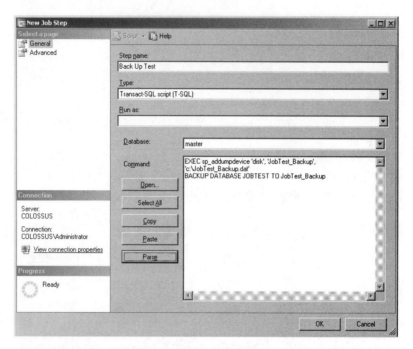

13. Click OK to create the step; you should now have two steps listed on the Steps page.

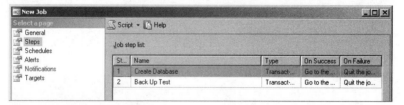

14. Move to the Schedules page, and click the New button to create a schedule that will instruct SQL Server when to fire the job.

15. In the Name box, enter **Create and Back Up Database**.

16. Select One Time from the Schedule Type drop-down list. Set the time to be five minutes from the time displayed in the system tray (usually at the bottom-right corner of your screen).

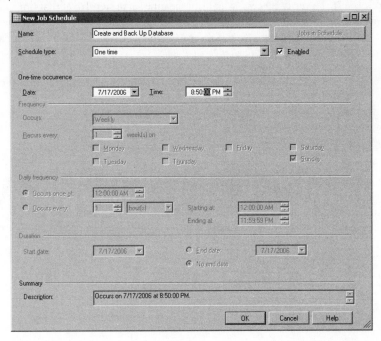

17. Click OK to create the schedule, and move to the Notifications tab.

18. On the Notifications page, check the boxes next to E-mail (if you configured Database Mail earlier) and Net Send, choosing Administrator as the operator to notify. Next to each, select When the Job Completes from the list box (this will notify you no matter what the outcome of the job is).

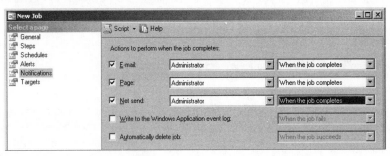

19. Click OK to create the job.

Criteria for Completion

This task is complete when you have successfully created a job that builds and backs up a database named JobTest. To verify success, wait until the time set in step 16; at that time, you should see a message pop up on your screen, notifying you of completion. You can then check for the existence of the JobTest database in SQL Server Management Studio (as shown in Figure 3.1) and the `c:\JobTest_Backup.dat` file.

FIGURE 3.1 You should see the JobTest database in Object Explorer after the job runs.

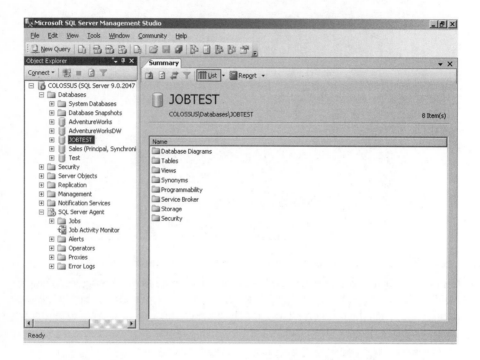

Task 3.4: Creating an Alert

An alert fires when an event (usually a problem) occurs on SQL Server; some examples are a full transaction log or incorrect syntax in a query. These alerts can then be sent to an operator so they can be addressed. Alerts are based on one of three features: an error number, an error severity level, or a performance counter.

All the errors that can occur in SQL Server are numbered (about 3,700 of them exist). Even with so many errors, there aren't enough. For example, suppose you want to fire an alert when a user deletes a customer from your Customers database. SQL Server doesn't have an alert with the structure of your database or your users' names; therefore, you have the ability to create new error numbers and generate an alert for such proprietary issues. You're allowed to create as many error messages as you want in SQL Server, starting with error number 50,001 (this is the starting number for all user-defined errors), which you fire using the RAISERROR() command.

You can make custom error messages dynamic by adding parameters. A *parameter* is a placeholder for information that is supplied when the error is fired. For example, "A customer has been deleted" always displays the same static text every time the error occurs; but if you use a parameter such as "Customer %1s has been deleted," you can use the RAISERROR() command with a parameter that looks like this—RAISERROR(50001,10,1,'Bob Smith')—to create the result "Customer Bob Smith has been deleted." Parameters can be more useful than static text; the parameters you can use are as follows:

- %1s and %s for strings (such as 'Bob Smith')
- %1d and %d for numbers

Each error in SQL Server also has an associated severity level, stating how serious the error is. Alerts can be generated by severity level. Table 3.1 lists the common levels.

TABLE 3.1   Severity Levels of Errors

Level	Description
10	This is an informational message caused by mistakes in the information that was entered by the user. It isn't serious.
11–16	These are all errors that can be corrected by the user.
17	This error is generated when the server runs out of resources, such as memory or hard disk space.
18	A nonfatal internal error has occurred. The statement will finish, and the user connection will be maintained.
19	A nonconfigurable internal limit has been reached. Any statement that causes this will be terminated.
20	A single process in the current database has suffered a problem, but the database itself is unscathed.
21	All processes in the current database are affected by the problem, but the database is undamaged.
22	The table or index that is being used is probably damaged. You should run DBCC to try to repair the object. (Alternatively, the problem may be in the data cache, which means a simple restart may suffice.)

TABLE 3.1   Severity Levels of Errors *(continued)*

Level	Description
23	This message usually means the entire database has been damaged somehow and you should check the integrity of your hardware.
24	Your hardware has failed. You'll probably need to get new hardware and reload the database from a backup.

You can also create performance alerts, which are based on the same performance counters you may have seen in the Windows Performance Monitor program. These counters provide statistics about various components of SQL Server and then act on them. A good example of when to use such an alert is with a full transaction log error.

You can also generate alerts based on Windows Management Instrumentation (WMI) events. WMI is Microsoft's implementation of web-based enterprise management, which is an industry initiative to make systems easier to manage by exposing managed components such as systems, applications, and networks as a set of common objects. SQL Server has been updated to work with WMI and to respond to WMI events.

Using WMI alerts, you can respond to events that you couldn't even see before. For example, you can create an alert to fire when an ALTER LOGIN command is issued. This can be useful for managing security. In addition, you can create an alert to fire when a CREATE TABLE command is run so you can keep track of storage on your database.

In this task, you'll create an alert based on a custom error message that uses parameters.

Scenario

You have a sales database on your SQL Server that contains customer information. Part of the information stored therein is the customer credit limit. Your sales manager wants to be notified when someone on his team tries to increase a customer's credit limit to greater than $10,000. You know no built-in error message will handle this task, so you decide to create a custom error message and fire it using the RAISERROR() command.

Scope of Task

Duration

This task should take approximately 15 minutes.

Setup

For this task, you need access to the machine you installed SQL Server 2005 on in Task 1.1 and the operator you created in Task 3.2.

Caveat

The Messenger service must be running for you to receive Net Send messages.

Procedure

In this task, you'll create a custom error message that accepts a string parameter and then create an alert based on the custom error message.

Equipment Used

For this task, you need access to the machine you installed SQL Server 2005 on in Task 1.1 and the operator you created in Task 3.2.

Details

Follow these steps to create an alert that is based on a custom error message:

1. Open a new SQL Server query by clicking the New Query button in SQL Server Management Studio.

2. Enter and execute the following code to create a new error that is logged to the Windows event log every time it fires:

```
USE master
GO
EXEC sp_addmessage @msgnum=50001, @severity=10,
    @msgtext=N' This is a custom error by %ls.', @with_log='TRUE'
GO
```

3. In Object Explorer, expand your server, and then expand SQL Server Agent.

4. Right-click Alerts, and select New Alert.

5. In the Name box, enter **Custom Alert**.

6. Select the Error Number radio button, and enter **50001** in the Error Number text box.

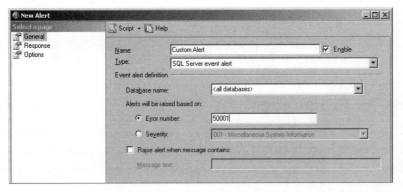

7. On the Response page, check the Notify Operators box, and check the E-mail, Pager, and Net Send boxes next to Administrator.

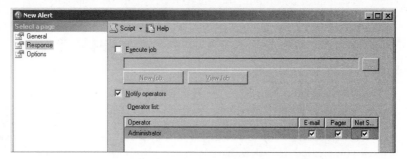

8. On the Options page, check the E-mail, Pager, and Net Send boxes to include the entire text of the error message in the alert, and click OK to create the alert.

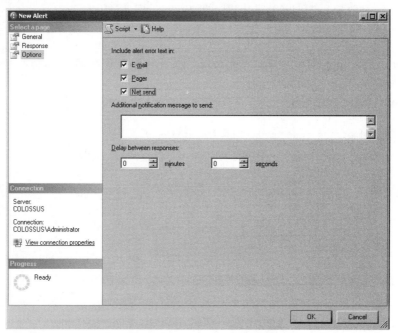

Criteria for Completion

This task is complete when you have successfully created an alert based on a custom error message that accepts a string parameter. Follow these steps to verify that you have been successful:

1. To test the new alert, open a new query, and execute the following code:

```
RAISERROR(50001,10,1,'SQL Guru')
```

2. When the e-mail and Net Send message opens, note the detail it gives you, and then click OK.

Task 3.5: Creating a Database Maintenance Plan

You need to perform many tasks to keep your databases running at peak performance at all times. Such tasks as index reorganizations, database file size reductions, and database and transaction log backups all need to happen on a regular basis to keep your server running smoothly. The trick is that most of these tasks should happen off-hours. You now know, of course, that you can just create jobs and schedule the tasks to run off-hours. The problem is that you'll have to create a number of jobs for each of your databases to keep them all up to par.

To avoid all the labor of creating multiple jobs for multiple databases, use the *Maintenance Plan Wizard*. You can use this handy tool to create jobs for all the standard maintenance tasks required to keep your database system running smoothly.

In this task, you'll create a database maintenance plan for all the databases on your system using the Maintenance Plan Wizard.

Scenario

As the database administrator for your company, you know how important it is to keep the database system running smoothly at all times. You know quite a few maintenance tasks need to be run regularly to keep the system tuned, such as index reorganizing, database and log backups, file maintenance, and so on. These tasks should be performed during off-peak hours, so you know you need to schedule all these tasks; however, you do not want to create separate jobs for each of these tasks. To make the task easier, you decide to use the Maintenance Plan Wizard.

Scope of Task

Duration

This task should take approximately 30 minutes.

Setup

For this task, you need access to the machine you installed SQL Server 2005 on in Task 1.1.

Caveat

Make sure you have SQL Server Integration Services (SSIS) running before starting this task.

Procedure

In this task, you'll create a database maintenance plan for all the databases on your server using the Maintenance Plan Wizard.

Equipment Used

For this task, you need access to the machine you installed SQL Server 2005 on in Task 1.1.

Details

Follow these steps to create a database maintenance plan:

1. In SQL Server Management Studio, expand Management, right-click Maintenance Plans, and select Maintenance Plan Wizard.

2. On the welcome screen, click the Next button.

3. On the Select a Target Server screen, enter **Maintenance Plan 1** in the Name box, enter a description if you'd like, select your default instance of SQL Server, and click Next.

4. On the Select Maintenance Tasks screen, check the boxes for all the available tasks except Execute SQL Server Agent Job, and click Next.

5. On the next screen, you can set the order in which these tasks are performed. Leave the default, and click Next.

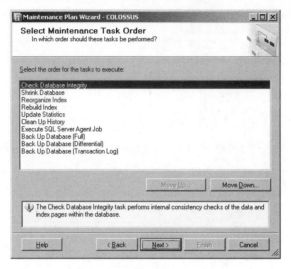

6. The next screen allows you to select the databases on which you want to perform integrity checks. When you click the drop-down list, you'll see several choices:

- All Databases: This encompasses all databases on the server in the same plan.
- All System Databases: This choice affects only the master, model, and MSDB databases.
- All User Databases: This affects all databases (including AdventureWorks) except the system databases.
- These Databases: This choice allows you to be selective about which databases to include in your plan.

For this task, select All Databases, click OK, and then click Next.

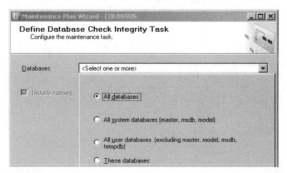

7. On the Define Shrink Database Task screen, select All Databases, click OK, and then click Next.

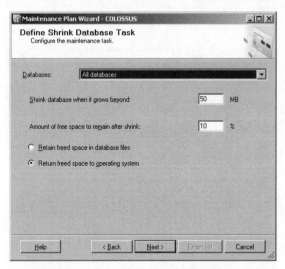

8. On the Define Reorganize Index Task screen, select All Databases from the Databases drop-down list, click OK, and then click Next.

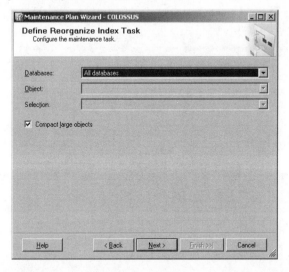

9. The Define Rebuild Index Task screen gives you a number of options for rebuilding your indexes:

- Reorganize Pages with the Default Amount of Free Space: This regenerates pages with their original fill factor.

- Change Free Space per Page Percentage To: This creates a new fill factor. If you set this to 10, for example, your pages will contain 10 percent free space.

Again, select All Databases, accept the defaults, click OK, and then click Next.

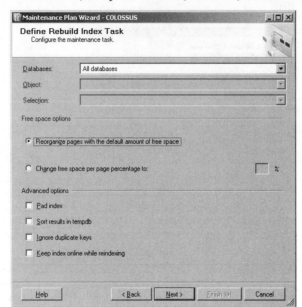

10. Next comes the Define Update Statistics Task screen. Again, select All Databases, click OK, and then click Next.

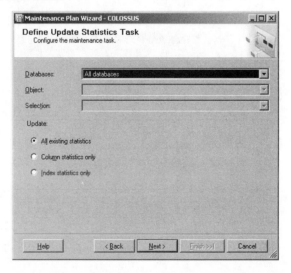

11. Next is the Define History Cleanup Task screen. All the tasks performed by the maintenance plan are logged in the MSDB database. This list is referred to as the *history*, and it can become quite large if you don't prune it occasionally. On this screen, you can set when

and how the history is cleared from the database so you can keep it in check. Again, accept the defaults, and click Next.

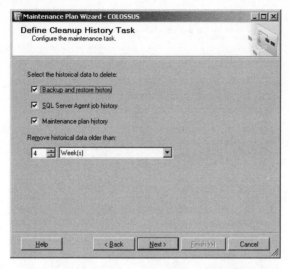

12. The next screen allows you to control how full backups are performed. Select All Databases from the drop-down list, accept the defaults, click OK, and then click Next.

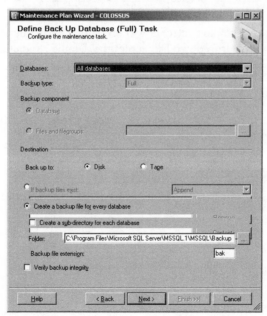

13. The next screen allows you to control how differential backups are performed. Select All Databases from the drop-down list, accept the defaults, click OK, and then click Next.

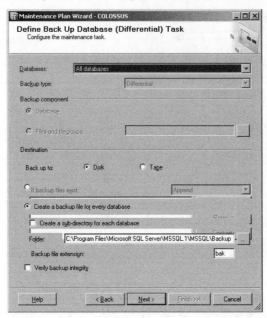

14. The next screen allows you to control how transaction log backups are performed. Select All Databases from the drop-down list, accept the defaults, and click Next.

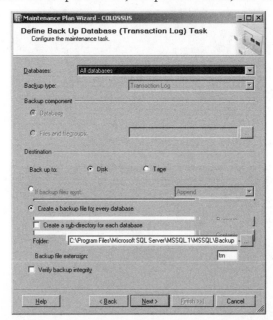

15. On the Select Plan Properties screen, click the Change button to create a schedule for the job.

16. Enter **Maintenance Plan 1 Schedule** for the schedule name, accept the rest of the defaults, and click OK to create the schedule.

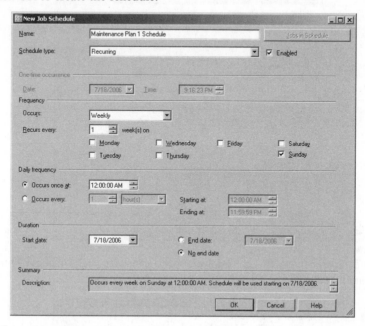

17. Click Next to continue.

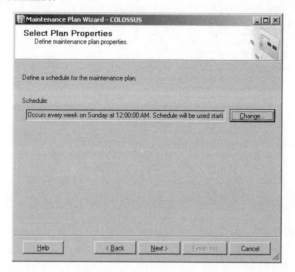

18. On the Select Report Options screen, you can write a report to a text file every time the job runs, and you can e-mail the report to an operator. In this case, write a report to C:\, and click Next.

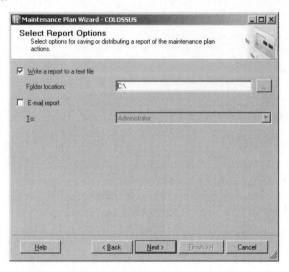

19. On the next screen, you can view a summary of the tasks to perform. Click Finish to create the maintenance plan.

20. Once SQL Server is finished creating the maintenance plan, you can click Close.

Criteria for Completion

This task is complete when you have successfully created a database maintenance plan for all the databases on the default instance of SQL Server using the Maintenance Plan Wizard. Follow these steps to verify that you are successful:

1. In SQL Server Management Studio, expand Management, and then expand Maintenance Plans. You should see Maintenance Plan 1 listed.

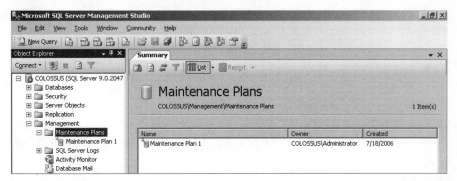

2. Double-click Maintenance Plan 1 to open Design view. You can view and modify all the options you set for the maintenance plan on this screen.

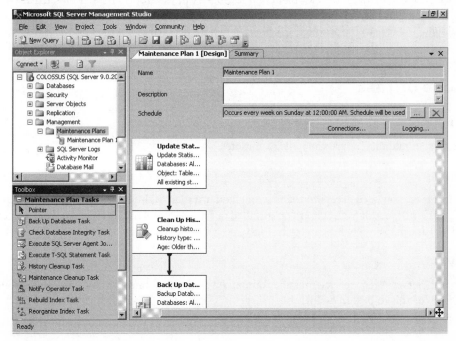

3. Close Design view.

Task 3.6: Using the Copy Database Wizard

You can use the *Copy Database Wizard* to copy or move a database and all its associated objects to another server. You might want to do that for one of several good reasons:

- If you are upgrading your server, the Copy Database Wizard is a quick way to move your data to the new system.
- You can use the wizard to create a backup copy of the database on another server, ready to use in case of emergency.
- Developers can copy an existing database and use the copy to make changes without endangering the live database.

The Copy Database Wizard will prove to be a valuable tool in your administrative functions, so in this task, you will use it to make a copy of the JobTest database created in Task 3.3.

Scenario

Your company has a SQL Server instance in production and another SQL Server instance that is reserved specifically for development and testing. Your developers have been hard at work on a new database for several weeks, and they are now ready to move the database from the development server to the production server. You have decided to use the Copy Database Wizard to accomplish the task.

Scope of Task

Duration

This task should take approximately 15 minutes.

Setup

For this task, you need access to the machine you installed SQL Server 2005 on in Task 1.1, the Second instance of SQL Server you installed in Task 1.2, and the JobTest database you created in Task 3.3.

Caveat

The SQL Server Agent service must be running on both the default instance and the Second instance for this to be successful.

Procedure

In this task, you'll copy the JobTest database from the default instance of SQL Server to the Second instance using the Copy Database Wizard.

Equipment Used

For this task, you need access to the machine you installed SQL Server 2005 on in Task 1.1, the Second instance of SQL Server you installed in Task 1.2, and the JobTest database you created in Task 3.3.

Details

Follow these steps to copy the JobTest database using the Copy Database Wizard:

1. Open SQL Server Management Studio by selecting it from the Microsoft SQL Server group under Programs on the Start menu, expand your server, and expand Databases.

2. Right-click the JobTest database, go to Tasks, and select Copy Database. You will see the welcome screen.

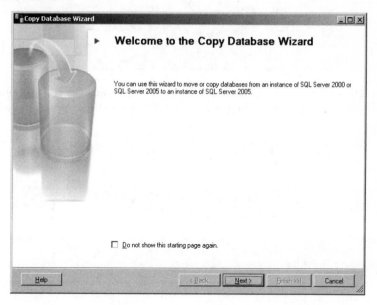

3. Click Next.

4. On the second screen, you are asked to select a source server. Select the default instance of your server and the proper authentication type (usually Windows Authentication), and click Next.

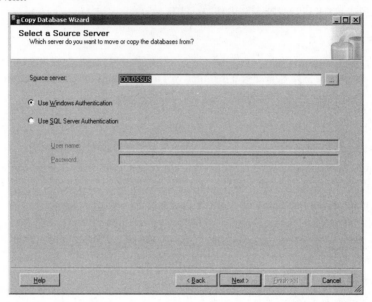

5. On the next screen, you need to select a destination, so click the ellipsis button, check the box next to the Second instance, and click OK. Choose the appropriate security, and click Next.

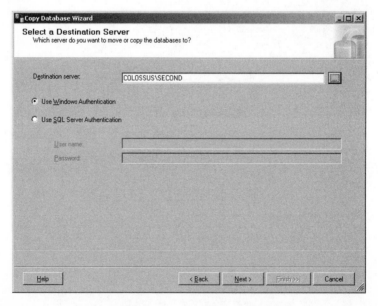

6. Next you are asked which mode you would like to use. Attach/detach is useful for copying databases between servers that are in remote locations from each other; it requires the database to be taken offline. The SQL Management Object transfer method allows you to keep the database online and gives you the flexibility to make a copy on the same server, so select the SQL Management Object Method option, and click Next.

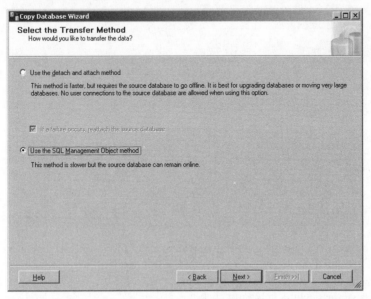

7. Next you are asked which database you would like to move or copy. Check the Copy box next to JobTest, and click Next.

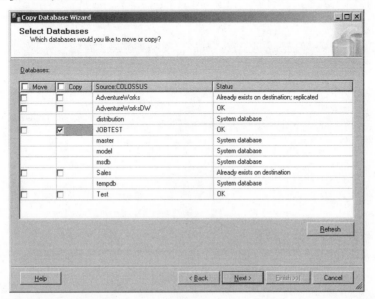

8. On the Configure Destination Database screen, accept the defaults, and click Next.

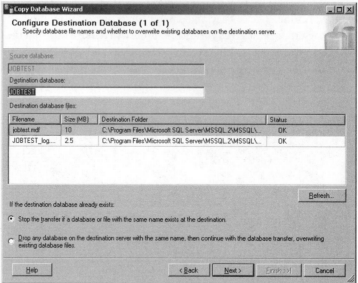

9. On the next screen, you are given the option to copy additional database objects. This is especially useful if the destination server does not have all the logins required to access the database or if additional stored procedures are used for business logic in your applications. Leave the defaults here, and click Next.

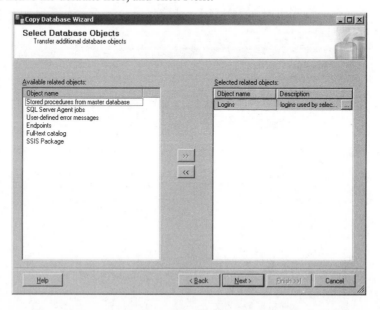

10. You now have the option to change the name of the package that will be created; this matters only if you plan to save the package and execute it later. Accept the defaults, and click Next.

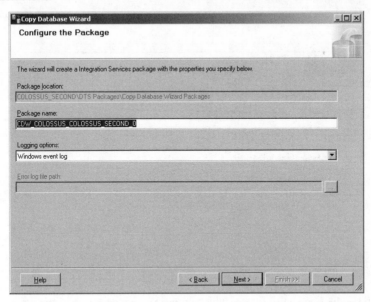

11. On the next screen, you are asked when you would like to run the SSIS job created by the wizard. Select Run Immediately, and click Next.

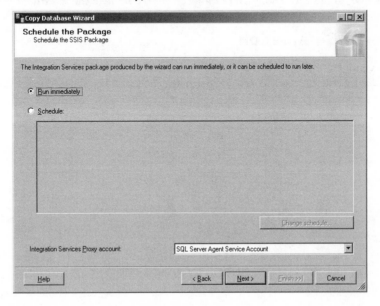

12. The final screen summarizes the choices you have made. Click Finish to copy the Test database.

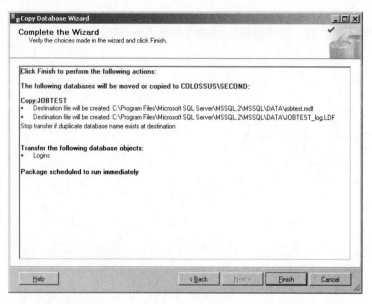

13. You will see the Log Detail screen, which shows you each section of the job as it executes. Clicking the Report button will show each step of the job and its outcome.

14. Click Close on the Performing Operation screen to complete the wizard.

Criteria for Completion

This task is complete when you have successfully copied the JobTest database from the default instance of SQL Server to the Second instance using the Copy Database Wizard. You should see the JobTest database listed in Object Explorer under Databases on the Second instance, as shown in Figure 3.2.

FIGURE 3.2   You should see the JobTest database on the Second instance if the Copy Database Wizard is successful.

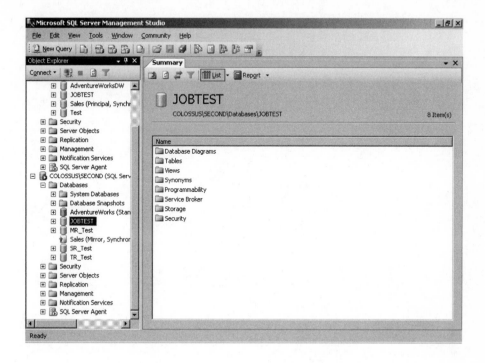

Phase

4

Monitoring and Troubleshooting SQL Server

Imagine for a moment you are the chief operating officer of a sizable company. It is your job to make sure the company runs smoothly and that everything gets done efficiently. How will you do this? You could just guess at it, randomly assigning tasks and then assuming they will get done. Imagine the chaos that would ensue if you used this approach. Nothing would get done. Some departments would have too much to do, and others would have nothing to do—and your company would go bankrupt.

A better approach would be to ask for reports from the various department managers and base your decisions on those reports. You might discover, for instance, that the accounting department has too much work and could use some help. Based on this report, you could hire more accountants. You might find that the production department has little to do because the sales department has not been doing a good job; based on this report, you could motivate sales to get to work so production would have something to do.

Now, instead of being in charge of the entire company's operations, you are in charge of your SQL Server. Here too, you need to make certain everything is getting done efficiently. Again, you could just guess at this and randomly assign tasks, but as already discussed, that is an invitation to disaster. Instead, you need to get reports from your department managers—and in this case, the department managers are the central processing unit (CPU), the disk subsystem, the database engine, and so on. Once you have these reports, you can assign tasks and resources accordingly.

Many system administrators don't perform monitoring functions because they think they don't have the time. Most of their time is spent on firefighting—that is, troubleshooting problems that have cropped up. However, it's safe to say that if the system administrators had taken the time to monitor their systems, those problems might never have arisen in the first place. That makes monitoring and optimization *proactive* troubleshooting, not *reactive*, as is the norm. So, you can see why it is important that I discuss the various methods and tools for getting the reports you need from SQL Server.

However, no matter how diligent you may be in monitoring your system, problems will arise from time to time. To deal with these problems, you need to have some troubleshooting skills, so I will also cover some methods for troubleshooting common problems.

As is best with most subjects, you'll start at the bottom and work your way up, so I'll discuss the Windows System Monitor first.

Task 4.1: Using Windows System Monitor

SQL Server cannot function properly if it does not have available system resources such as ample memory, adequate processor power, fast disks, and a reliable network subsystem. If these systems do not work together, the overall system will not function properly. For example, if the memory is being overused, the disk subsystem slows down, because the memory has to write to the pagefile (which is on the disk) far too often. To keep this from happening, you need to monitor the health of the subsystems; you can do this using System Monitor.

System Monitor comes with Windows and is located in the Administrative Tools section of the Start menu (the tool is labeled Performance). Four views are available for your use:

Graph This view displays a graph of system performance. As values change, the graph will spike or dip accordingly.

Report The report view looks like what you might get on a piece of paper, except that the values here change with system use.

Alert With alert view, you can tell System Monitor to warn you when something bad is looming on the horizon, perhaps when the use of the central processing unit (CPU) is almost—but not quite yet—too high. This type of warning gives you time to fix potential problems before they become actual problems.

Log The log view is for record keeping. With log view, you can monitor your system over a time period and view the information later, as opposed to viewing it in real time (the default).

With each of these views, you monitor objects and counters. An *object* is part of the system, such as the processor or the physical memory. A *counter* displays the statistical information about how much that object is being used. For example, the % Processor Time counter under the Processor object will tell you how much time your processor spends working. Table 4.1 lists common counters and their recommended values.

 WARNING To see the Network Segment: % Network Utilization counter, you must install the Network Monitor Agent on the Services tab of the Network Control Panel.

You can monitor SQL Server as well as Windows objects using System Monitor, because SQL Server provides its own objects and counters. The process for monitoring SQL Server is the same as it is with Windows—you just add different objects and counters. Table 4.2 describes the SQL Server counters you will be using most often.

TABLE 4.1   Common Counters and Values in System Monitor

Object	Counter	Use	Recommended Value	Recommendations
Processor	% Processor Time	The amount of time the processor spends working	Less than 75%	If this is too high, you should off-load some processes to another server or purchase a multiprocessor machine.
Memory	Pages/Sec	The number of times per second that data had to be moved from random access memory (RAM) to disk, and vice versa	Fewer than 5	If this is too high, it means your system is compensating for a lack of RAM by paging to disk. You should add more RAM if this is too high.
Memory	Available Bytes	The amount of physical RAM available	More than 4MB	This number should be low, because Windows uses as much RAM as it can grab for file cache.
Memory	Committed Bytes	The amount of RAM committed to use	Less than physical RAM	If this is higher than the physical RAM, then you should consider adding more RAM.
PhysicalDisk	% Disk Time	The amount of time the disk is busy reading or writing	Less than 50%	If this is higher than 50%, you should consider off-loading some processes to another machine or adding disks to your array.
Network Segment	% Network Utilization	The amount of network bandwidth being used	Less than 30%	If this is too high, then you should consider segregating your network with a router or bridge to decrease broadcast traffic.

TABLE 4.2   Most Frequently Used SQL Server System Monitor Counters

Object	Counter	Use	Recommendations
SQLServer:Buffer Manager	Buffer Cache Hit Ratio	How much data is being retrieved from cache instead of disk.	This should be in the high 90s. If it is too low, then you may need to add more RAM to your system.
SQLServer:Buffer Manager	Page Reads/Sec	Number of data pages that are read from disk each second.	This should be as low as possible.
SQLServer:Buffer Manager	Page Writes/Sec	Number of data pages that are written to disk each second.	This should be as low as possible.
SQLServer: General Statistics	User Connections	Number of user connections. Each of these connections will take some RAM.	Use this to predict how much memory you will need for your system when you add new users.
SQLServer: Memory Manager	Total Server Memory (KB)	Total amount of memory that SQL Server has been dynamically assigned.	Use this when determining whether you have enough RAM to add more processes, such as replication, to a SQL Server.
SQLServer:SQL Statistics	SQL Compilations/ Sec	Number of compiles per second.	This should be as high as possible.

I can't give you an exact number for many of these SQL Server counters because each machine is different. You will have to collect a baseline of data to compare against for yourself.

In this task, you will work with Windows System Monitor to monitor objects and counters.

Scenario

As the lead database administrator (DBA) for your company, you understand how important it is to keep SQL Server up and running at top speed. You want to make sure all the subsystems on the server are working in harmony and none is being overloaded. The best way to accomplish that goal is to view the data in Windows System Monitor on a regular basis.

Scope of Task

Duration

This task should take approximately 15 minutes.

Setup

For this task, you need access to the machine you installed SQL Server 2005 on in Task 1.1.

Caveat

This task doesn't have any caveats.

Procedure

In this task, you will work with the graph and report views in Windows System Monitor.

Equipment Used

For this task, you need access to the machine you installed SQL Server 2005 on in Task 1.1.

Details

Follow these steps to work with Windows System Monitor:

1. Log on to Windows as Administrator.

2. From the Start menu, select Programs ➢ Administrative Tools ➢ Performance. Notice that the graph is already populated with counters.

3. On the toolbar, click the Add button (it looks like a + sign) to open the Add Counters dialog box.

4. In the Performance Object box, select Memory.

5. In the Select Counters from List box, select Available Bytes, and click Add.

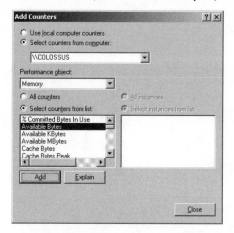

6. Click Close, and notice the graph being created on the screen.

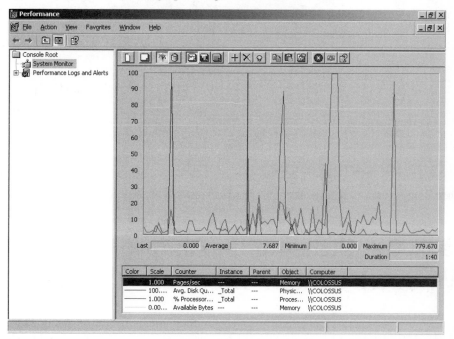

7. Press Ctrl+H, and notice the current counter changes color. This can make the chart easier to read.

8. On the toolbar, click the View Report button (it looks like a sheet of paper), and notice how the same data appears in report view.

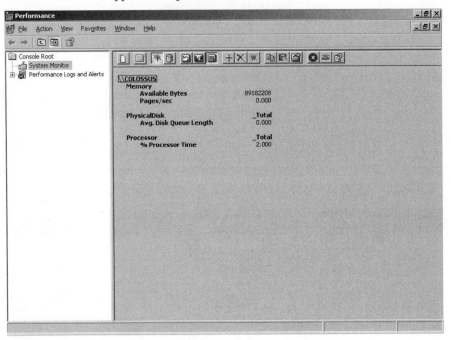

Criteria for Completion

This task is complete when you have familiarized yourself with Windows System Monitor.

Task 4.2: Creating an Alert in Windows System Monitor

It goes without saying that you cannot be in front of the computer staring at Windows System Monitor 24/7. At the least, you need a few hours of sleep! Kidding aside, you need to have Windows notify you when your system encounters a potential problem. That is what the alert view in Windows System Monitor does.

As mentioned in the previous task, you use alert view to have System Monitor warn you when something is about to become a problem, not after it has already blossomed into a catastrophe. A good example is the Memory: Pages/Sec counter. When this counter is more than 5 for a sustained period, then you do not have enough random access memory (RAM), and you need to add more. By monitoring this closely and having Windows alert you in time, your users will never know that there was an issue.

In this task, you will create an alert in Windows System Monitor.

Scenario

As the lead database administrator (DBA) for your company, you understand how important it is to keep SQL Server up and running at top speed. You want to make sure all the subsystems on the server are working in harmony and none is being overloaded. The best way to accomplish that goal is to view the data in Windows System Monitor on a regular basis. You need to be notified if a subsystem suddenly becomes overloaded as well, so you decide to create some alerts in Windows System Monitor to keep you updated.

Scope of Task

Duration

This task should take approximately 15 minutes.

Setup

For this task, you need access to the machine you installed SQL Server 2005 on in Task 1.1.

Caveat

In this task, you will create an alert that notifies you when the Processor: % Processor Time counter is less than 70 percent (which is just an arbitrary value that we use in this task). In production, this would be more than 75 percent.

Procedure

In this task, you will create an alert in Windows System Monitor.

Equipment Used

For this task, you need access to the machine you installed SQL Server 2005 on in Task 1.1.

Details

Follow these steps to work with Windows System Monitor:

1.   Log on to Windows as Administrator.
2.   From the Start menu, select Programs ➤ Administrative Tools ➤ Performance.
3.   In the left pane, expand Performance Logs and Alerts, right-click Alerts, and select **New Alert Settings**.
4.   Enter **Test Alert** in the Name box, and click OK.
5.   In the Alert Settings dialog box, enter **Test Alert** in the Comment field.
6.   Click Add.
7.   Select the Processor object and the % Processor Time counter, and click Add; then click Close.
8.   Select Under from the Alert When Value Is drop-down list, enter **70** for Limit, and click OK. This will generate an alert if the processor is not busy 70 percent of the time. In the real world, you would set this to more than 70 percent, thus warning you just before it becomes a serious problem.
9.   Click OK to create the alert.

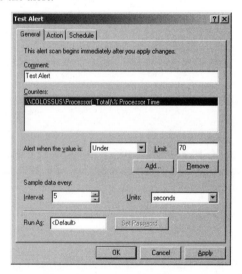

Criteria for Completion

This task is complete when you have created an alert that notifies you when the Processor: % Processor Time counter is less than 70 percent, which you should see in Event Viewer as outlined in the earlier task details. Follow these steps to verify:

1.   To view the alerts, open Event Viewer, and look for them in the Application log.

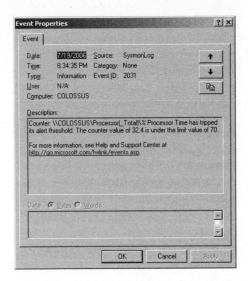

2. Watch the alerts generated for a short time, then select the alert, and finally press the Delete key. If asked whether you want to continue deleting a running alert, click OK.

3. Exit System Monitor and Event Viewer.

Task 4.3: Creating a SQL Server Performance Alert

SQL Server performance alerts are based on the same performance counters you used in Windows System Monitor in the previous task. These counters provide statistics about various components of SQL Server and then act on them. A good example of when to use such an alert is with a full transaction log error.

When a transaction log fills to 100 percent, no users can access the database, so they can't work. Some companies lose substantial amounts of money every hour their users aren't working, and it could take some time before you can bring the database to a usable state by clearing the transaction log. Therefore, you should find the problem before it happens by clearing the transaction log when it reaches a certain percentage, say 70 percent.

To see the capability of performance alerts in action, in this task you'll create an alert that fires when the transaction log for the AdventureWorks database is less than 100 percent full.

Scenario

As the lead database administrator (DBA) for your company, you understand how important it is to keep SQL Server up and running at top speed, and you want to make certain that all the databases are available at all times. You have had some trouble with the Sales database, which is heavily used. Occasionally under heavy usage, the transaction log fills to 100 percent, and the users are locked out. You can't find a reliable pattern for when this happens, but you still need to prevent it. You have decided that the best way to keep the log from filling to capacity is to create a performance alert that runs a backup job to clear the log before it gets to 100 percent full.

Scope of Task

Duration

This task should take approximately 15 minutes.

Setup

For this task, you need access to the machine you installed SQL Server 2005 on in Task 1.1, the AdventureWorks database installed with the sample data, and the operator you created in Task 3.2.

Caveat

In this task, you will create an alert that fires when the log is less than 100 percent full. On your production systems, you should set such an alert to fire when the log is about 70 percent full and then fire a job that will back up (and thus clear) the transaction log. You will also need to have the Messenger service running to receive the Net Send message.

Procedure

In this task, you'll create an alert that fires when the transaction log for the AdventureWorks database is less than 100 percent full, and you will then disable the alert.

Equipment Used

For this task, you need access to the machine you installed SQL Server 2005 on in Task 1.1, the AdventureWorks database installed with the sample data, and the operator you created in Task 3.2.

Details

Follow these steps to create a performance alert in SQL Server Management Studio:

1. Open SQL Server Management Studio, expand your server, and then expand SQL Server Agent.
2. Right-click Alerts, and select New Alert.
3. In the Name box, enter **Performance Alert**.
4. In the Type list, select SQL Server Performance Condition Alert.
5. In the Object box, select SQLServer:Databases.
6. In the Counter box, select Percent Log Used.

7. In the Instance box, select AdventureWorks.

8. Make sure Alert If Counter is set to Falls Below.

9. In the Value box, enter **100**.

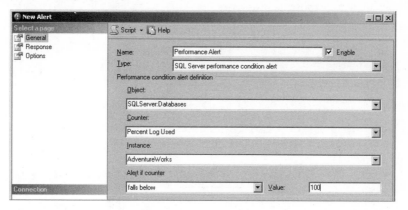

10. Select the Response page, check the Notify Operators box, and check the Net Send box next to your operator name.

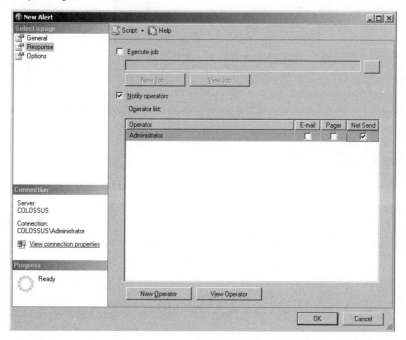

11. Click OK to create the alert.

12. When the Net Send message opens, note the detail that is provided, and click OK to close the message.

Because you probably don't want that error popping up every few minutes, you need to disable it:

1. In SQL Server Management Studio, under Alerts in SQL Server Agent, double-click Performance Alert to expose its properties.

2. Uncheck the Enable box, and click OK to apply the changes.

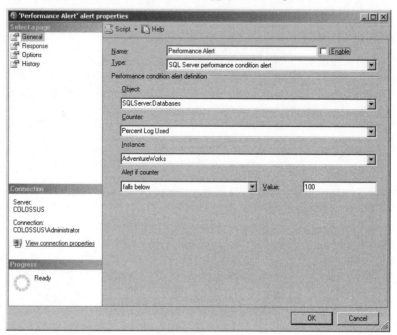

Criteria for Completion

This task is complete when you have created a performance alert that notifies you when the transaction log of the AdventureWorks database is less than 100 percent full. You will see a Net Send message similar to the one in Figure 4.1.

FIGURE 4.1 A Net Send message will open when the performance alert fires.

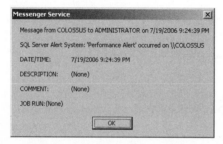

Task 4.4: Creating a WMI Alert

Windows Management Instrumentation (WMI) is Microsoft's implementation of web-based enterprise management, which is an industry initiative to make systems easier to manage by exposing managed components such as systems, applications, and networks as a set of common objects. SQL Server has been updated to work with WMI and respond to WMI events. But with all the techno-babble out of the way, what does this mean to you?

Using WMI alerts, you can respond to events that you couldn't even see before. For example, you can create an alert to fire when an ALTER LOGIN command is issued. This can be useful for managing security. In addition, you can create an alert to fire when a CREATE TABLE command is run so you can keep track of storage on your database. The only limitation is your imagination—so you need to know how to create WMI alerts.

You'll create a WMI alert in this task that fires when a new database is created.

Scenario

You are the database administrator (DBA) for a medium-sized company that employs several developers, many of whom create SQL Server objects on a regular basis. Management has implemented a change control program to keep track of what objects are changed and when, and management wants all the developers to follow this new protocol. You have been asked to help make sure no database objects are changed in the production environment without a change control document in place and approved. You could prevent the developers from modifying production objects, but you would have to remove the permissions they need to do their jobs, so you decide to create a WMI alert to notify yourself and management when a production object is modified so you can check for a corresponding change request.

Scope of Task

Duration

This task should take approximately 15 minutes.

Setup

For this task, you need access to the machine you installed SQL Server 2005 on in Task 1.1 and the operator you created in Task 3.2.

Caveat

You must have the Messenger service running to receive the Net Send message.

Procedure

In this task, you will create a WMI alert that fires when a new database is created. You will then disable the alert.

Equipment Used

For this task, you need access to the machine you installed SQL Server 2005 on in **Task 1.1** and the operator you created in Task 3.2.

Details

Follow these steps to create a WMI alert in SQL Server Management Studio:

1. Open SQL Server Management Studio, expand your server, and then expand SQL Server Agent.

2. Right-click Alerts, and select New Alert.

3. In the Name box, enter **WMI Alert**.

4. In the Type list, select WMI Event Alert.

5. Make sure Namespace is set to `\\.\root\Microsoft\SqlServer\ServerEvents\ MSSQLSERVER`.

6. Enter this query in the Query box:

```
SELECT * FROM CREATE_DATABASE
```

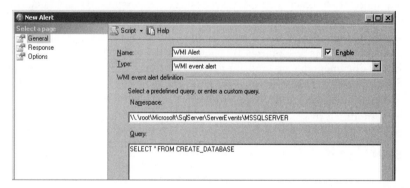

7. Select the Response page, check the Notify Operators box, and check the Net Send box next to your operator name.

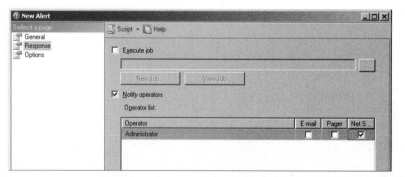

8. On the Options page, check the Net Send box under Include Alert Error Text In, and click OK to create the alert.

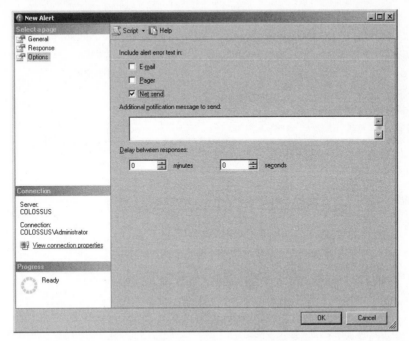

9. Open a new SQL Server query in SQL Server Management Studio by clicking the New Query button.

10. Enter and execute the following code to fire the new alert:

```
USE Master
GO
CREATE DATABASE WMITest
ON PRIMARY
(
    NAME = N'WMITest',
    FILENAME = N'C:\WMITest.mdf' ,
    SIZE = 3072KB ,
    MAXSIZE = UNLIMITED,
    FILEGROWTH = 1024KB
)
LOG ON
(
    NAME = N'WMITest_log', FILENAME = N'C:\WMITest_log.ldf' ,
    SIZE = 504KB ,
```

```
    MAXSIZE = UNLIMITED,
    FILEGROWTH = 10%
)
```

11. When the Net Send message opens, note the detail that is provided, and click OK to close the message (it may take a few seconds for the message to open).

12. To disable the alert, open it, uncheck the Enable box, and click OK.

Criteria for Completion

This task is complete when you have created a performance alert that notifies you when someone has created a new database. You will see a Net Send message similar to the one in Figure 4.2.

FIGURE 4.2   A Net Send message will open when the WMI alert fires.

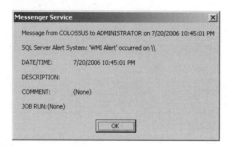

Task 4.5: Running a Trace in Profiler

When running a company, once you have the management team working in harmony, you can focus your attention on the rest of the workforce. As in any company, the employees need to be monitored to make sure they are doing their fair share of work. In this analogy, the queries that are run on SQL Server would be the employees who need to be monitored, and Profiler is the tool you need to do the work.

Profiler allows you to monitor and record what is happening inside the database engine. You do this by performing a *trace*, which is a record of data that has been captured about events. Traces are stored in a table, a trace log file, or both, and they can be either shared (viewable by everyone) or private (viewable only by the owner).

The actions you will be monitoring, called *events*, are anything that happens to the database engine, such as a failed login or a completed query. These events are logically grouped into *event classes* in Profiler so they will be easier for you to find and use. Some of these events are useful for maintaining security, and some are useful for troubleshooting problems, but most of these events are used for monitoring and optimizing. The following event classes are available:

Cursors   A cursor is an object that is used to work with multiple rows of data by moving through them one row at a time. This event class monitors events that are generated by cursor usage.

Database   This is a collection of events to monitor automatic changes in size for data and log files.

Errors and Warnings   The events in this class monitor errors and warnings such as a failed login or a syntax error.

Locks   When users access data, that data is locked so other users cannot modify data someone else is reading. These events monitor the locks placed on your data.

Objects   You can monitor this class of events to see when objects (such as tables, views, or indexes) are opened, closed, or modified in some way.

Performance   These events display Showplan event classes as well as event classes produced by data manipulation operators.

Scans   Tables and indexes can be scanned, which means SQL Server must read through every entry in the object to find the data for which you are looking. The events in this class monitor these object scans.

Security Audit   These events monitor security. Failed logins, password changes, role changes, and so on, are contained in this category.

Server   This category contains classes that monitor server control and memory change events.

Sessions   When a user connects to SQL Server, that user is said to have *started a session* with the server. This event class monitors user sessions.

Stored Procedures   A stored procedure is a collection of Transact-SQL code that is stored on the server and is ready to be executed. This event class monitors events that are triggered by the use of stored procedures.

Transactions   A transaction is a group of Transact-SQL commands that are viewed as a unit, meaning either they must all be applied to the database together or all of them fail. This event class monitors SQL Server transactions (including anything that happens to a transaction log where transactions are recorded) as well as transactions that go through the Distributed Transaction Coordinator (DTC).

TSQL   This event class monitors any Transact-SQL commands that are passed from the client to the database server.

User Configurable   If the other events in Profiler do not meet your needs, you can create your own event to monitor with these user-configurable events. This is especially handy for custom applications you may create.

OLEDB   OLEDB is an interface that developers can use to connect to SQL Server. This event class monitors OLEDB-specific events.

Broker   Service Broker is a new component in SQL Server 2005 that provides asynchronous message queuing and delivery. The Broker event class monitors events generated by Service Broker.

Full Text   Full-text indexing gives you flexibility in querying SQL Server by letting you search for phrases, word variations, weighted results, and so on. These indexes are controlled by a separate service (msftesql). Using this event class, you can monitor events generated by the full-text index service and its indexes.

Deprecation   Over the years, many commands have been deprecated in SQL Server. One such example is the DUMP statement, which was used in earlier versions of SQL Server to back up databases and logs but is no longer a valid command. The Deprecation event class helps you track down procedures and programs that are using deprecated functions and commands so you can update them.

Progress Report   This class of events helps you monitor the progress of long-running commands, such as online index operations.

When you create a trace, it is based on a *trace template*. A *template* is a predefined trace definition that you can use to create a trace out of the box, or you can modify it to fit your needs. You can choose from several templates:

Blank   This template has no configuration at all. It is a blank slate you can use to create a completely unique trace definition.

SP_Counts   You can use this template to see how many stored procedures are started, which database ID they are called from, and which server process ID (SPID) called the stored procedure.

Standard   This template records logins and logouts, existing connections (at the time of the trace), completed remote procedure calls (RPCs), and completed Transact-SQL batches.

TSQL   This records the same events as the Standard template except this template displays only the EventClass, TextData, SPID, and StartTime data columns. This is useful for tracking which queries are being run, when they are being run, and who is running them.

TSQL_Duration   This tracks which queries are being executed and how long those queries take. This is especially useful for finding queries and stored procedures with poor performance.

TSQL_Grouped   You can use this template to discover what applications are being used to connect to SQL Server and who is using those applications. This template tracks queries that are being run and groups them by application name, then Windows username, then SQL Server username, and then process ID.

TSQL_Replay   Trace files can be replayed against a server, meaning that every action in a trace file can be executed as if it were coming from a user. This template is especially useful for replaying against a server to find the cause of a crash or some other unexpected event.

TSQL_SPs   You can use this template to find out who is running stored procedures and what those stored procedures do.

Tuning   You can use this specifically for creating a trace file for the Database Engine Tuning Advisor, which I will discuss later in this phase.

In this task, you'll get some hands-on experience with Profiler by creating and running a trace.

Scenario

You are the database administrator (DBA) for a medium-sized company with several SQL Server users. Recently your users have started complaining that they are having trouble retrieving data from SQL Server. Some users cannot access the data they need at all, and others can access it, but it is slow. You realize that this could be any number of problems ranging from network connectivity to security issues. It could even be a combination of these problems. You realize that the best way to troubleshoot this problem is to run a trace in Profiler.

Scope of Task

Duration

This task should take approximately 15 minutes.

Setup

For this task, you need access to the machine you installed SQL Server 2005 on in Task 1.1 and the AdventureWorks database installed with the sample data.

Caveat

This task doesn't have any caveats.

Procedure

In this task, you will configure and run a trace in Profiler.

Equipment Used

For this task, you need access to the machine you installed SQL Server 2005 on in Task 1.1 and the AdventureWorks database installed with the sample data.

Details

Follow these steps to create and run a trace in Profiler:

1. From the Start menu, select Programs ➤ Microsoft SQL Server 2005 ➤ Performance Tools ➤ SQL Server Profiler.

2. From the File menu, select New Trace.

3. Connect to your default server instance using the proper authentication; this opens the Trace Properties dialog box.

4. In the Trace Name box, enter **Monitor**.

5. Use the Standard (default) template.

6. Check the Save to File box, and click Save to accept the default name and location. Leave the Enable File Rollover box checked and the Server Processes Trace Data box unchecked.

7. Check the Save to Table box, log on to your default server instance, and fill in the following:

    -   Database: **AdventureWorks**

    -   Owner: **dbo**

    -   Table: **Monitor**

8. Click OK once you have made these changes.

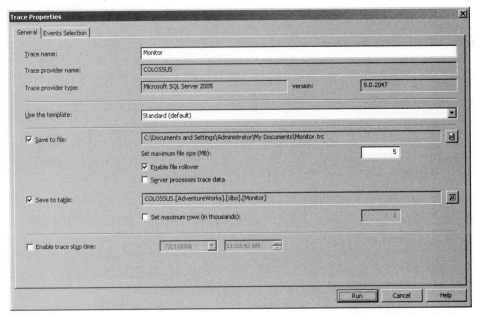

9. Click the Events Selection tab, and check the Show All Events box toward the bottom of the tab.

10. In the Events grid, expand Security Audit (if it is not already expanded), and check the box to the left of Audit Schema Object Access Event. This will monitor the opening and closing of objects, such as tables.

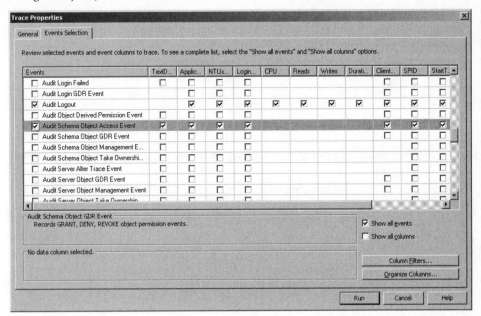

11. Click Run to start the trace.

12. Leave Profiler running, and open a new SQL Server query in SQL Server Management Studio.

13. Execute the following query:

```
USE AdventureWorks
SELECT * FROM Person.Contact
```

14. Switch to Profiler, and click the Pause button (double blue lines). In Profiler, notice the amount of data that was collected.

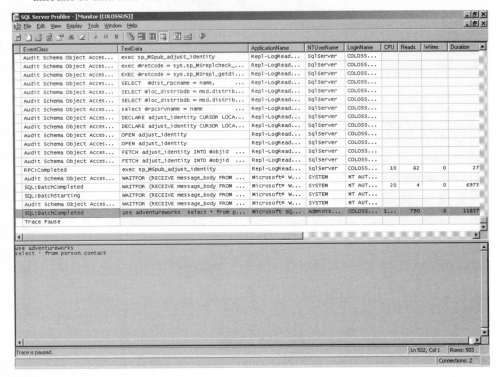

15. Click the Stop button (the red box) to stop the trace.

16. Close Profiler and SQL Server Management Studio.

> When the Server Processes Trace Data box is checked, SQL Server processes the trace. This can slow server performance, but no events are missed. If the box is unchecked, the client processes the trace data. This results in faster performance, but some events may be missed under a heavy server load.

Criteria for Completion

This task is complete when you have created and run a trace in Profiler. You should see a list of database activity as discussed earlier in the task details.

Task 4.6: Creating a Workload in Profiler

If one musical instrument in an orchestra is out of tune, the entire symphony sounds bad, and the performance is ruined. In the same way, if even one SQL Server database is out of tune, it could slow down the entire system. Perhaps an index was created using the wrong columns, or maybe users have started querying different data over time, which would require the creation of new indexes. If any of this is true, your databases need tuning. To do that, you need to use the *Database Engine Tuning Advisor*.

Before you can run the Database *Engine* Tuning Advisor, you need to create a workload. You get this by running and saving a trace in Profiler based on the Tuning template. It is best to get this workload during times of peak database activity to make sure you give the advisor an accurate load.

In this task, you will create a workload file to use with the Database *Engine* Tuning Advisor in the next task.

Scenario

You have a SQL Server 2005 instance that has been running well for several months. Over the past couple of weeks, though, users have started complaining about performance. They tell you that queries are taking an excessive amount of time to return data. After doing some research into the problem, you realize the users have begun to query on columns that are not indexed, and some of the indexes currently in place may not be used any longer. You know that the most efficient way to fix this problem is by using the Database Engine Tuning Advisor; however, before you can do that, you need to create a workload file.

Scope of Task

Duration

This task should take approximately 15 minutes.

Setup

For this task, you need access to the machine you installed SQL Server 2005 on in Task 1.1, the AdventureWorks database installed with the sample data, and the Monitor table you created in Task 4.5.

Caveat

This task doesn't have any caveats.

Procedure

In this task, you will create a workload file by configuring a trace in Profiler based on the Tuning trace template.

Equipment Used

For this task, you need access to the machine you installed SQL Server 2005 on in Task 1.1, the AdventureWorks database installed with the sample data, and the Monitor table you created in Task 4.5.

Details

Follow these steps to create a workload in Profiler:

1. First you need to remove the indexes from the test table, so open SQL Server Management Studio, and expand Databases ➢ AdventureWorks ➢ Tables.
2. Right-click Monitor, and select Modify.
3. Right-click the key icon by the RowNumber column, and select Remove Primary Key.
4. Click the Save button on the toolbar to remove the indexes from the table.
5. To stop any excess traffic on the server, right-click SQL Server Agent in Object Explorer, select Stop, then click OK.
6. From the Start menu, select Programs ➢ Microsoft SQL Server 2005 ➢ Performance Tools ➢ Profiler.
7. From the File menu, select New Trace to open the Trace Properties dialog box.
8. Connect to your default server instance using the proper authentication.
9. In the Trace Name box, enter **Tuning**.
10. Use the Tuning template.
11. Check the Save to File box, and click Save to accept the default name and location. Leave the Enable File Rollover box checked and the Server Processes Trace Data box unchecked.

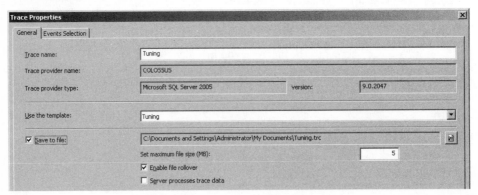

12. Click Run to start the trace.

13. Leave Profiler running, and open a new SQL Server query in SQL Server Management Studio.

14. Execute the following query (make sure to insert your username in the WHERE clause):

```
USE AdventureWorks
SELECT textdata FROM monitor
WHERE NTUserName = 'Your_User_Name'
```

15. Switch to Profiler, click the Stop button (red box), and then close Profiler.

Criteria for Completion

This task is complete when you have created a workload file in Profiler. You should see a list of database activity, as shown in Figure 4.3.

FIGURE 4.3   You should see a list of database activity when you run the workload trace.

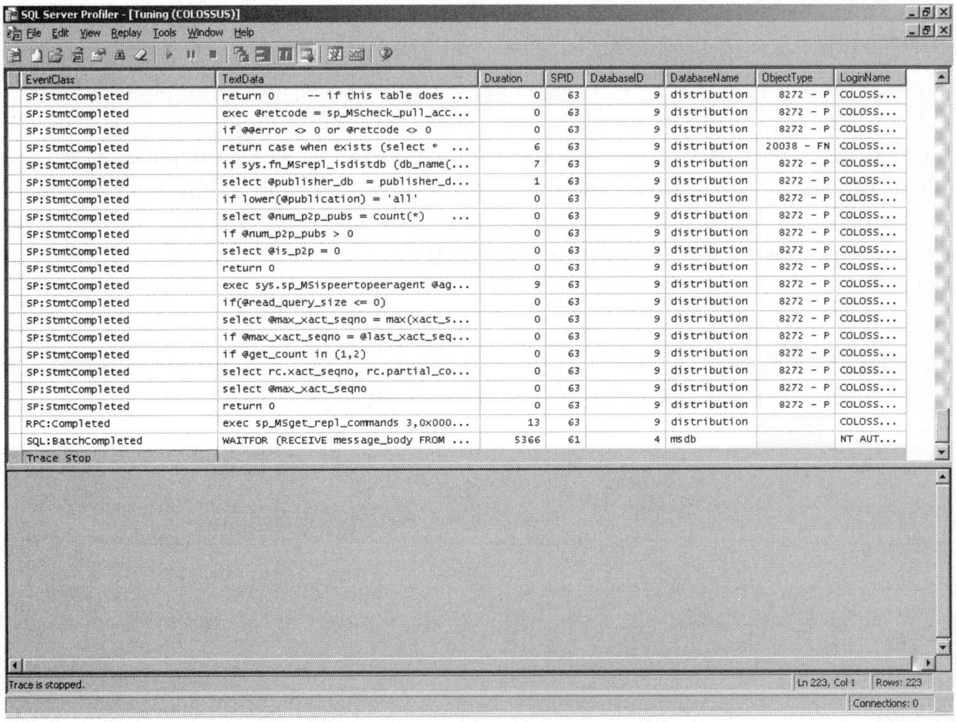

Task 4.7: Using the Database Engine Tuning Advisor

You already know the importance of keeping a database tuned. If anything is out of tune, so to speak, the entire server will suffer for it. The first step in tuning a database is to create a workload file based on the Tuning template, as you did in the previous task. The next step is to run the Database Engine Tuning Advisor.

This tool will parse the workload file you provide and compare the activity recorded therein against the existing indexes in the database. If the database has all the indexes needed to run at top speed, then the Database Engine Tuning Advisor makes no recommendations. If, on the other hand, you need to make changes, the Database Engine Tuning Advisor will present you with the proposed changes and allow you to implement them on the spot or schedule them for later.

In this task, you will use the Database Engine Tuning Advisor to tune the AdventureWorks database based on the workload file you created in Task 4.6.

Scenario

You have a SQL Server 2005 instance that has been running well for several months. Over the past couple of weeks, though, users have started complaining about performance. They tell you queries are taking an excessive amount of time to return data. After doing some research into the problem, you realize that the users have begun to query on columns that are not indexed, and some of the indexes currently in place may not be used any longer. Because you have already created a workload file, you are ready to tune the database using the Database Engine Tuning Advisor.

Scope of Task

Duration

This task should take approximately 15 minutes.

Setup

For this task, you need access to the machine you installed SQL Server 2005 on in Task 1.1, the AdventureWorks database installed with the sample data, the Monitor table you created in Task 4.5, and the workload file you created in Task 4.6.

Caveat

This task doesn't have any caveats.

Procedure

In this task, you will tune the AdventureWorks database using the Database Engine Tuning Advisor and the workload file you created in Task 4.6.

Equipment Used

For this task, you need access to the machine you installed SQL Server 2005 on in Task 1.1, the AdventureWorks database installed with the sample data, the Monitor table you created in Task 4.5, and the workload file you created in Task 4.6.

Details

To run the Database Engine Tuning Advisor, follow these steps:

1. From the Start menu, select Programs ➤ Microsoft SQL Server 2005 ➤ Performance Tools ➤ Database Engine Tuning Advisor.

2. Connect to your server using the appropriate authentication method. This will create a new session in the advisor.

3. In the Session Name box, enter **Tuning Session**.

4. In the Workload section, click the Browse button (it looks like a pair of binoculars), and locate the `Tuning.trc` trace file created earlier.

5. In the databases and tables grid, check the box next to AdventureWorks.

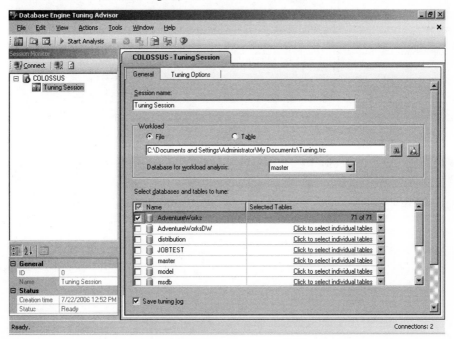

6. Switch to the Tuning Options tab. From here you can instruct the advisor what physical changes to make to the database; specifically, you can have the advisor create new indexes (clustered and nonclustered) and partition the database.

7. Leave the Limit Tuning Time option checked and set for the default time; this prevents the advisor from taking too many system resources.

8. Leave the default options for Physical Design Structures (PDS) to Use in Database, Partitioning Strategy to Employ, and Physical Design Structures (PDS) to Keep in Database.

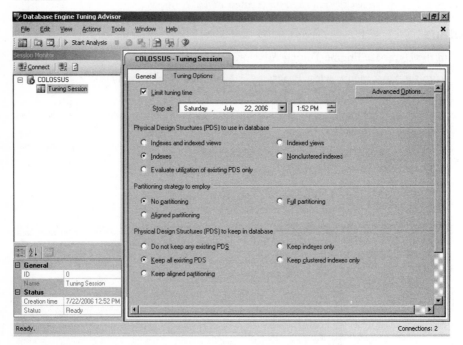

9. Click the Advanced Options button. From here you can set these options:

    ▪ Define Max. Space for Recommendations (MB) will set the maximum amount of space used by the recommended physical performance structures.

    ▪ All Recommendations Are Offline will generate recommendations that may require you to take the database offline to implement the change.

- Generate Online Recommendations Where Possible will return online recommendations even if a faster offline method is possible. If there is no online method, then an offline method is recommended.

- Generate Only Online Recommendations will return only online recommendations.

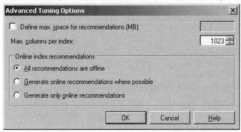

10. Click Cancel to return to the advisor.

11. Click the Start Analysis button on the toolbar.

12. You should see a progress status screen during the analysis phase.

13. After analysis is complete, you will be taken to the Recommendations tab; you should see a recommendation for creating an index on the Monitor table.

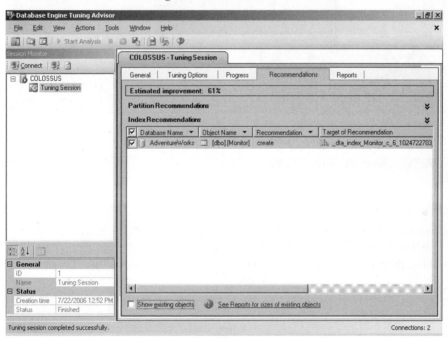

14. You can also check the Reports tab for more detailed information about the analysis process. Select Statement Detail Report from the Select Report drop-down list as an example.

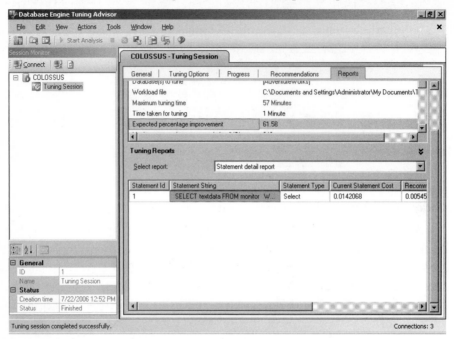

15. To apply these recommendations, select Apply Recommendations from the Actions menu.

16. In the dialog box that opens, click Apply Now, and click OK.

17. When the index has been created, click Close.

18. Close the Database Engine Tuning Advisor.

Criteria for Completion

This task is complete when you have used the Database Engine Tuning Advisor to create an index on the Monitor table in the AdventureWorks database using the Tuning.trc workload file created in Task 4.6. You should see a new index on the Monitor table. Follow these steps to verify:

1. Open SQL Server Management Studio, expand your server, and then select Databases ➢ AdventureWorks ➢ Tables ➢ Monitor ➢ Indexes.

2. You should see a new index listed.

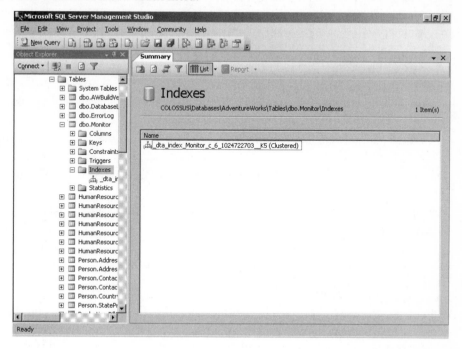

Task 4.8: Identifying and Rectifying the Cause of a Block

Obviously, you do not want other users to be able to change data while you are reading or modifying it. This would cause confusion and inaccuracies in your database, and your system would soon go from being a database server to being a large paperweight. To keep this from happening, SQL Server automatically places locks on the data that is being accessed to limit what other users can do with that data. SQL Server has several types of locks; shared locks and exclusive locks are the most important to understand:

▪ *Shared* locks are placed on data that is being accessed for read purposes. In other words, when a user executes a SELECT statement, SQL Server places a shared lock on the data requested. Shared locks allow other users to access the locked data for reading but not for modifying.

- *Exclusive* locks are placed on data that is being modified. This means when a user executes an INSERT, UPDATE, or DELETE statement, SQL Server uses an exclusive lock to protect the data. Exclusive locks do not allow other users to access the locked data for any purpose; the data is exclusively available to the user who placed the lock.

You won't deal with other locks as often (if ever), but it is good to know they exist:

- *Update* locks indicate that a user may want to update data. This prevents a type of deadlock where two users are trying to update data but neither of them can get an exclusive lock because the other user has a shared lock on the data.

- *Intent* locks indicate SQL Server wants to place a lock lower in the database hierarchy, such as at the table level.

- *Schema* locks are for when Data Definition Language (DDL) statements, such as ALTER TABLE, are executed.

- *Bulk update* locks are used when bulk copy operations are in progress or when the TABLOCK hint is used on a query.

SQL Server does a great job of dynamically setting these locks, so you don't need to be concerned with setting them yourself. What you do need to be concerned with is making sure your queries are properly written so SQL Server does not place locks that get in the users' way. The primary cause of this is deadlocks.

Deadlocks occur when users try to place exclusive locks on each other's objects (as shown in Figure 4.4). For example, User1 places an exclusive lock on Table1 and then tries to place an exclusive lock on Table2. User2 already has an exclusive lock on Table2, and User2 tries to put an exclusive lock on Table1. This condition could cause SQL Server to enter an endless loop of waiting for the locks to be released, but fortunately an algorithm built into SQL Server looks for and rectifies this problem. SQL Server picks one of the users (called the *victim* in SQL Server terminology) and kills their query. The user whose query was killed will receive an error message stating they are the victim of a deadlock and should try their query again later.

FIGURE 4.4 Deadlocks degrade system performance.

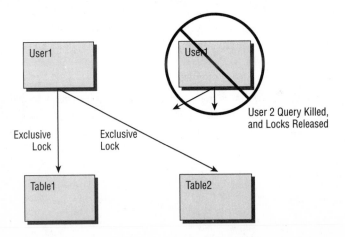

This can cause aggravation among the users because it slows their work. You can avoid deadlocks by monitoring SQL Server using one of three methods:

- Use Profiler to monitor the Lock:Deadlock and Lock:Deadlock Chain events in the Locks event class.
- Check the Current Activity folders under Management in Enterprise Manager.
- Use the `sp_lock` stored procedure to find out what locks are in place.

When you find the cause of the deadlock, you can have your developers rewrite the offending queries. Of course, that takes time, and you need to get your users running again right away. You can find which user is blocking other users by querying the `sys.dm_exec_requests` system view. Once you find the offending session, you can terminate it with the `KILL` command.

In this task, you will see how to use `sys.dm_exec_requests` and the `KILL` command to rectify a block.

Scenario

You have a SQL Server instance that has been running fine for several months. Recently, though, your developers created some new stored procedures and pushed them into production. When only a few users are connected to the system, everything runs fine, but when the traffic starts to pick up, users start complaining that they cannot access data. The most common complaint is that when the user tries to retrieve data, the system seems to hang and the query never completes. You recognize this as a block, and you decide to troubleshoot it using the `sys.dm_exec_requests` system view and the `KILL` command.

Scope of Task

Duration

This task should take approximately 20 minutes.

Setup

For this task, you need access to the machine you installed SQL Server 2005 on in Task 1.1, the AdventureWorks database installed with the sample data, and the Monitor table you created in Task 4.5.

Caveat

This task doesn't have any caveats.

Procedure

In this task, you will simulate a blocking condition using the `TABLOCKX` and `HOLDLOCK` query hints. This tells SQL Server to place an exclusive lock on the table and hold the lock until the query completes, which will block other users from accessing the table in question. You will then query the sys.dm_exec_requests system view to find the blocking session ID and use the KILL command to end the session and release the lock.

Equipment Used

For this task, you need access to the machine you installed SQL Server 2005 on in Task 1.1, the AdventureWorks database installed with the sample data, and the Monitor table you created in Task 4.5.

Details

To simulate a block, troubleshoot it, and rectify it, follow these steps:

1. To start a locking session, open a new query in SQL Server Management Studio, and execute this command:

```
BEGIN TRAN
SELECT * FROM monitor WITH (TABLOCKX, HOLDLOCK)
```

2. Now to create a blocked session, open a new query, and execute this code:

```
UPDATE monitor SET textdata = 'test'
WHERE rownumber = 1
```

3. Notice that the second query does not complete because the first query is holding an exclusive lock on the table. To find the session that is doing the blocking, open a third query window.

4. In the third query window, query the sys.dm_exec_requests system view for any session that is being blocked with this code:

```
SELECT session_id, status, blocking_session_id
FROM sys.dm_exec_requests
WHERE blocking_session_id > 0
```

5. The blocking_session_id is the session causing the problem. To end it, execute the KILL command with the blocking_session_id value. For example, if blocking_session_id is 53, you would execute this:

```
KILL 53
```

6. Switch to the second query (from step 2); it should be complete with one row affected.

Criteria for Completion

This task is complete when you have simulated a block, queried the sys.dm_exec_requests system view to find the errant session, and used the KILL command to end it. If you were successful, the query from step 6 in the "Details" section will complete with one row affected.

Task 4.9: Using the Dedicated Administrator Connection

It is rare, but SQL Server can stop responding to normal queries and appear to be frozen. How could this happen? Consider that when you bought the system that houses SQL Server, you likely planned for future growth and usage. No matter how much time and effort you put into this plan, though, some companies just outgrow their servers too quickly, and the servers can't handle the workload. In a scenario like this, it is possible that SQL Server might stop responding to normal queries. To troubleshoot this issue, or any kind of problem where SQL Server just isn't responding to normal calls, you need the *Dedicated Administrator Connection* (DAC).

The DAC is a special diagnostics connection that is always available for connection, even under normal operating circumstances. As the name implies, only administrators (members of the sysadmin server role) can connect to the DAC to run diagnostic queries and troubleshoot problems. So, how does it work?

By default, SQL Server listens for normal queries on TCP port 1433, so when a user runs a SELECT query, it is transmitted to the server over port 1433. The DAC listens, by default, on TCP port 1434, so it is not cluttered with user traffic. In other words, it is always free and available for connections. Because the DAC is always available, it always consumes some system resources, but these are kept to a minimum.

Because the DAC consumes minimal resources and is meant to be used only for diagnostic functions, some limitations exist on what you can do with it:

- To ensure available resources, only one DAC connection is allowed per server. If you try to open a DAC connection to a server that already has a DAC connection open, you will get error 17810, and the connection will be denied.

- You can't run any parallel commands or queries from within the DAC. For example, you cannot run BACKUP or RESTORE.

- Because of resource constraints, the DAC is not available in SQL Server 2005 Express Edition.

- Because of the limited resources available, you should not run complex queries in the DAC, such as large queries with complex joins.

- By default, you cannot access the DAC from a remote machine; you must be on the server. You can change this by setting the remote admin connections option to 1 by using the sp_configure stored procedure, like this:

```
sp_configure 'remote admin connections', 1
GO
RECONFIGURE
GO
```

That seems like a lot of restrictions, so you may be wondering what you *are* allowed to do. The DAC is especially good for these tasks:

- Querying dynamic management views:

  - You can query `sys.dm_exec_requests` to find blocking queries.

  - You can query `sys.dm_os_memory_cache_counters` to check the health of the system memory cache.

  - You can query `sys.dm_exec_sessions` for information about active sessions.

- Querying catalog views

- Running basic `DBCC` commands:

  - You can use `DBCC FREEPROCCACHE` to remove all elements from the procedure cache.

  - You can use `DBCC FREESYSTEMCACHE` to remove all unused entries from all caches.

  - You can use `DBCC DROPCLEANBUFFERS` to remove all clean buffers from the buffer pool.

  - You can use `DBCC SQLPERF` to retrieve statistics about how the transaction log space is used in all databases.

- Using the `KILL` command to end an errant session

You can see that this is a powerful weapon in your troubleshooting arsenal, but how do you use it? In this task, you will work with the DAC.

Scenario

You have a SQL Server 2005 instance that has been running well for several months. Just this morning, though, your developers pushed some new stored procedures into production. A few hours later, users started complaining that they could not connect to SQL Server to retrieve data. While trying to investigate the problem, you find that you cannot connect to SQL Server using SQL Server Management Studio either. You know that the only method left for troubleshooting is the DAC.

Scope of Task

Duration

This task should take approximately 15 minutes.

Setup

For this task, you need access to the machine you installed SQL Server 2005 on in Task 1.1.

Caveat

This task doesn't have any caveats.

Procedure

In this task, you will connect to the DAC and run a query.

Equipment Used

For this task, you need access to the machine you installed SQL Server 2005 on in Task 1.1.

Details

To connect to the DAC and run a query, follow these steps:

1. Open a command prompt on your server.

2. The following command connects to the server specified with the -S parameter using a trusted connection as specified by the -E parameter. The -A parameter specifies the DAC, or an administrative connection. Run the following command now:

   ```
   Sqlcmd -S (local) -A -E
   ```

3. You should see a 1> prompt. From here you can enter a query. Type the following, and hit Enter:

   ```
   SELECT session_id, status, blocking_session_id
   FROM sys.dm_exec_requests
   ```

4. You should now see a 2> prompt. Type **GO**, and hit Enter to execute the query.

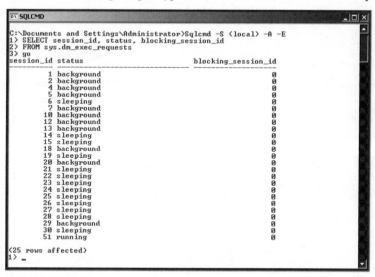

5. You should now be back at the 1> prompt. To exit the DAC, enter **Exit**, and hit Enter.

6. To connect to the DAC in SQL Server Management Studio, close all open copies of SQL Server Management Studio.

7. Open SQL Server Management Studio, connect to the default instance, and open a new query.

8. From the Query menu, hover over Connection, and click Change Connection.

9. To connect to the local machine, enter **ADMIN:** in front of the server name in the Server Name text box, and click Connect.

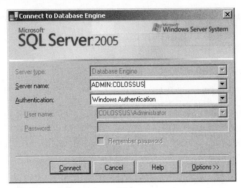

10. Execute this query in the new query window:

```
SELECT session_id, status, blocking_session_id
FROM sys.dm_exec_requests
```

11. You should see a list of sessions in the results grid.

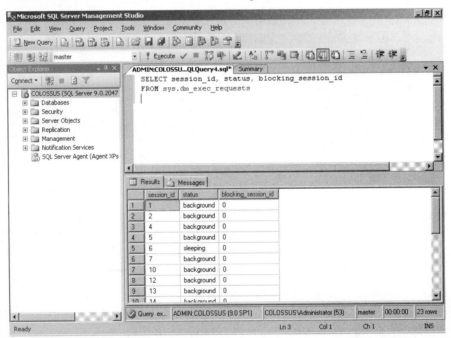

12. Close SQL Server Management Studio.

Criteria for Completion

This task is complete when you have connected to the DAC using both the command line and SQL Server Management Studio. You should see results from each query as outlined in the "Details" section of this task.

Index

Note to the reader: Throughout this index **boldfaced** page numbers indicate primary discussions of a topic. *Italicized* page numbers indicate illustrations.

Q

R

SYBEX | SERIOUS SKILLS.

From book smarts to Street Smarts.

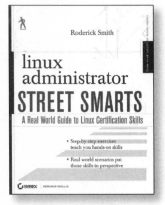

Roderick Smith

linux
administrator
STREET SMARTS
A Real World Guide to Linux Certification Skills

- Step-by-step exercises
  teach you hands-on skills
- Real world scenarios put
  those skills in perspective

ISBN10: 0-470-08348-4
ISBN13: 978-0-470-08348-2 • US $29.99
November 2006

James Pyles

pc technician
STREET SMARTS
A Real World Guide to CompTIA A+ Skills

- Step-by-step exercises
  teach you hands-on skills
- Real world scenarios put
  those skills in perspective

ISBN10: 0-470-08458-8
ISBN13: 978-0-470-08458-8 • US $29.99
December 2006

Joseph Jorden

SQL server
2005 DBA
STREET SMARTS
A Real World Guide to SQL Server 2005 Certification Skills

- Step-by-step exercises
  teach you hands-on skills
- Real world scenarios put
  those skills in perspective

ISBN10: 0-470-08349-2
ISBN13: 978-0-470-08349-9 • US $29.99
November 2006

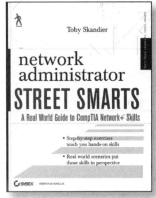

Toby Skandier

network
administrator
STREET SMARTS
A Real World Guide to CompTIA Network+ Skills

- Step-by-step exercises
  teach you hands-on skills
- Real world scenarios put
  those skills in perspective

ISBN10: 0-470-04724-0
ISBN13: 978-0-470-04724-8 • US $29.99
August 2006

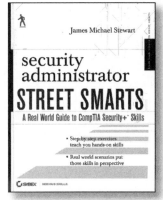

James Michael Stewart

security
administrator
STREET SMARTS
A Real World Guide to CompTIA Security+ Skills

- Step-by-step exercises
  teach you hands-on skills
- Real world scenarios put
  those skills in perspective

ISBN10: 0-470-10258-6
ISBN13: 978-0-470-10258-9 • US $29.99
February 2007

Hit the ground running with the street-smart training you'll find in the new *Street Smarts* series
from Sybex. These practical books organize key information around the actual day-to-day tasks and
scenarios you'll face in the field—then teach you the hands-on skills you need to complete those
tasks. And because the exercises in each book are based upon exam objectives from leading technology
certifications, you can also use each *Street Smarts* as a lab manual for certification prep.

Visit www.sybex.com

Wiley, the Wiley logo, and the Sybex logo are registered trademarks of John Wiley & Sons, Inc. and/or its affiliates.

SYBEX
An Imprint of WILEY
Now you know.